Best-Loved Stories of the LDS People Volume 2

Best-Loved Stories of the LDS People Volume 2

Edited by Jay A. Parry, Jack M. Lyon,
and Linda Ririe Gundry

DESERET BOOK COMPANY
SALT LAKE CITY, UTAH

Also available from Deseret Book

BEST-LOVED POEMS OF THE LDS PEOPLE

BEST-LOVED STORIES OF THE LDS PEOPLE

BEST-LOVED HUMOR OF THE LDS PEOPLE

Library of Congress Cataloging-in-Publication Data

Best-loved stories of the LDS people / edited by Jay A. Parry, Jack M. Lyon, Linda Ririe Gundry.

p. cm.

Includes bibliographical references and index.

ISBN 1-57345-574-1 (hardcover)

1. Church of Jesus Christ of Latter-day Saints—History—19th century—Sources. 2. Mormon Church—History—19th century—Sources. 3. Mormons—History—19th century—Sources. I. Parry, Jay A. II. Lyon, Jack M. III. Gundry, Linda Ririe.

BX8611.B36 1999

289.3'32—dc21 97-24195

CIP

Printed in the United States of America 72082-6516

10 9 8 7 6 5 4 3 2 1

Contents

Example

Faith

Faithfulness

Family

Healing

Humor

Integrity

Love

Missionary Work

Prayer

Prophecy

Protection

Revelation

Temple Work

Testimony

The Restoration

Word of Wisdom

PREFACE

Elder Bruce R. McConkie once said, "We have in the Church an untapped, almost unknown, treasury of inspiring and faith promoting stories" (*New Era,* July 1978, 4). As we have compiled this second volume of *Best-Loved Stories of the LDS People,* we have come to know something of the truth of Elder McConkie's statement, for we have found many hundreds of stories that teach, edify, and inspire.

Even as we were getting the first volume ready for press, we found ourselves saying things like, "Did we include that story of President Kimball and the little boys sitting on the front row? How could we have overlooked that? Is there still time to get it into the book?"

Unfortunately, there came a time when we did have to stop adding stories, and even many of our favorites had to be left out. Fortunately, however, Deseret Book's management and publishing staff have graciously allowed us to compile this second volume, including our unused favorites and adding many more stories that are either best-loved or deserve to be. In particular, we'd like to thank Ronald A. Millett, Sheri L. Dew, Kent S. Ware, Jennifer Adams, Patricia J. Parkinson, Ronald O. Stucki, Sheryl Gerber, Keith Hunter, and Bronwyn Evans.

In compiling these stories we have standardized and modernized some of the spelling, capitalization, and punctuation for ease of reading.

We hope you enjoy this new collection of timeless stories, and that you find many ways to use them in talks, lessons, and family home evenings. Thus will the Church's "untapped, almost unknown treasury" be brought to light again.

Callings

A Delinquent Elder

EZRA TAFT BENSON

At a stake presidency's meeting in Boise, Idaho, years ago, we were trying to select a president for the weakest and smallest elders quorum in the stake. Our clerk had brought a list of all the elders of that quorum, and on the list was the name of a man whom I had known for some years. He came from a strong Latter-day Saint family, but he wasn't doing much in the Church. If the bishop made a call to do some work on the chapel, he'd usually respond, and if the elders wanted to play softball, you would sometimes find him out playing with them. He did have leadership ability; he was president of one of the service clubs and was doing a fine job.

I said to the stake president, "Would you authorize me to go out and meet this man and challenge him to square his life with the standards of the Church and take the leadership of his quorum? I know there is some hazard in it, but he has the ability."

The stake president said, "You go ahead, and the Lord bless you."

After Sunday School I went to this man's home. I'll never forget the look on his face as he opened the door and saw a member of his stake presidency standing there. He hesitantly invited me in; his wife was preparing dinner, and I could smell the aroma of coffee coming from the kitchen. I asked him to have his wife join us, and when we were seated, I told him why I had come. "I am not going to ask for your answer today," I told him. "All I want you to do is to promise me that you will think about it, pray about it, think about it in terms of what it will mean to your family, and then I'll be back to see you next week. If you decide not to accept, we'll go on loving you," I added.

The next Sunday, as soon as he opened the door I saw there had been a change. He was glad to see me, and he quickly invited me in and called his wife to join us. He said, "Brother Benson, we have done as you said. We've thought about it and we've prayed about it, and we've decided to accept the call. If you brethren have that much confidence in me, I'm willing to square my life with the standards of the Church, a thing I should have done a long time ago." He also said, "I haven't had any coffee since you were here last week, and I'm not going to have any more."

He was set apart as elders quorum president, and attendance in his quorum began going up—and it kept going up. He went out, put his arm around the inactive elders, and brought them in. A few months later I moved from the stake.

Years passed, and one day on Temple Square in Salt Lake City, a man came up to me, extended his hand, and said, "Brother Benson, you don't remember me, do you?"

"Yes, I do," I said, "but I don't remember your name."

He said, "Do you remember coming to the home of a delinquent elder in Boise seven years ago?" And then, of course, it all came back to me. Then he said, "Brother Benson, I'll never live long enough to thank you for coming to my home that Sunday afternoon. I am now a bishop. I used to think I was happy, but I didn't know what real happiness was."

Ezra Taft Benson, *God, Family, Country,* 186–88.

"I DREAMED THAT I WAS IN THE PRESIDENT'S OFFICE"

HENRY EYRING

In May 1860, after having labored in the Indian Territory four and a half years, I [Henry Eyring] started for Utah, where I arrived August 29, 1860. At that time the Cherokee Mission was under the direct charge of the Presidency in Utah, but it was very difficult in those days to get any news from there. I had had charge of the mission for over two years, and altogether had been in that field nearly four and a half years; hence I began to think that possibly my mission might come to a close before long. Getting no news of any kind from Utah, I enquired of the Lord and He answered me in a dream, as follows: I dreamed that I was in the President's office in Salt Lake City, and that I addressed President Young, saying: "I have come of my own accord, but if I have not stayed long enough, I am willing to return and complete my mission." The President answered: "It is all right, you have stayed long enough." On the strength of this dream I started for Utah; and when I met the President, I said to him: "President Young, I have come without being sent for; if this was not right, I am willing to go back and finish my mission." He answered pleasantly: "It is all right, we have been looking for you."

Andrew Jenson, *LDS Biographical Encyclopedia,* 1:311.

"I WAS NO LONGER AFRAID"

ANTONIA FLORES

One time many years ago, the branch president [in the Tacna Branch of the Peru Lima Mission] interviewed me to call me as Relief Society president. I was very afraid to be Relief Society president. I just didn't see how I could handle such a job and was afraid to tell him yes. Later that day, I remembered the principle of fasting and prayer. I fasted and prayed about accepting this position that I was so afraid of.

In the night, I had a revelation. I dreamed that I was walking, carrying a great weight in my hands. I had been walking a long time and was tired from carrying such a heavy weight. Then I saw our Lord Jesus Christ, and he took the weight out of my hands and invited me, saying, "Come, follow me." The next morning I felt wonderful; the fear had left me. I hurried to the branch president to tell what had happened, that I was no longer afraid and was sure it was right, and so I have been able to continue working in the Relief Society several years as president with two wonderful counselors.

Antonia Flores, in Leon R. Hartshorn, comp., *Remarkable Stories from the Lives of Latter-day Saint Women,* 2:87–89.

CHARACTER

A Check for One Hundred Fifty Dollars

HEBER J. GRANT

I want to reprint a poem that nearly sixty years ago was repeated to me in Idaho, or, rather, it was not repeated as a poem; it was sung as a song by the late Francis M. Lyman.

It so happened that from Tooele I had to travel thirty-six miles to Salt Lake City and then on through Davis County, Weber County, and up to Brigham City, and then two and three-fourths days' journey west out to Oakley, to what was then a branch of the Grantsville Ward of the Tooele Stake of Zion over which I presided. (The first motion I made as an apostle was to present that whole country to the Box Elder Stake of Zion.) Now, when I was on that trip, Brother Lyman sang a song to me, and that very night I sat down and asked him to repeat it to me while I wrote it down, and the next day I learned it:

Let each man learn to know himself;
To gain that knowledge let him labor
To improve those failings in himself
Which he condemns so in his neighbor.

How lenient our own faults we view,
And conscience' voice adeptly smother;
Yet, oh, how harshly we review
The selfsame failings in another!

And if you meet an erring one
Whose deeds are blamable and thoughtless,

Consider, ere you cast the stone,
If you yourself are pure and faultless.

Oh, list to that small voice within,
Whose whisperings oft make men confounded,
And trumpet not another's sin;
You'd blush deep if your own were sounded.

And in self-judgment if you find
Your deeds to others are superior,
To you has Providence been kind,
As you should be to those inferior.

Example sheds a genial ray
Of light which men are apt to borrow;
So first improve yourself today
And then improve your friends tomorrow.

I did some work for a man once, and he sent me a check for five hundred dollars with a letter apologizing for not sending me a thousand. Subsequently, I did for another individual some work which was ten times harder, involved ten times more labor and a great deal more time; and he sent me a check for one hundred fifty dollars, and told his friends he had rewarded me handsomely.

I wrote him a letter about as follows: "My dear friend: Enclosed find your check. Please take it and go to 'H,'" and then I drew a long line, but never added the '1's' and I never mailed the letter. Subsequently, I showed that check to a dear friend of mine, first explaining the work I had done and asking him how much it was worth. He said: "Ten thousand, three hundred dollars."

I pulled the check out of the drawer and handed it to him. I said: "It is only ten thousand, one hundred fifty dollars short."

He said to me: "Mr. Grant, you are a young man. 'Old men for counsel and young men for war'; I want you to give me your word of honor that you will take my advice."

I said: "I will make no such promise, but if I can take it without violating my conscience, I will try."

He said, "O your conscience will be all right. Deposit that check quickly."

Then he said: "Did that man intend to insult you?"

I said: "No. He told my friends he had rewarded me handsomely."

To this he replied, "A man's a fool who takes an insult that isn't intended. I have prolonged your life; I have rendered you a great service, because you could never look at that check but what you wanted to swear, and I believe it is worse to keep it in than to let it out. I have heard that anger creates a fluid in the body that poisons the blood and shortens the length of life. Now, you have promised to do what I say, if you can in good conscience. When you go home tonight get down on your knees and say: 'O Lord, I am a man who can generally express myself so that everybody understands me; I am not usually at a loss for words; I have sufficient vocabulary so that I can generally talk my ideas into the other fellow. But, O Lord, tonight I am utterly and absolutely at a loss to find the words to express my gratitude to you that when you made me you gave me a bigger heart than you gave that fellow who sent me a check for one hundred fifty dollars.'"

I immediately opened the drawer where I kept scores of copies of this poem, which I have distributed from Japan to the Hawaiian Islands, from the midnight sun country down to Italy, and all over the United States—I immediately took this poem out and gave it to this man, and said: "I have not had sense enough to learn but one-half of the words; this part I have overlooked:

> And in self-judgment if you find
> Your deeds to others are superior,
> To you has Providence been kind
> As you should be to those inferior."

Those four lines have been of more value to me since that man pointed out to me the force of them. Why, I had been preaching that poem and distributing it and had not learned to apply it to myself. I have since tried to remember this, and commend these lines to all my friends and brethren.

Improvement Era, March 1941, 137.

Love for Animals

LLEWELYN R. McKAY

Father [David O. McKay] hates to see an animal mishandled, or to know that one is suffering or killed unnecessarily. As a small boy, I observed my first lesson in this regard. We were walking up the hill on 21st Street, Ogden, and were halfway up the block after leaving Washington Avenue. There we observed a man whipping his horses unmercifully as the team vainly attempted to pull a wagon load of coal out of a rut in the road. The driver swore and cursed as he cracked his whip over their heads and cut the creatures' backs. Father watched only for a second before he strode up to the driver and said, "Hold on there a minute, young man; you can't expect these horses to pull with their heads held up so high!" And without waiting for an answer, he unhooked the checkreins, loosened them several inches, then turned to the driver who was still swearing—but in lower tones:

"Now turn your team to the left, keep a tight hold on the reins, and command the team sternly—but without the whip!"

The man was about to answer but thought better of it after looking into father's determined eyes and did as he was told. The faithful horses lowered their heads and pulled the load out of the hole. Father came back to where I was standing on the sidewalk and said, "Some people shouldn't be allowed to drive horses, because they don't show as much sense as the horses!"

Llewelyn R. McKay, comp., *Home Memories of President David O. McKay,* 126.

THE BADGER

LLEWELYN R. McKAY

One morning I was helping father [David O. McKay] irrigate a patch of potatoes at the Dry Hollow farm. Duke, my large Belgian police dog, was scouting around the neighboring field and suddenly set up a loud barking. I left my work to investigate the cause and discovered that Duke had cornered a badger. The poor little fellow was standing his ground, and his sharp claws kept the dog at a distance. Unwittingly, I walked behind the animal to get a better look at him. Afraid I was about to attack him, the badger turned quickly to face me. That off-guard turn was all that Duke needed. In a flash, he pounced on the poor little creature and, with a firm grip on its neck, shook it to its death.

I carried the dead animal back to father. His face fell as I showed him the animal, and he said, "Why did you let your dog kill it? It is a harmless creature, and there was no need to take its life. Who knows, it may even have some babies which now will starve to death in their hole!"

I have never needlessly killed an animal since that time!

Llewelyn R. McKay, comp., *Home Memories of President David O. McKay,* 129–30.

"HE DIDN'T REALLY LOVE ME"

JAYNANN PAYNE

We will never forget that sweet young girl of sixteen who came to live with us one summer for the remaining months of her unwed pregnancy. My husband is an attorney and was handling the adoption of her baby. She hadn't wanted to marry the boy who was the father of her unborn child. She had been beguiled and had partaken of the bitter fruit.

In September she gave birth to a beautiful little boy, and the day she was to leave the hospital, Dean and I had to go to Salt Lake City. We stopped at the hospital long enough to meet the couple who were adopting the baby. Under hospital rules, this young mother, sixteen years old, had to take her beautiful nine-pound boy from the arms of the nurse and hand him over to my husband, who then stepped outside the room and gave the baby to the adopting parents. It tore me apart to watch her and to see that young couple leave with her baby.

She said to me, "Sister Payne, he lied to me when he said nobody would get hurt, and that because we loved each other, anything we did was alright. He didn't really love me. That is why I didn't marry him, because he wasn't worthy to be the father of my little boy. It's all a great big lie, and I don't want to live a lie!

"Oh, if only I had known five minutes before I was immoral how I would feel five minutes after I gave my baby away!"

For this girl not to have thought ahead about the consequences of her actions and not to have realized that lust is the mere image of love is indeed heartbreaking. It is so important to keep in tune, keep in touch, to receive the Spirit each and every day. We never know what is going to happen; and if we make the commitment in our private rooms, by the side of our beds, to our Father in heaven, of what we want to be in life—what we will do and what we won't do—and then ask for his help in keeping our commitments, he will help us in public and private.

BYU Speeches, 10 February 1970; as quoted in Leon R. Hartshorn, *Remarkable Stories from the Lives of Latter-day Saint Women,* 2:203.

Conversion

"I Directly Read It through Twice"

ZERA PULSIPHER

When I was about twenty-one I married a very agreeable companion, lived with her about one year when she died leaving one child which we named Harriett. After the death of my wife (Polly, or Mary, Randell) I had some anxiety about [my wife's] state and condition, consequently in answer to my desires in a few weeks she came to me in vision and appearing natural looked pleasant as she ever did and sat by my side and assisted me in singing a hymn—beginning thus: "That glorious day is drawing nigh when Zion's Light Shall Shine." This she did with a seeming composure. This vision took away all the anxiety of my mind concerning her in as much as she seemed to enjoy herself well. This hymn which she introduced and sang with me applied to the great work of the last dispensation of the fullness of times. This transpired about ten years before Joseph Smith had discovered the first revelation of the work of the last days. My mind became calm as respecting her condition in the spirit world. . . .

I [eventually] removed to Onondaga County in the state of New York. I then lost my only son by the fall of a tree which caused much grief to me in that place.

I had many agreeable friends and good society there. I bought a farm and built a mill. I also built a meetinghouse for the Baptist Church which I was then associated with [as their minister]. In the summer of 1831 I heard a minister say that an ancient record or Golden Bible [had come forth] in Manchester near Palmyra which remark struck me like a shock of electricity [and] at the same time thought it might be something that would give light to my mind upon principles that I had been thinking of for years and many times I had remarked that if the pure church with its gifts and graces was not on the earth, if so I had not found it. But I should be happy enough to find it in my day.

. . . In the fall of 1831 there was a Book of Mormon brought in to town. I succeeded in getting it. I directly read it through twice, gave it a thorough investigation and believed it was true, and the winter following Jerod [Jared] Carter came. . . . As soon as he came into town I, with two Methodist preachers, went to see him. After a reasonable introduction I questioned him upon the principles of the ancient gospel with all its gifts belonging to it. I asked him if he believed it; he answered in the affirmative. I asked him if he had ever laid hands on the sick and they had recovered. Yes, he said, he had in many instances.

He preached the following evening to a crowded congregation, held up the Book of Mormon and declared it to be a revelation from God. I could not gain-say anything he had said. He sat down and gave liberty for remarks; the congregation seemed to be in amaze, not knowing what to think of what they had heard. I arose and said to the congregation that we had been hearing strange things, and if true they were of the utmost importance to us. If not true it was one of the greatest impositions, and as the preacher had said that he had got his knowledge from heaven and was nothing but a man and I the same, that I had just as good a right to obtain that blessing as he; therefore I was determined to have that knowledge for myself, which I considered it my privilege, from that time I made it a matter of fervent prayer.

I think about the seventh day as I was thrashing in my barn with doors shut, all at once there seemed to be a ray of light from heaven, which caused me to stop work for a short time, but soon began it again. Then in a few minutes another light came over my head, which caused me to look up. I thought I saw the angels with the Book of Mormon in their hands in the attitude of showing it to me and saying, "this is the great revelation of the last days in which all things spoken of by the prophets must be fulfilled." The vision was so open and plain that I began to rejoice exceedingly, so that I walked the length of my barn crying "Glory Hal-la-lu-ya to God and the Lamb forever."

For some time it seemed a little difficult to keep my mind in a proper state of reasonable order, I was so filled with the joys of heaven. But when my mind became calm I called the church together, and informed them of what I had seen. I told them of my determination to join the Church of Latter Day Saints, which I did, and a large body of my church went with me. I was ordained to the office of an elder and went to preaching with considerable success at home and abroad. I had the privilege of baptizing Wilford Woodruff on the 31st of December, 1833, at Richland, New York.

Zera Pulsipher, Autobiography.

"I Was Cautious in Religious Matters"

Lorenzo Dow Young

In November, 1829, I removed to a place called Hector Hill. In February, 1831, my father, my brothers Joseph and Brigham, and Heber C. Kimball came to my house. They brought with them the Book of Mormon. They were on their way to visit some Saints in Pennsylvania. Through fear of being deceived, I was quite cautious in religious matters. I read and compared the Book of Mormon with the Bible, and fasted and prayed that I might come to a knowledge of the truth. The Spirit seemed to say, "This is the way; walk ye in it." This was all the testimony I could get at the time; it was not altogether satisfactory.

The following May, Elder Levi Gifford came into the neighborhood and desired to preach. My brother, John, belonged to the Methodist church, and had charge of their meetinghouse which was in the neighborhood. I obtained from him permission for Elder Gifford to preach in it. The appointment was circulated for a meeting the same evening.

This was on Saturday evening, and the circuit preacher of that district was to hold a meeting there on Sunday. Elder Midbury, the circuit preacher, attended the meeting. The house was crowded. As soon as Elder Gifford had concluded his discourse, Elder Midbury arose to his feet and said: "Brethren, sisters and friends: I have been a preacher of the gospel for twenty-two years; I do not know that I have been the means of converting a sinner, or reclaiming a poor backslider; but this I do know, that the doctrine the stranger has preached to us tonight is a deception, that Joe Smith is a false prophet, and that the Book of Mormon is from hell."

After talking awhile in this strain, he concluded. I immediately arose to my feet and asked the privilege of speaking, which was granted. I said that Elder Midbury, in his remarks, entirely ignored the possibility of more revelation, and acknowledged that he had been a preacher of the gospel for twenty-two years, without knowing that he had been the means of converting a sinner, or of reclaiming a poor backslider. But still he claimed to know that the doctrine he had just heard was false, that Joseph Smith was an impostor, and that the Book of Mormon was from hell. "Now, how is it possible," I asked, "for him to know these things unless he has received a revelation?"

When I sat down a strong man, by the name of Thompson, who was well known in the neighborhood as a belligerent character, stepped up to Elder Gifford and demanded the proofs of the authenticity of the Book of Mormon.

Elder Gifford replied, "I have said all I care about saying tonight."

Then said Mr. Thompson, "We will take the privilege of clothing you with a coat of tar and feathers, and riding you out of town on a rail."

In the meantime, four or five others of like character came to the front.

Acting under the impulse of the moment—true to the instincts of my nature to protect the weak against the strong, I stepped between Elder Gifford and Mr. Thompson. Looking the latter in the eye, I said, "Mr. Thompson, you cannot lay your hand on this stranger to harm a hair of his head, without you do it over my dead body."

He replied by mere threats of violence, which brought my brother John to his feet.

With a voice and manner, that carried with it a power greater than I had ever seen manifested in him before, and, I might say, since, he commanded Mr. Thompson and party to take their seats. He continued, "Gentlemen, if you offer to lay a hand on Mr. Gifford, you shall pass through my hands, after which I think you will not want any more tonight." Mr. Thompson and party quieted down and then took their seats. . . .

In the spring of 1831 there was a two-days' meeting of the Saints, about six miles from where I lived, in the state of Pennsylvania. I attended it, and became fully convinced of the divine origin of the latter-day work.

In the summer of 1831, I settled up my business and started for the latter-day Zion, in the state of Missouri. On my way out of the state of New York, I visited Elder J. P. Green, in the town of Avon.

As I arrived there on Saturday, he said, "Brother Lorenzo, I am very glad you have come. I have an appointment to preach at 10 o'clock, eight miles from here, but I am very unwell and not able to fill it. I want you to do it for me."

I rather ridiculed the idea, saying, "You want me to preach as a Mormon elder, when I have not even joined the Church?"

He still desired me to go, and said, "it will be all right."

E. M. Green, the son of J. P. Green, accompanied me, with a revelation on the organization of the Church, which his father directed him to read to the congregation.

Arriving at the place appointed, I found the house full, and a Baptist preacher in the stand. I introduced myself to the minister; he invited the congregation to sing, and I prayed, and E. M. Green read the revelation. I arose and commenced to speak. The good Spirit was with me, and I had much freedom. I talked about one hour and a quarter. At the close I gave anyone the privilege of speaking who wished to. The Baptist minister arose and bore his testimony, that what they had heard was true Bible doctrine, and could not be questioned.

After meeting, several persons gathered around me and wished to be baptized. Knowing that I had not received authority to administer the ordinance, I put them off, telling them that when Elder Green came to fill the next appointment that had been made for him, he would baptize them. Among those who requested baptism, at that time, were the brothers Joseph and Chandler Holbrook, and Mary Ann Angell, now the relict [widow] of President Brigham Young.

On the following morning I told Elder Green that, inasmuch as I had believed in the gospel for some time, and had preached as a "Mormon" elder, I thought it was time that I was baptized. He administered the ordinance, and ordained me an elder. I then went on my way rejoicing.

Fragments of Experience, 33–36.

"BROUGHT FORTH BY AN ANGEL'S HAND"

MAY BOOTH TALMAGE

Zina [Diantha Young] was about 13 years old. Living as they did within about sixty miles of the hill Cumorah, they were familiar with the current rumors concerning the bringing forth of the Book of Mormon. Her parents were soon converted to our faith, and the following year Hyrum Smith and David

Whitmer visited their home, bringing with them a copy of the first edition of the Book of Mormon. Aunt Zina says: "When I entered the room and read the title of the book that was lying on the window sill, my whole soul was filled with joy. Without opening it I clasped it to my heart and exclaimed, 'O Truth, Truth, Truth!' I knew it had been brought forth by an angel's hand and the feeling that possessed me was one of supreme ecstasy. From that moment until the present I have never had a doubt of its divinity."

Before these brethren left her home she received the ordinance of baptism at the hands of Hyrum Smith.

Young Woman's Journal, June 1901, 256.

A TESTIMONY OF THE BOOK OF MORMON

EDWARD W. TULLIDGE

The following experience of Abigail Leonard, a venerable and respected lady, now in her eighty-second year of life, will also be of interest in this connection. She says:

"In 1829 Eleazer Miller came to my house, for the purpose of holding up to us the light of the gospel, and to teach us the necessity of a change of heart. He did not teach creedism, for he did not believe therein. That night was a sleepless one to me, for all night long I saw before me our Saviour nailed to the cross. I had not yet received remission of my sins, and, in consequence thereof, was much distressed. These feelings continued for several days, till one day, while walking alone in the street, I received the light of the spirit.

"Not long after this, several associated Methodists stopped at our house, and in the morning, while I was preparing breakfast, they were conversing upon the subject of church matters, and the best places for church organization. From the jottings of their conversation, which I caught from time to time, I saw that they cared more for the fleece than the flock. The Bible lay on the table near by, and as I passed I occasionally read a few words until I was impressed with the question: 'What is it that separates two Christians?'

"For two or three weeks this question was constantly on my mind, and I read the Bible and prayed that this question might be answered to me.

"One morning I took my Bible and went to the woods, when I fell upon my knees, and exclaimed: 'Now, Lord, I pray for the answer of this question, and I shall never rise till you reveal to me what it is that separates two Christians.' Immediately a vision passed before my eyes, and the different sects passed one after another by me, and a voice called to me, saying: 'These are built up for gain.' Then, beyond, I could see a great light, and a voice from above called out: 'I shall raise up a people, whom I shall delight to own and bless.' I was then fully satisfied, and returned to the house.

"Not long after this a meeting was held at our house, during which every one was invited to speak; and when opportunity presented, I arose and said: 'Today I come out from all names, sects and parties, and take upon myself the name of Christ, resolved to wear it to the end of my days.'

"For several days afterward, many people came from different denominations and endeavored to persuade me to join their respective churches. At length the associated Methodists sent their presiding elder to our house to preach, in the hope that I might be converted. While the elder was discoursing I beheld a vision in which I saw a great multitude of people in the distance, and over their heads hung a thick, dark cloud. Now and then one of the multitude would struggle, and rise up through the gloomy cloud; but the moment his head rose into the light above, the minister would strike him a blow, which would compel him to retire; and I said in my heart, 'They will never serve me so.'

"Not long after this, I heard of the 'Book of Mormon,' and when a few of us were gathered at a neighbor's we asked that we might have manifestations in proof of the truth and divine origin of this book, although we had not yet seen it. Our neighbor, a lady, was quite sick and in much distress. It was asked that she be healed, and immediately her pain ceased, and health was restored. Brother Bowen defiantly asked that he might be slain, and in an instant he was prostrated upon the floor. I requested that I might know of the truth of this book, by the gift and power of the Holy Ghost, and I immediately felt its presence. Then, when the Book of Mormon came, we were ready to receive it and its truths. The brethren gathered at our house to read it, and such days of rejoicing and thanksgiving I never saw before nor since. We were now ready for baptism, and on or about the 20th of August, 1831, were baptized."

Edward W. Tullidge, *The Women of Mormondom,* 160–63.

Courage

"I Suddenly Saw the Mob"

AMANDA SMITH

We sold our beautiful home in Kirtland for a song, and traveled all summer to Missouri—our teams poor, and with hardly enough to keep body and soul together. We arrived in Caldwell county, near Haun's Mill, nine wagons of us in company. Two days before we arrived we were taken prisoners by an armed mob that had demanded every bit of ammunition and every weapon we had. We surrendered all. They knew it, for they searched our wagons. A few miles more brought us to Haun's Mill. . . . My husband pitched his tent by a blacksmith's shop. Brother David Evans made a treaty with the mob that they would not molest us. He came just before the massacre and called the company together and they knelt in prayer. I sat in my tent. Looking up I suddenly saw the mob coming—the same that took away our weapons. They came like so many demons or wild Indians. Before I could get to the blacksmith's shop door to alarm the brethren, who were at prayers, the bullets were whistling amongst them.

I seized my two little girls and escaped across the mill-pond on a slab-walk. Another sister fled with me. Yet though we were women, with tender children, in flight for our lives, the demons poured volley after volley to kill us. A number of bullets entered my clothes, but I was not wounded. The sister, however, who was with me, cried out that she was hit. We had just reached the trunk of a fallen tree, over which I urged her, bidding her to shelter there where the bullets could not reach her, while I continued my flight to some bottom land.

When the firing had ceased I went back to the scene of the

massacre, for there were my husband and three sons, of whose fate I as yet knew nothing. As I returned I found the sister in a pool of blood where she had fainted, but she was only shot through the hand. Farther on was lying dead Brother McBride, an aged white-haired revolutionary soldier. His murderer had literally cut him to pieces with an old corn-cutter. . . . Passing on I came to a scene more terrible still to the mother and wife. Emerging from the blacksmith shop was my eldest son, bearing on his shoulders his little brother Alma. "Oh! my Alma is dead!" I cried, in anguish. "No, mother; I think Alma is not dead. But father and brother Sardius are killed!"

What an answer was this to appall me! My husband and son murdered; another little son seemingly mortally wounded; and perhaps before the dreadful night should pass the murderers would return and complete their work! But I could not weep then. The fountain of tears was dry; the heart overburdened with its calamity, and all the mother's sense absorbed in its anxiety for the precious boy which God alone could save by his miraculous aid.*

It was night now. There were none left from that terrible scene, throughout that long, dark night, but about half a dozen bereaved and lamenting women, and the children. Eighteen or nineteen, all grown men excepting my murdered boy and another about the same age, were dead or dying; several more of the men were wounded, hiding away, whose groans through the night too well disclosed their hiding places, while the rest of the men had fled, at the moment of the massacre, to save their lives. The women were sobbing, in the greatest anguish of spirit; the children were crying loudly with fear and grief at the loss of fathers and brothers. . . .

[After caring for Alma's wounds,] it was then I found vent to my feelings in tears, and resigned myself to the anguish of the

*For the story of the healing of Alma Smith's hip, see "I Was Directed as by a Voice," page 125.

hour. And all that night we, a few poor, stricken women, were thus left there with our dead and wounded. All through the night we heard the groans of the dying. Once in the dark we crawled over the heap of dead in the blacksmith's shop to try to help or soothe the sufferers' wants; once we followed the cries of a wounded brother who hid in some bushes from the murderers, and relieved him all we could. It has passed from my memory whether he was dead in the morning or whether he recovered.

Next morning brother Joseph Young came to the scene of the massacre. "What shall be done with the dead?" he inquired, in horror and deep trouble. There was not time to bury them, for the mob was coming on us. Neither were there left men to dig the graves. All the men excepting the two or three who had so narrowly escaped were dead or wounded. It had been no battle, but a massacre indeed. "Do anything, Brother Joseph," I said, "rather than leave their bodies to the fiends who have killed them." There was a deep dry well close by. Into this the bodies had to be hurried, eighteen or nineteen in number. No funeral services could be performed, nor could they be buried with customary decency. The lives of those who in terror performed the last duty to the dead were in jeopardy. Every moment we expected to be fired upon by the fiends who we supposed were lying in ambush waiting [for] the first opportunity to dispatch the remaining few who had escaped the slaughter of the preceding day. . . .

I cannot leave the tragic story without relating some incidents of those five weeks when I was a prisoner with my wounded boy in Missouri, near the scene of the massacre, unable to obey the order of extermination. All the Mormons in the neighborhood had fled out of the state, excepting a few families of the bereaved women and children who had gathered at the house of Brother David Evans, two miles from the scene of the massacre. To this house Alma had been carried after that fatal night. In our utter desolation, what could we women do but pray? Prayer was our only source of comfort; our Heavenly Father our only helper. None but he could save and deliver us.

One day a mobber came from the mill with the captain's fiat: "The captain says if you women don't stop your d———d prayer he will send down a posse and kill every d———d one of you!" And he might as well have done it, as to stop us poor women praying in that hour of our great calamity. Our prayers were hushed in terror. We dared not let our voices be heard in the house in supplication. I could pray in my bed or in silence, but I could not live thus long. This godless silence was more intolerable than had been that night of the massacre. I could bear it no longer. I pined to hear once more my own voice in petition to my Heavenly Father. I stole down to a corn field, and crawled into a stalk of corn. It was as the temple of the Lord to me at that moment. I prayed aloud and most fervently.

When I emerged from the corn a voice spoke to me. It was a voice as plain as I ever heard one. It was no silent, strong impression of the spirit, but a voice, repeating a verse of the Saint's hymn:

> That soul who on Jesus hath leaned for repose,
> I cannot, I will not, desert to its foes;
> That soul, though all hell should endeavor to shake,
> I'll never, no never, no never forsake!

From that moment I had no more fear. I felt that nothing could hurt me. Soon after this the mob sent us word that unless we were all out of the state by a certain day we should be killed. The day came, and at evening came fifty armed men to execute the sentence. I met them at the door. They demanded of me why I was not gone? I bade them enter and see their own work. They crowded into my room and I showed them my wounded boy. They came, party after party, until all had seen my excuse. Then they quarreled among themselves and came near fighting. At last they went away, all but two. These I thought were detailed to kill us. Then the two returned.

"Madam," said one, "have you any meat in the house?"

"No," was my reply.

"Could you dress a fat hog if one was laid at your door?"

"I think we could!" was my answer. And then they went and caught a fat hog from a herd which had belonged to a now exiled brother, killed it and dragged it to my door, and departed. These men, who had come to murder us, left on the threshold of our door a meat offering to atone for their repented intention.

Yet even when my son was well I could not leave the state, now accursed indeed to the Saints. The mob had taken my horses, as they had the drove of horses, and the beeves, and the hogs, and wagons, and the tents, of the murdered and exiled. So I went down into Daviess county (ten miles) to Captain Comstock, and demanded of him my horses. There was one of them in his yard. He said I could have it if I paid five dollars for its keep. I told him I had no money. I did not fear the captain of the mob, for I had the Lord's promise that nothing should hurt me. But his wife swore that the mobbers were fools for not killing the women and children as well as the men—declaring that we would breed up a pack ten times worse than the first.

I left without the captain's permission to take my horse, or giving pay for its keep; but I went into his yard and took it, and returned to our refuge unmolested. Learning that my other horse was at the mill, I next yoked up a pair of steers to a sled and went and demanded it also. Comstock was there at the mill. He gave me the horse, and then asked if I had any flour. "No; we have had none for weeks." He then gave me about fifty pounds of flour and some beef, and filled a can with honey. But the mill, and the slaughtered beeves which hung plentifully on its walls, and the stock of flour and honey, and abundant spoil besides, had all belonged to the murdered or exiled Saints. Yet was I thus providentially, by the very murderers and mobocrats themselves, helped out of the state of Missouri.

The Lord had kept his word. The soul who on Jesus had leaned for succor had not been forsaken even in this terrible hour of massacre, and in that infamous extermination of the "Mormons" from Missouri in the years 1838–39.

Andrew Jenson, *LDS Biographical Encyclopedia,* 2:793–97.

"APPLYING ICE WATER TO MY WOUNDS"

JOHN TAYLOR

I do not remember the time that I stayed at Carthage, but I think three or four days after the murder [of Joseph and Hyrum Smith], when Brother Marks with a carriage, Brother James Allred with a wagon, Dr. Ellis, and a number of others on horseback, came for the purpose of taking me to Nauvoo. I was very weak at the time, occasioned by the loss of blood and the great discharge of my wounds [incurred at Carthage], so when my wife asked me if I could talk I could barely whisper no. Quite a discussion arose as to the propriety of my removal, the physicians and people of Carthage protesting that it would be my death.

It was finally agreed, however, that I should go; but as it was thought that I could not stand riding in a wagon or carriage, they prepared a litter for me. I was carried downstairs and put upon it. A number of men assisted to carry me, some of whom had been engaged in the mob. As soon as I got downstairs, I felt much better and strengthened, so that I could talk; I suppose the effect of the fresh air.

I found that the tramping of those carrying me produced violent pain, and a sleigh was produced and attached to the end of Brother James Allred's wagon, a bed placed upon it, and I propped up on the bed. Mrs. Taylor rode with me, applying ice water to my wounds. As the sleigh was dragged over the prairie, which was quite tall, it moved very easily and gave me very little pain.

When I got within five or six miles of Nauvoo the brethren commenced to meet me from the city, and they increased in number as we drew nearer until there was a very large company of people of all ages and both sexes, principally, however, men.

For some time there had been almost incessant rain, so that in many low places on the prairie it was from one to three feet deep in water, and at such places the brethren whom we met took hold of the sleigh, lifted it, and carried it over the water; and when we arrived in the neighborhood of the city, where the roads were excessively muddy and bad, the brethren tore down the fences, and we passed through the fields.

Never shall I forget the differences of feeling that I experienced between the place that I had left and the one that I had now arrived at. I found myself very much better after my arrival at Nauvoo than I was when I started on my journey, although I had traveled eighteen miles.

Joseph Smith, *History of the Church,* 7:117–19.

"SHALL I EVER BE FREE AGAIN IN THIS LIFE?"

PARLEY P. PRATT

After months of captivity in a Missouri dungeon], and half way between hope and despair, I spent several days in fasting and prayer, during which one deep and all absorbing inquiry, one only thought, seemed to hold possession of my mind. . . . It was not how long shall I suffer; it was not when or by what means I should be delivered; but it was simply this: Shall I ever, at any time, however distant it may be, or whatever I may suffer first; shall I ever be free again in this life, and enjoy the society of my dear wife and children, and walk abroad at liberty, dwell in society and preach the gospel, as I have done in bygone years?

Let me be sure of this and I care not what I suffer. To circumnavigate the globe, to traverse the deserts of Arabia, to wander amid the wild scenes of the Rocky Mountains to accomplish so desirable an object, would seem like a mere trifle if I could only be sure at last. After some days of prayer and fasting, and seeking the Lord on the subject, I retired to my bed in my lonely chamber at an early hour, and while the other prisoners and the guard were chatting and beguiling the lonesome hours in the upper apartment of the prison, I lay in silence, seeking and expecting an answer to my prayer, when suddenly I seemed carried away in the spirit, and no longer sensible to outward objects with which I was surrounded. A heaven of peace and calmness pervaded my bosom; a personage from the world of spirits stood before me with a smile of compassion in every look, and pity mingled with the tenderest love and sympathy in every expression of the countenance. A soft hand seemed placed within my own, and a glowing cheek was laid in tenderness and warmth upon mine. A well-known voice saluted me, which I readily recognized as that of the wife of my youth, who had for near two years been sweetly sleeping where the wicked cease from troubling and the weary are at rest. I was made to realize that she was sent to commune with me, and answer my question.

Knowing this, I said to her in a most earnest and inquiring tone: Shall I ever be at liberty again in this life and enjoy the society of my family and the Saints, and preach the gospel as I have done? She answered definitely and unhesitatingly: "YES!" I then recollected that I had agreed to be satisfied with the knowledge of that one fact, but now I wanted more.

Said I: Can you tell me how, or by what means, or when I shall escape? She replied: "THAT THING IS NOT MADE KNOWN TO ME YET." I instantly felt that I had gone beyond my agreement and my faith in asking this last question, and that I must be contented at present with the answer to the first.

Her gentle spirit then saluted me and withdrew. I came to myself. The doleful noise of the guard . . . again grated on my ears, but Heaven and hope were in my soul.

Next morning I related the whole circumstance of my vision to my two fellow prisoners, who rejoiced exceedingly. This may seem to some like an idle dream, or a romance of the imagination; but to me it was, and always will be, a reality, both as it regards what I then experienced and the fulfillment afterwards.

Parley P. Pratt, *Autobiography of Parley P. Pratt,* 204–5.

"ARMED WITH WEAPONS YOU KNOW NOT OF"

ANDREW JENSON

The mob gathered to the number of one hundred, all fully armed. They took from Elder Patten his walking stick and a penknife, and went through with a mock trial; but would not let the defendants produce any witnesses; and without suffering them to say a word in defense, the judge pronounced them guilty of the charge preferred. Brother Patten, being filled with the Holy Ghost, arose to his feet, and by the power of God bound them fast to their seats while he addressed them. He rebuked them sharply for their wicked and unjust proceedings. Brother Parrish afterwards said, "My hair stood up straight on my head, for I expected to be killed." When Patten closed, the Judge addressed him, saying, "You must be armed with concealed weapons, or you would not treat an armed court as you have this." Patten replied, "I am armed with weapons you know not of, and my weapons are the Holy Priesthood and the power of God. God is my friend, and he permits you to exercise all the power you have, and he bestows on me all the power I have."

Andrew Jenson, *LDS Biographical Encyclopedia,* 1:78.

MOB OR NO MOB

LUCY MACK SMITH

We proceeded on our journey [from Palmyra to Kirtland, in 1831], and arrived at Buffalo on the fifth day after leaving Waterloo.

Here we found the brethren from Colesville, who informed us that they had been detained one week at this place, waiting for the navigation to open. Also, that Mr. Smith [Joseph Smith, Sr.] and Hyrum had gone through to Kirtland by land, in order to be there by the first of April.

I asked them if they had confessed to the people that they were "Mormons." "No, indeed," they replied, "neither must you mention a word about your religion, for if you do you will never be able to get a house, or a boat either."

I told them I should tell the people precisely who I was; "and," continued I, "if you are ashamed of Christ, you must not expect to be prospered; and I shall wonder if we do not get to Kirtland before you."

While we were talking with the Colesville brethren, another boat landed, having onboard about thirty brethren, among whom was Thomas B. Marsh, who immediately joined us, and, like the Colesville brethren, he was decidedly opposed to our attending to prayer, or making known that we were professors of religion. He said that if our company persisted in singing and praying, as we had hitherto done, we should be mobbed before the next morning.

"Mob it is, then," said I, "we shall attend to prayer before sunset, mob or no mob."

Lucy Mack Smith, *History of Joseph Smith by His Mother,* 198–202.

"Don't Come Back until You Come in the Right Spirit"

John A. Widtsoe

About 1896, Moses Thatcher, an apostle of the Church, was suspended from service in the Quorum of the Twelve Apostles. Brother Thatcher, a man of unusual gifts and most charming personality, was very popular in his home town of Logan, as throughout the Church. His suspension caused widespread discussion, and many of his intimate Logan friends felt that he had been treated unjustly, and took his side against the action of the authorities of the Church. The temporary upheaval was tempestuous. Men's feelings ran high. While the excitement was at its height, two of the ward elders called at the Widtsoe home as ward teachers. The widow's two sons were home, and the whole family assembled to be instructed by the visiting teachers. Soon the visitors began to comment on the "Thatcher episode," as it was called, and explained how unjustly Brother Thatcher had been treated. [My mother] answered not a word, but there was a gathering storm in her stern eyes and high-held head.

After some minutes of listening to the visitors find fault with the Quorum of the Apostles with respect to Brother Thatcher, she slowly rose from her chair and as slowly walked to the entrance door of the house, which she threw wide open. With eyes now blazing she turned to the two brethren and said: "There is the door. I want you to leave this house instantly. I will not permit anyone in this house to revile the authorities of the Church, men laboring under divine inspiration. Nor do I wish such things spoken before my sons whom I have taught to love the leaders of the Church. And don't come back until you come in the right spirit to teach us the gospel. Here is the door. Now, go!" The visitors hurried out shamefacedly, for the widow had chastised them thoroughly. In defense of the gospel, Sister Widtsoe knew no fear.

John A. Widtsoe, *In the Gospel Net,* 97–98.

"I LICKED HIM GOOD AND PLENTY"

CHARLES W. NIBLEY

The first time I ever remember seeing Joseph F. Smith was in the then little village of Wellsville, in the year 1867. He was twenty-eight years of age, and had recently been chosen [as] one of the twelve apostles. President Brigham Young and company were making a tour of the northern settlements, and the new apostle, Joseph F. Smith, was among the number. I heard him preach in the old meetinghouse at Wellsville, and I remarked at the time what a fine specimen of young manhood he was—strong, powerful, with a beautiful voice, so full of sympathy and affection, so appealing in its tone, that he impressed me, although I was a youth of but eighteen. He was a handsome man.

At that time I was clerking in a little store owned by Father Ira Ames, one of the old Kirtland veterans of the Church. Apostle

George A. Smith was one of that company and he was entertained at Brother Ames' home, where I also lived. I recall that at the dinner table, Father Ames asked George A. who of the Smiths this young man Joseph F. was.

George A. replied that he was Hyrum's son; his mother, Mary Fielding Smith.

Brother Ames remarked that he looked like a likely young fellow, and George A. replied in about these words:

"Yes, I think he will be all right. His father and mother left him when he was a child, and we have been looking after him to try and help him along. We first sent him to school, but it was not long before he licked the schoolmaster, and could not go to school. Then we sent him on a mission, and he did pretty well at that. I think he will make good as an apostle."

Some years ago I related this incident to President Smith, and he told me that the reason he had trouble with the schoolmaster was that the schoolmaster had a leather strap with which he used to chastise the children. He was a rather hard-hearted schoolmaster, one of the olden type that believed in inflicting bodily punishment.

President Smith said: "My little sister was called up (Aunt Martha, now living in Provo) to be punished. I saw the school master bring out the leather strap, and he told the child to hold out her hand. I could not stand for that. I just spoke up loudly and said, 'Don't whip her with that,' and at that he came at me and was going to whip me, and instead of him whipping me, I licked him good and plenty."

At the time of this incident, Joseph F. (for, by that name he was affectionately called) was about fifteen years of age. But he was a strong, powerful youth, and his big heart could not tolerate such punishment, especially if it bordered on the cruel, to be inflicted upon a little child.

Improvement Era, January 1919, 191–92.

"You Have One More Chance!"

LLEWELYN R. McKAY

Father [David O. McKay] has always had the courage to stand up for his convictions. Even when a boy, his determination to hold his ground when he was convinced he was right was always evident. An incident is told by Thomas E. McKay that happened during a Fourth of July baseball game between Huntsville and Eden. Keen rivalry had always existed between these two teams, and on this holiday the grandstand was packed, and feelings were tense. During the seventh inning one of the Huntsville players was forced to leave the game because of an injury, and David O. was drafted to take his place although he was much younger than the players on the regular team. It was an exciting moment for him because the score was tied and had been for several innings.

David O. was a good batter and received a cheer when his turn came around. As the playing proceeded, the umpire called the second strike. The pitcher on the Eden team, however, claimed that it was the third strike. He was a large, burly fellow with a quick temper, and he was known to be a bully and quite a pugilist. He picked up a baseball bat, and coming up to David O. he waved the bat menacingly and demanded, "Get out of there, kid, or I will crack this on your head!"

Immediately a hush came over the spectators who anxiously awaited the outcome. Thomas E. claims that he was shaking in his boots to see his brother in such a predicament. However, his older brother was up to the situation. In a cool tone he said, "The umpire called only two strikes; so go back to your pitcher's box and try to get me out; you have one more chance!"

By this time John Allen, one of the best players, came strolling over with a bat in his hand as though he were waiting for his turn at the plate. The pitcher looked at the determination on David O.'s face and at John Allen's warning glance and decided to continue the game. His next throw was a swift straight ball. David O. connected and made a two-base hit. The next batter hit a single, and father was able to make home plate safely. This brought a thunderous applause from the spectators because this was the deciding run of the game. Although father's friends congratulated him on making the run, the true congratulations were in their hearts because he stood up to a bigger man in spite of all odds and because he refused to be bullied when he knew that he was right.

Llewelyn R. McKay, comp., *Home Memories of President David O. McKay,* 162–63.

EXAMPLE

"Some Remarkable Influence"

CHARLES DICKENS

I go aboard my emigrant ship. . . . But nobody is in an ill-temper, nobody is the worse for drink, nobody swears an oath or uses a coarse word, nobody appears depressed, nobody is weeping, and down upon the deck in every corner where it is possible to find a few square feet to kneel, crouch, or lie in, people, in every unsuitable attitude for writing, are writing letters.

Now, I have been in emigrant ships before this day in June. And these people are so strikingly different from all other people in like circumstances whom I have never seen, that I wonder aloud, "What would a stranger suppose these emigrants to be!"

The vigilant bright face of the weather-browned captain of the *Amazon* is at my shoulder, and he says, "What, indeed! The most of these came aboard yesterday evening. They came from various parts of England in small parties that had never seen one another before. Yet they had not been a couple of hours onboard, when they established their own police, made their own regulations, and set their own watches at all the hatchways. Before nine o'clock, the ship was as orderly and as quiet as a man-of-war! . . .

"A stranger would be puzzled to guess the right name of these people, Mr. Uncommercial," says the captain.

"Indeed he would."

"If you hadn't known, could you ever have supposed—?"

"How could I! I should have said they were in their degree the pick and flower of England."

"So should I," says the captain.

"How many are they?"

"Eight hundred in round numbers." . . . Eight hundred Mormons.

I afterwards learned that a dispatch was sent home by the captain before he struck out into the wide Atlantic, highly extolling the behavior of these emigrants, and the perfect order and propriety of all their social arrangements. . . . But I went onboard their ship to bear testimony against them if they deserved it, as I fully believed they would; to my great astonishment they did not deserve it; and my predispositions and tendencies must not affect me as an honest witness. I went over the *Amazon*'s side, feeling it impossible to deny that, so far, some remarkable influence had produced a remarkable result, which better known influences have often missed.

Charles Dickens, *The Uncommercial Traveller,* 200–11.

A STUDENT'S DETERMINATION

LLEWELYN R. McKAY

When father [David O. McKay] was president of Weber Academy, a student came into his office and said, "President McKay, it looks as if I shall have to withdraw from school for awhile, for I am unable to make ends meet financially. I shall return again later, however, because I am determined to get an education. For the time being, I shall have to find full-time work."

That lad was Aaron W. Tracy, and father learned that he was an orphaned boy who lived alone in a small back room. He walked many miles to school and kept himself in food, clothes, and tuition costs by accepting all available, odd jobs.

"My boy," father said, "you are absolutely right in wanting an education, and if you are determined to continue until graduation, let us see if we can't work something out. Now my wife needs someone to help out around the house, and we have a spare room upstairs in our home where you can sleep and thus save room rent. Why don't you move in with us?"

Aaron seemed grateful for the opportunity, and the next day he became one of the family.

"I have never had anyone who helped me out so much," mother has often stated. "On Saturdays, Aaron turned the washing machine for me, and I usually had seven to ten fillings. I often asked Aaron, 'Aren't you getting tired?' and he would always answer in the negative, even though I knew he was quite weary after doing the outside chores."

In the summer Aaron worked on the farm from early until late. Father said of him, "I like that boy; he always does a job right! He is determined to make good; you mark my word, he will reach his goal with such determination."

And he did. The inspiration he received from sitting in father's classes gave him the desire to become a teacher also, so after he was graduated from Weber, he continued on with his education.

I was a member of the student body at Weber Normal College when he became president of that institution, and his leadership and inspiration gained the respect and love of all students.

All of his students are thankful that this young orphan boy had enough determination to continue on to his objective against many odds. We shall always remember him as one of our great teachers!

Llewelyn R. McKay, comp., *Home Memories of President David O. McKay,* 136.

SEVEN LITTLE BOYS

SPENCER W. KIMBALL

Long years ago when I was in the presidency of the St. Joseph Stake in Arizona, one Sabbath day I filled an assignment in the Eden Ward. The building was a small one, and most of the people were close to us as we sat on the raised platform about a foot and a half above the floor of the building itself.

As the meeting proceeded, my eye was attracted to seven little boys on the front seat of the chapel. I was delighted that they were in this ward conference. I made a mental note, then shifted my interest to other things. Soon my attention was focused on the seven little boys again.

It seemed strange to me that each of the seven raised his right leg and put it over the left knee, and then in a moment all would change at the same time and put the left leg over the right knee. I thought it was unusual, but I just ignored it.

In a moment or two, all in unison brushed their hair with their right hands; then all seven boys leaned lightly on their wrists and supported their faces by their hands, and then simultaneously they went back to the crossing of their legs again.

It all seemed so strange, and I wondered about it as I was trying to think of what I was going to say in the meeting. And then suddenly it came to me like a bolt of lightning: These boys were mimicking me!

That day I learned the lesson of my life—that we who are in positions of authority must be careful indeed, because others watch us and find in us their examples.

Ensign, November 1974, 79.

Faith

"Let Her Have All That There Is"

JOHN HENRY EVANS

One day a woman came to see the President [Charles C. Rich]. The wife of one of the Battalion boys, she told him with copious tears that she had nothing for her children to eat. This was before any government money had come into the community through the soldiers. I shall let Mrs. Rich tell the story:

My husband turned to me and said, "Let this Sister have some flour, Sarah." This was a puzzle to me, knowing that we did not have twenty pounds of flour in the house, and none in the place to buy, even if we had the money to buy it with. So I said, "We haven't twenty pounds of flour in the house and none that can be bought." He looked at me and smiled. "Sarah," he said, "let her have all that there is in the house, and trust in the Lord to provide for us."

I did as he bade me, but wondered how our own children were to eat. When the sister was gone, Mr. Rich said, "I know, Sarah, that the Lord will open the way for us to live. So don't feel uneasy." I too began to ask the Lord to open the way for us.

Along toward the evening we saw some covered wagons coming down the hill toward the house. They stopped in front, and the men came in. One of them proved to be Brother Sidwell, who had been with Brother Benson and who had called on us in the East. Brother Sidwell said he wanted to stop with us overnight, and my husband told him he could. He then turned to Mr. Rich and said to him, "The Spirit tells me you are out of money, and tells me to help you." And he handed Mr. Rich fifty dollars. Mr. Rich handed the money to me, saying, "Now you see the Lord has opened the way for us to get flour." He was overcome with gratitude.

With understanding our situation, Brother Sidwell informed us that "we have enough bread in our wagons for tonight and the morning." He told us also they had a wagon load of flour a little way back, which would reach here either tonight or in the morning, so that we might be supplied with breadstuff.

On this we burst into tears, to think the Lord had so blessed us for our kindness to the poor sister and her children.

When the wagon load of flour arrived, Mr. Rich not only laid in a supply for ourselves, but got a lot to give out to others that were sick and poor in the place. The man with the flour also let us have some groceries. He was a wealthy bachelor on his way to Winter Quarters. When, later on, we went to Winter Quarters to begin our journey to the West, he assisted us and others to start to the mountains.

John Henry Evans, *Charles Coulson Rich: Pioneer Builder of the West,* 125–26.

"He Felt Repaid in Blessings"

AUTHOR UNKNOWN

Brother L——— arrived in Nauvoo from England, his native country, in March, 1844. He was an excellent mechanic, had held good situations and been in good circumstances in the "old country," and his skill as a workman was such as to command ready employment and high wages in any of the large cities of America, had such been his object.

But he had embraced the gospel and received a testimony of its truth, and afterwards the spirit of gathering with the Saints, which enabled him to brook the taunts and ridicule heaped upon him by friends and relatives for his unpopular faith, and resist the pleading of aged parents, who were loath to part with him.

His faith and zeal were such that he had left friends and property and all that he had formerly held dear, and come to America that he might be with the chosen people of God and assist in building up Zion.

He was ambitious to labor upon the temple, and applied for work immediately upon his arrival in Nauvoo. When informed that there was plenty of work but nothing to pay with, he replied that pay was no consideration.

He took hold with a determination, and worked with all the energy with which the young, strong and enthusiastic nature was capable from that time until the work upon the temple ceased, upwards of two years, and during that time only received in cash for his services the small amount of fifty cents.

Many a time he felt the pangs of hunger, and went to his work fasting rather than join with his family in eating the last ration of food in their possession, but the Lord sustained him by His Spirit, gave him joy in his labors and provided a way for more food to be obtained to sustain the lives of himself and his family.

He and his young wife had a habit of appealing to the Almighty in prayer when in an extremity, and they invariably found comfort in so doing, and generally had their prayers answered.

Upon one occasion, their infant child was dangerously sick, and they felt the want of twenty-five cents to procure some medicine with. Where to get it they did not know, and so, as usual, they prayed to the Lord to open their way to obtain it. They felt an assurance on arising from their knees that their prayer would be answered, but they knew not how. Soon afterwards the husband happened to feel some hard substance in the waistband of his pants, and called his wife's attention to it, wondering what it could be. The pants were almost new. They had been made to order for him only a short time before. There was no hole in the band, and it seemed that, whatever it was, it must have been inserted between the pieces of cloth when the pants were being made, and yet he thought it strange that he had not discovered it before.

To solve the mystery, a few stitches were cut, and the waistband opened, when, lo! there were two new ten cent pieces and one five cent piece—just the amount of money they required to buy medicine with.

Lest the money might have been lost by the tailor who made the pants, a very poor man who lived neighbor to them, he took it to him and asked him, but that impecunious individual said he knew it could not be his, for he had never had a cent of money in his possession for months.

They accepted it as a gift from the Lord, bought the medicine their child needed and he was soon well.

When the work on the temple was nearing completion, the food supply for the family became entirely exhausted, and there seemed no prospect of obtaining any more without quitting the work on the temple and going elsewhere for employment. That, of course, Brother L——— was averse to doing, and in this, as in other cases of extremity, he and his wife retired to their bedroom to lay the matter before the Lord. They had scarcely finished their prayer when a knock was heard at the door. On opening it, they found a man there who said he desired a particular job of work done, which he did not feel like entrusting to anyone else but Brother L———. However, he was in no particular hurry for it, it need not be done till the work on the temple was completed, but he wanted to arrange and pay for it then, as he was going on a foreign mission. "But," said he, "I have nothing to pay you for it but wheat; can you use that?"

It was the very thing the family stood most in need of; it was gratefully accepted and regarded as a direct answer to their prayer, and within a short time the wheat was ground and a good supply of flour returned from it. . . .

With such manifestations as these of God's goodness, he was encouraged to continue in his labors upon the temple of God, and when it was so far completed that the holy ordinances for which it was designed could be performed in it, he felt repaid in the blessings which he therein received for all his efforts towards its construction.

Fragments of Experience, 83–85, 87.

"COULD IT NOT BE A TEMPTATION?"

W. W. CLUFF

In the year 1866, Elders Joseph F. Smith, Franklin W. Young and myself had been traveling as missionaries on the island of Hawaii laboring about ten months in the Helo and Koohala Conferences, on the north and east side of the island. A conference of all the elders laboring in that mission was called to meet on the island of Lanai. It required five dollars each to pay our fare from our field of labor to the place of conference. In starting from Helo and traveling by land to Upolu, a distance of about one hundred and fifty miles, we would visit about ten branches of the Church. At each of these we held meetings and reminded the Saints that we were on our way to conference, and that we required so much money to pay our passage across the channel to Lanai. Money among the natives was scarce and difficult to get. When we left Waipio, the last and largest branch on the way, we had only received seventy-five cents in money and five or six goat-skins, worth twelve and a half cents each. While it looked very discouraging, we had faith that by doing all we could the Lord would open the way for us to attend the conference with our brethren.

On leaving Wimea, fifty miles from Upolu, where we would embark on the vessel, the road forked, one going north and one going west. About three miles west on the road, a family of Saints lived; with this family we had left some of our books and clothes, and to go that way would take us three miles out of our way. I being considered the best walker, it was decided that I should go that way and the brethren continue on the direct route.

I had not proceeded more than a mile when I found a man's coat lying in the middle of the road; picking it up I found a money purse in one of the pockets, containing some papers and three five dollar gold pieces. Being just the amount we needed and finding them as I did, the first impression was that it was a Godsend. There being no one in sight, I started across the country to intersect the brethren, thinking I would bury the coat with all it contained except the money, in a deep ravine, and cover it over with lava rock. I had not gone fifty yards when another thought suggested itself, and I asked myself the questions:

Do you really think the finding of the coat was a Godsend? Could it not be a temptation? It certainly belonged to some person to whom the papers might be valuable. With these thoughts and reflections, and that the Lord would not bestow a blessing at the expense of another of His children, my conscience smote me, and, still seeing no one in sight, I turned back to the road and proceeded to the house where our things were left. Only the woman was at home; to her I related the finding of the coat, and, taking out the pocket book, showed her the money and papers which proved to be of great value to the owner, a white man who lived about fifty miles east, and of whose hospitality we had a number of times partaken. As a guard against the woman keeping the money, I let her see me take a memorandum of the money and papers, and also told her I would write to the owner. On overtaking the brethren, I told them about finding the coat and the fifteen dollars we needed to pay our passage, and asked them if they did not think it a Godsend; they replied that it really looked like it.

"I thought so, too, at first, but on second thought I feared it might be a temptation, in our straitened circumstances," I replied.

"True, it is not the way the Lord would come to our aid," they said.

On explaining what I did with the coat and contents, they expressed great pleasure and satisfaction, approving heartily my actions. That night we stopped with a white man by the name of Lincoln who had married a native woman who was a member of our Church. We had stopped there a number of times before. Mr. Lincoln had always made us welcome.

The next morning we bade the family good-bye and started on our journey, our host following us out of the house, saying:

"If you are going to your conference, on Lanai, you will want money to pay your fares, here is five dollars for each of you, if you will accept it." We did accept it with heartfelt thanks both to Mr. Lincoln and to our Father in Heaven, believing He had put it into his heart to give us just the amount of money we required. In proceeding on our way, we all felt and acknowledged that this really was a Godsend, as Mr. Lincoln and his family had never before given us money, and during our stay this time not a word had been said about our needing money to pay our passage to Lanai. We recognized that the Lord had really heard and answered our prayers.

Edwin F. Parry, *Sketches of Missionary Life,* 122–28.

"HE FASTED, AND HE PRAYED"

MATTHEW COWLEY

Two boys in New Zealand graduated from a high school down there. The principal came to me and he said, "President Cowley, these two boys should go on in their education. Use your influence with them." Then he told me this story about one of them.

"This young man came to me one day. He was living in the dormitory. He was what they called the monitor. It wasn't a native high school, but he was a native. He came to me one day, and he said, 'Mr. Hogan, I want to go home for three days.' I said, 'Why, you can't go home, you have a job here. What do you want to go home for?' He said, 'Well, I am preparing to take my matric,' [as they call it down there, matriculation examination for entrance into a university]. He said, 'I want to go home for three days and fast and pray.'

"I was astonished. I excused myself and went to my office and called up one of your members, one of our native members, and I said, 'Listen to me, do you people have in your Church something you call fasting?' He said, 'Yes.' I said, 'What do you do it for?' 'When we want a blessing, we fast and pray.' I said, 'Well, I have read about it in the Bible, but I have never heard of anybody doing it.' I went back to the young man and said, 'You go home for three days.' He went home, and he fasted, and he prayed, and he was the top man in passing his matric examination."

So he and his cousin went on to the university—one to study dentistry and one to study medicine. They came home after a few weeks. I was surprised to see them at one of our conferences because the university was on a different island. I said, "What are you doing here?" They said, "We are through." I said, "What do you mean?" They said, "We don't get any encouragement from our people. They tell us we are only Maoris. We can't learn anything; they tell us to go out and cut scrub and make some money; so we are not going back."

There immediately flashed in my mind that boy's fasting and praying for three days so that he could matriculate for a university. I knew they were not to leave, so I said, "Well, if that's the way you feel about it, I am going to call you on a mission and advance you in the priesthood." After the meeting I went out and put them into a room and ordained each an elder. I set them apart as missionaries in the New Zealand mission. They said, "Where are we going on this mission?" I said, "You are going down to the university. When you are not studying medicine and dentistry, you are to preach the gospel every opportunity you get." They went back. They certainly preached the gospel, and they made a good job out of it because the first year I was invited by the dean of the medical school to come down there and talk to the graduates. . . . Well, one of them is a doctor now, and the other one is a dentist. Come to think about it, I have never released them from those missions yet.

Matthew Cowley, *Matthew Cowley Speaks,* 280–81.

"YOU TRUSTED IN MONEY; BUT I TRUSTED IN GOD"

PHILO DIBBLE

When Joseph [Smith] first came to Nauvoo, then called Commerce, a Mr. White, living there, proffered to sell him his farm for twenty-five hundred dollars, five hundred dollars of the amount to be paid down, and the balance one year from that time. Joseph and the brethren were talking about this offer when some of them said: "We can't buy it, for we lack the money." Joseph took out his purse, and, emptying out its contents, offered a half dollar to one of the brethren, which he declined accepting, but Joseph urged him to take it, and then gave each of the other brethren a similar amount, which left him without any. Addressing the brethren, he then said: "Now you all have money, and I have none; but the time will come when I will have money and you will have none!" He then said to Bishop Knight: "You go back and buy the farm!"

Brother Knight went to White, but learned from him that he had raised the price one hundred dollars, and returned to Joseph without closing the bargain. Joseph again sent him with positive orders to purchase, but Brother Knight, finding that White had raised the price still another hundred dollars, again returned without purchasing. For the third time then Joseph commanded him to go and buy the farm, and charged him not to come back till he had done so.

When Bishop Knight got back to White, he had raised another hundred on the place, making the whole amount twenty-eight hundred dollars. However, the bargain was closed and the obligations drawn up, but how the money was going to be raised neither Brother Knight nor the other brethren could see. The next morning Joseph and several of the brethren went down to Mr. White's to sign the agreement and make the first payment on the land. A table was brought out with the papers upon it, and Joseph signed them, moved back from the table and sat with his head down, as if in thought for a moment. Just then a man drove up in a carriage and asked if Mr. Smith was there. Joseph hearing it, got up and went to the door. The man said, "Good morning, Mr. Smith; I am on a speculation today. I want to buy some land, and thought I would come and see you." Joseph then pointed around where his land lay, but the man said: "I can't go with you today to see the land. Do you want any money this morning?"

Joseph replied that he would like some, and when the stranger asked "How much?" he told him "Five hundred dollars."

The man walked into the house with Joseph, emptied a small sack of gold on the table, and counted out that amount. He then handed to Joseph another hundred dollars, saying: "Mr. Smith, I make you a present of this!"

After this transpired, Joseph laughed at the brethren and said: "You trusted in money; but I trusted in God. Now I have money and you have none."

Early Scenes in Church History, 95–96.

"I WILL PAY HIS EXPENSES"

HEBER J. GRANT

It has been said that the tenderest part of the human anatomy, of the male variety of the species, is the pocket; and I think there is little doubt of it, from my experience with mankind. The laws of the gospel of Jesus Christ are most exacting on the pockets of men, and our Church expects more from its members in this regard than any church upon the face of the earth.

I remember reading of an incident where a man away up in northern Scandinavia, in that cold, hard country, where it is difficult to make a living, heard an elder proclaim the gospel of Jesus Christ again restored to the earth—faith in the Lord Jesus Christ, repentance, baptism by immersion for the remission of sins, and the laying on of hands for the gift of the Holy Ghost, and that Joseph Smith was a prophet of the true and the living God. He received the witness in his heart to the truthfulness of this message, and he went down into the waters of baptism. He soon received the spirit of gathering, and he gathered from Scandinavia to Utah. After he had been here a little while the bishop called on him and said: "You do not pay any tithing."

"Why, I never heard about tithing."

And the bishop taught him the law of tithing, that one-tenth of all that he made belonged to the Church for the spread of the gospel and the building up of the work at home and abroad.

This man was shocked at the outrageous "tax" of the Church, as he termed it, but he said: "The gospel is true, and I guess I ought to live all the laws." After a great struggle he finally decided to comply with this law, and he honestly paid his tithing.

The bishop later came to him and said: "You do not pay any fast-day donation to take care of the poor," and the man said, "For the love of heaven, isn't ten percent of all you make enough to take care of the poor?"

"No," the bishop said; "but we do not ask you to give a dollar. All we ask is that you fast, that you fail to partake of food for two meals once a month—you are not asked for any money, but simply to give to us the equivalent of what you save. You can consult your doctor, and you will find that this is beneficial to your health to fast for a couple of meals once a month."

Well, he said, he did not know about that, but he finally concluded he ought to do his share for the poor, so he fasted, and in fasting he partook of the Spirit of the Lord that is given to us when we fast and pray to God; and he rejoiced in paying his fast-day donation.

Pretty soon the bishop came to him and said, "We need a new ward meetinghouse."

"Well, let the Church build it—the tithing ought to be enough for that."

The bishop said, "No, the Church will not build it, but the Church will give one dollar for each two dollars that we give. You know we need a new meetinghouse, in which to worship the Lord."

He kicked and kicked hard, to use a slang phrase, but finally concluded that they needed a new meetinghouse, and he wanted to do his share.

Next the bishop came around and said, "We need a Church academy, so our children may not only be educated in the things of the world—the sciences, arts, literature and so on—but in the things of God;" and he finally persuaded him to donate for an academy.

Then he came and said to this man: "We need a stake meetinghouse." He complained again, but finally donated for a stake house.

Then the bishop came around and said: "Here, brother, we are making an extra effort to complete the Salt Lake Temple, and we want a very large and splendid donation from you. You have been very prosperous; the Lord has blessed you since you came to this land."

He hemmed and hawed and complained, but he finally gave the donation, because in the meantime he had learned this glorious principle of vicarious labor for the dead. Some people ridicule that principle; they say it is absurd, it is ridiculous that we, the living, can do work for the dead. People may ridicule this principle, but the very foundation of all Christianity is based upon the vicarious labor and the death of our Lord Jesus Christ for us. So this man finally contributed for the temple. The academy was soon completed, and his boy attended and in due time graduated with honor.

Then the bishop called on him and said: "That boy of yours has graduated; he has made a fine record, and we would like him to go on a mission to his father's native land. It will cost you about $25 a month to send him and take care of him."

To this the man replied: "Bishop, that is the straw that breaks the camel's back. I paid tithing; I paid fast-day donations; I paid for a ward house; I paid for a stake house; I paid for an academy; I paid for the completion of the temple; but if the Church wants my boy, whom I had expected to bring me in at least seventy-five dollars a month now that he has graduated, they will have to pay his expenses or he will not go on a mission."

"Well," the bishop said, "that will be all right, he will not go, because the Church is not paying the expenses. All they will do for him is to bring him home free of charge when his mission is completed. They will do that, they will bring him home again. That will be the limit."

"Well, then," he said, "he will never go."

The bishop said, "All right. Let us dismiss the subject and talk on something else." They talked on for about an hour. The bishop went around and around, and finally he came to the native land of this man, the country from which he had come, as well as his relatives and friends. Then he said: "By the way, whom do you love more than anybody else on the earth, except your own flesh and blood, your own family?"

"Why," he said, "Bishop, more than any other person that draws the breath of life I love the man who came to me, away up in the midnight-sun country of Scandinavia, and brought to me the gospel of the Lord Jesus Christ, the man who came there with the Spirit of the living God, who touched my heart, and melted my very soul, and implanted in my being a knowledge that God lives, that Jesus is the Christ, that Joseph Smith was a prophet of the true and the living God; I love him beyond my power to tell."

The bishop then said, "Wouldn't you like somebody to love that boy of yours just as you love that elder?"

"Bishop," he said, "you have conquered me fair and square. The boy can go. I will pay his expenses."

Conference Report, October 1919, 24.

A THOUSAND DOLLARS IN GOLD DUST

ORSON F. WHITNEY

H[eber C. Kimball] often took his children into his confidence, giving them practical lessons in the virtues he desired them to cultivate. His son David H. relates the following:

"One day President Young made a call upon father for $1,000, for some public purpose, and not having the ready cash, he was at a loss to know where to get it. At his suggestion we went down in the garden and bowed ourselves in prayer, father calling upon the Lord to direct him in the matter. We then arose and started down the street, and he remarked that the Lord would answer our prayer and direct him aright. When even with Godbe's corner, William Godbe came out of his store and told him that, in looking through his safe, he had come across about $1,000 in gold-dust, belonging to him, which his son Heber P. had left there for him some time before, though father until then knew nothing about it."

Orson F. Whitney, *The Life of Heber C. Kimball,* 428.

"THE BREAKING OF DAY HAS FOUND ME ON MY KNEES"

SPENCER W. KIMBALL

My beloved brethren, this is the great day of my life. [President Kimball had just been sustained to the Council of the Twelve.] I have seen hands raised many times in my life, but never have they meant quite so much as they meant today when you raised your hands to sustain and support me.

I feel extremely humble in this calling that has come to me. Many people have asked me if I was surprised when it came. That, of course, is a very weak word for this experience. I was completely bewildered and shocked. I did have a premonition that this call was coming, but very brief, however. On the eighth of July, when President J. Reuben Clark called me, I was electrified with a strong presentiment that something of this kind was going to happen. As I came home at noon, my boy was answering the telephone and he said, "Daddy, Salt Lake City is calling."

I had had many calls from Salt Lake City. They hadn't ever worried me, like this one did. I knew that I had no unfinished business in Salt Lake City, and the thought came over me quickly, "You're going to be called to an important position." Then I hurriedly swept the thought from my mind, because it seemed so unworthy and so presumptuous. I had convinced myself that such a thing was impossible by the time I heard President Clark's voice a thousand miles away saying: "Spencer, this is Brother Clark speaking. The brethren have just called you to fill one of the vacancies in the Quorum of the Twelve Apostles."

Like a bolt of lightning it came. I did a great deal of thinking in the brief moments that I was on the wire. There were quite a number of things said about disposing of my business, moving to headquarters, and other things to be expected of me. I couldn't repeat them all; my mind seemed to be traveling many paths all at once—I was dazed, almost numb with the shock; a picture of my life spread out before me. It seemed that I could see all of the people before me whom I had injured, or who had fancied that I had injured them, or to whom I had given offense, and all the small, petty things of my life. I sensed immediately my inability and limitations and I cried back, "Not me, Brother Clark! You can't mean that!" I was virtually speechless. My heart pounded fiercely.

I recall two or three years ago, when Brother Harold B. Lee was giving his maiden address as an apostle of the Lord Jesus Christ from this stand, he told us of his experience through the night after he had been notified of his call. I think I now know something about the experience he had. I have been going through it for twelve weeks. I believe the brethren were very kind to me in announcing my appointment when they did so that I might make the necessary adjustments in my business affairs, but perhaps they were more inspired to give me the time I needed for a long period of purification, for in those long days and weeks I did a great deal of thinking and praying and fasting and praying. Conflicting thoughts surged through my mind—voices seeming to say, "You can't do the work. You are not worthy. You have not the ability"—and always finally came the triumphant thought: "You must do the work assigned—you must make yourself able, worthy, and qualified." And the battle raged on.

I remember reading that Jacob wrestled all night, "until the breaking of the day," for a blessing; and I want to tell you that for eighty-five nights I have gone through that experience, wrestling for a blessing. Eighty-five times, the breaking of the day has found me on my knees praying to the Lord to help me and strengthen me and make me equal to this great responsibility that has come to me. I have not sought positions nor have I been ambitious. Promotions have continued to come faster than I felt I was prepared for them.

I remember when I was called to be a counselor in the stake presidency. I was in my twenties. President Grant came down to help bury my father, who was the former stake president, and to reorganize the stake. I was the stake clerk. I recall that after I had been chosen, some of my relatives came to President Grant, unbeknownst to me, and said, "President Grant, it's a mistake to call a young man like that to a position of responsibility and make an old man of him and tie him down." Finally, after some discussion, President Grant said very calmly, but firmly, "Well, Spencer has been called to this work, and he can do as he pleases about it," and, of course, when the call came, I accepted it gladly, and I have received great blessings therefrom.

Conference Report, October 1943, 15–16.

"THIS AMOUNT WILL DOUBLE IN YOUR HANDS"

WILLIAM C. RYDALCH

For some time previous to the spring of 1860, my wife and I had been endeavoring to save means whereby we might obtain a team, harness and wagon. By the greatest thrift, economy and careful management, we finally found ourselves in possession of five hundred dollars, of which we were both justly proud, as money was much harder to obtain then than now. I immediately went to Salt Lake City, with this sum in my pocket, to purchase the much coveted outfit, but said nothing to anyone of my purpose, so that no one but my wife was aware that I had the money with me.

Soon after I arrived in the city I met President Heber C. Kimball on the sidewalk just below the *Deseret News* office. He shook hands with me and then said, "Brother Rydalch, will you loan me the five hundred dollars you have in your pocket?"

I looked at him with astonishment and dismay, as the thoughts ran swiftly through my mind of the sacrifices made by my wife and myself to save this amount; of the months of toil and industry it represented; but knowing him to be a man of God, I hesitated only for an instant, and then told him he could have it. At the same time I took from my pocket the twenty-five twenty-dollar gold pieces and handed them to him.

He blessed me and then said: "Brother Rydalch, I promise you that in less than three months this amount will double in your hands."

He turned and walked away, leaving me marveling at the strangeness of circumstance, and thinking of the possibilities of the promise being fulfilled, which he had made me. I returned home feeling confident that all would come out right, but I felt rather doubtful of convincing my wife of this fact, as I knew it would be a great disappointment to her.

About two weeks after this occurred I again went to Salt Lake, and upon meeting Brother Kimball he informed me that he had a span of mules in his stable that he had taken on a debt and asked me if I would look at them and take them on the five hundred dollars, if they suited me.

I went and looked at them and found them to be just what I wanted. I returned to the house and told him I would take them. He then asked me what I would allow him for them. I told him I did not wish to put a price on another man's property. He wanted to know if two hundred dollars was too much. I answered that it was not, and took them. He also said he had a set of lead harnesses which could go with them at forty dollars. This was a pretty good price, but I took it. He then spoke of the running gears of a new wagon, the box of which had been demolished by an accident while crossing the Big Mountain. He said I could have it for eighty dollars. This I agreed to take without any hesitation whatever, as it was a good bargain. He thought his son Heber P. had an extra box that would fit it. This he obtained for me and it fitted exactly. I went home as proud a man as could be found anywhere, as I had now the very articles which I had been saving my money to buy, all first-class, and Brother Kimball was still owing me one hundred and eighty dollars.

In about three weeks from this time I received a letter from James Lemmons who lived at Bountiful, Davis County, desiring me to look out for a good pair of mules for him that would do for leaders in crossing the plains, as he was going East to purchase goods for Hooper & Eldredge. I informed him by return mail that I had just the animals he wanted, and that he must come to

Grantsville immediately, or they might be sold. He came, was well suited with them and offered me four cows, five heifers and a fine Durham bull. These cattle I had then in my possession, as I was taking care of them for him. They were all in good condition, and some of the cows had calves.

We soon closed the bargain, he taking the mules and turning over the stock to me the same day. These cattle I considered well worth five hundred dollars in cash and I would not have sold them for that amount.

Soon after I went back to the city and met Brother Kimball at his home, but said nothing about what had taken place. He said Brother Henry Houtz was owing him one hundred and fifty dollars and he had a good horse which he wanted him to take for that amount. He asked me if I wanted him. I did not want a horse, but as he rather insisted on my going to see it I went. I found it to be an excellent animal, and decided to take him. I turned him into a good pasture and let him remain about two weeks, when an officer named Calapsey, from Camp Floyd, belonging to the commissary department, and who happened to be at Grantsville buying hay and grain, rode up to my house and inquired of me if I knew where he could purchase a good cavalry horse. I informed him that I was in possession of just what he was looking for. In a short time I sold him the animal for three hundred dollars, it being just what he wanted.

Several days after this I met President Kimball again at his home, and while there he mentioned the thirty dollars he was still owing me. He said he would like to pay me out of his store. This met with my approval and he gave me goods which were well worth seventy-five dollars, including a shawl worth at least fifty dollars, which was in constant use for twenty years. It had been about two months since President Kimball made the prediction which had been literally fulfilled, and I had fully realized one thousand dollars through the transaction.

Juvenile Instructor, 15 April 1892, 249–50.

"SOMETHING TOLD ME TO TURN UP THIS WAY"

AUTHOR UNKNOWN

At one time during her husband's [David O. McKay's] absence [while he was serving a mission], Emma Ray was in financial difficulty. She needed a sum of money to pay some obligations. She had exhausted all her resources without being able to raise the money. Finally, the night before the money was due, with tears rolling down her cheeks, she knelt by her bed and prayed with all her heart that Heavenly Father would show her a way to obtain this needed sum.

The next morning there was a knock at the door. The visitor was Brother John Hall, a member of her stake presidency. Since he had never paid a social call on her before, she was somewhat surprised to see him when she opened the door. His first words were, "Sister McKay, do you need me? When I was down at the corner, something told me to turn up this way."

"I should say I do. Won't you come in and sit down?" She then related her problem and the ways she had tried to solve it. He promptly produced his checkbook from his pocket and wrote her the needed amount.

"But, President Hall, I have no collateral, and I don't know when I can repay you."

"Never mind, David O. will see to it when he returns."

Her letters across the world, always optimistic, always encouraging, assured her missionary that he needn't worry about family affairs or his loved ones. All was well.

Relief Society Magazine, July 1967, 488–89.

TWO CHILDREN BEHIND THE IRON CURTAIN

DAVID O. McKAY

On Sunday, June 29, 1952, Sister McKay and I were in Berlin, Germany, near the Iron Curtain. Arrangements had been made for a meeting of the Saints, investigators, and friends in the "Mercedes Palast" theater, the largest hall in North Berlin.

Prior to the meeting I had received word through the presidency of the East German Mission that one of the members of the Church in that mission—a sister—had lost her husband and eldest son under communist rule. She had been driven from her home, and was subsequently exposed to the rigors of the weather and lack of nutrition until she finally became paralyzed and had been confined to her bed for five years. She had heard of my coming to Berlin, and being unable to travel herself, she expressed the desire that her two little children—a boy and a girl about ten and twelve years of age—be sent over to meet the President of the Church.

This good sister said: "I know if I send my children to shake hands with President McKay, and then they come home and take my hand—if I can hold their little hands in mine—I know that I shall get better."

Arrangements were made for them to take the trip. Some of the Saints contributed to the clothing of the little children, and the missionaries contributed to pay their expenses.

I asked the mission president to point out these little children as they came to the meeting. Two little children among thousands who were assembled! Anticipating meeting them, I took a new handkerchief, and when that little girl and boy came along, I went to them and shook their hands, and said, "Will you take this handkerchief to your mother with my blessing?" I later learned that after I had shaken hands with them, they would not shake hands with anyone else, for they did not want to touch anyone with their hands until they got back to their mother.

We heard no more about it; however, the incident was well-known throughout the crowd. I saw the children again in the conference house that night. They were sleeping on the top floor of the mission home—sweet little darlings!

When Sister McKay returned to Salt Lake City, she wrote to the mission president's wife and asked her to find out how the mother of the two little children was getting along. In her reply, the mission president's wife said, "This sister thanks the Lord every day for the blessing and the handkerchief which President McKay sent through her two children, and she has the faith that she will fully recover, and I believe so, too. Immediately after the children came home, her feet and toes began to get feeling in them, and this feeling slowly moved up into her legs, and now she gets out of bed alone and seats herself on a chair, and then, with her feet and the chair, works all the way around to the kitchen sink, where she has the children bring her the dishes to wash, and other things, and is very thankful that she is able to help now."

That is the faith of a mother in the Russian zone. God bless her, and bless all who are over there!

David O. McKay, *Cherished Experiences,* 149–51.

A Little Encouragement

EMMA RAY RIGGS McKAY

Children respond favorably to praise. Let me give you an example. The first and only year I taught school, the principal came into my room the first day, which was midyear, and, pointing out a child twelve years of age, he said, before the whole roomful of pupils, "You'll have to watch out for that boy; he is the worst boy in school. He drove Miss B. away by throwing a bottle of ink at her."

What a blow for the boy, and for me, too! I thought, "Now Earl will show me that that record is true by being his worst. I'll try to nip it in the bud."

I wrote a little note, saying, "Earl, I think the principal was mistaken about your being a bad boy. I trust you and know you are going to help me make this room the best in school." As I walked down the aisle I slipped it to him without anyone's noticing. I saw his face light up, and afterwards his mother told me that he brought the note home and said in an excited tone, "Read this, Mother, but don't destroy it, for I want to wear it next to my heart." He was one of my best behaved boys the remainder of the year. Praise brings good results, not cruel criticism nor abuse.

Emma Ray Riggs McKay, *The Art of Rearing Children Peacefully,* 10–11.

"To Him That Believeth . . ."

PARLEY P. PRATT

After making our escape into the county of Clay—being reduced to the lowest poverty—I made a living by day labor, jobbing, building, or wood cutting, till some time in the winter of 1834, when a general conference was held at my house, in which it was decided that two of the elders should be sent to Ohio, in order to counsel with President [Joseph] Smith and the Church at Kirtland, and take some measures for the relief or restoration of the people thus plundered and driven from their homes. The question was put to the conference: "Who would volunteer to perform so great a journey?"

The poverty of all, and the inclement season of the year made all hesitate. At length Lyman Wight and myself offered our services, which were readily accepted. I was at this time entirely destitute of proper clothing for the journey; and I had neither horse, saddle, bridle, money nor provisions to take with me; or to leave with my wife, who lay sick and helpless most of the time.

Under these circumstances I knew not what to do. Nearly all

had been robbed and plundered, and all were poor. As we had to start without delay, I almost trembled at the undertaking; it seemed to be all but an impossibility; but "to him that believeth all things are possible." I started out of my house to do something towards making preparation; I hardly knew which way to go, but I found myself in the house of brother John Lowry, and was intending to ask him for money; but as I entered his miserable cottage in the swamp, amid the low, timbered bottoms of the Missouri river, I found him sick in bed with a heavy fever, and two or three others of his family down with the same complaint, on different beds in the same room. He was vomiting severely, and was hardly sensible of my presence. I thought to myself, "Well, this is a poor place to come for money, and yet I must have it; I know of no one else that has got it; what shall I do?" I sat a little while confounded and amazed. At length another elder happened in; at that instant faith sprung up in my heart; the Spirit whispered to me, "Is there anything too hard for the Lord?" I said to the elder that came in: "Brother, I am glad you have come; these people must be healed, for I want some money of them, and must have it."

We laid hands on them and rebuked the disease; brother Lowry rose up well; I did my errand, and readily obtained all I asked. This provided in part for my family's sustenance while I should leave them. I went a little further into the woods of the Missouri bottoms, and came to a camp of some brethren, by the name of Higbee, who owned some horses; they saw me coming, and, moved by the Spirit, one of them said to the other, "There comes Brother Parley; he's in want of a horse for his journey—I must let him have old Dick;" this being the name of the best horse he had. "Yes," said I, "brother, you have guessed right; but what will I do for a saddle?" "Well," says the other, "I believe I'll have to let you have mine." I blessed them and went on my way rejoicing.

I next called on Sidney A. Gilbert, a merchant, then sojourning in the village of Liberty—his store in Jackson County having been broken up, and his goods plundered and destroyed by the mob. "Well," says he, "Brother Parley, you certainly look too shabby to start a journey; you must have a new suit; I have got some remnants left that will make you a coat," etc. A neighboring tailoress and two or three other sisters happened to be present on a visit, and hearing the conversation, exclaimed, "Yes, Brother Gilbert, you find the stuff and we'll make it up for him." This arranged, I now lacked only a cloak; this was also furnished by Brother Gilbert.

Brother Wight was also prospered in a similar manner in his preparations. Thus faith and the blessings of God had cleared up our way to accomplish what seemed impossible. We were soon ready, and on the first of February we mounted our horses, and started in good cheer to ride one thousand or fifteen hundred miles through a wilderness country. We had not one cent of money in our pockets on starting.

Parley P. Pratt, *Autobiography of Parley P. Pratt,* 87–89.

"WHAT IS THE BOY WORTH?"

SARAH M. KIMBALL

My eldest son was born in Nauvoo, November 22, 1841; when the babe was three days old a little incident occurred which I will mention. The walls of the Nauvoo Temple were about three feet above the foundation. The Church was in need of help to assist in raising the temple walls. I belonged to The Church of Jesus Christ of Latter-day Saints: my husband did not belong to the Church at that time. I wished to help on the temple, but did not like to ask my husband (who owned considerable property) to help for my sake.

My husband came to my bedside, and as he was admiring our three days' old darling, I said, "What is the boy worth?" He replied, "O, I don't know; he is worth a great deal." I said, "Is he worth a thousand dollars?" The reply was, "Yes, more than that if he lives and does well." I said, "Half of him is mine, is it not?" "Yes, I suppose so." "Then I have something to help on the temple." He said pleasantly, "You have?" "Yes, and I think of turning my share right in as tithing." "Well, I'll see about that."

Soon after the above conversation Mr. Kimball met the Prophet Joseph Smith, president of the Church, and said, "Sarah has got a little the advantage of me this time; she proposes to turn out the boy as Church property."

President Smith seemed pleased with the joke, and said, "I accept all such donations, and from this day the boy shall stand recorded, Church property." Then turning to Willard Richards, his secretary, he said, "Make a record of this, and you are my witness." Joseph Smith then said, "Major [my husband was a major in the Nauvoo Legion], you now have the privilege of paying $500 and retaining possession, or receiving $500 and giving possession." Mr. Kimball asked if city property was good currency, and the President replied that it was. Then said Mr. Kimball, "How will that reserve block north of the temple suit?" President Smith replied, "It is just what we want." The deed was soon made out and transferred to the Church.

President Smith later said to me, "You have consecrated your firstborn son, for this you are blessed of the Lord. I bless you in the name of the Lord God of Abraham, of Isaac, and of Jacob. And I seal upon you all the blessings that pertain to the faithful.

Your name shall be handed down in honorable remembrance from generation to generation.

"Your son shall live and be a blessing to you in time, and an honor and glory to you throughout the endless eternities to come. He shall be girded about with righteousness and bear the helmet and the breastplate of war. You shall be a blessing to your companion, and the honored mother of a noble posterity. You shall stand as a savior to your father's house, and receive an everlasting salvation, which I seal upon you by the gift of revelation and by virtue and authority of the holy priesthood vested in me, in the name of Jesus Christ."

Sarah M. Kimball, in Augusta Joyce Crocheron, comp., *Representative Women of Deseret,* 25–26.

"I READ THE BIBLE FROM COVER TO COVER"

SPENCER W. KIMBALL

Let me tell you of one of the goals I made when I was still but a lad. When I heard a Church leader from Salt Lake City tell us at conference that we should read the scriptures, and I recognized that I had never read the Bible, that very night at the conclusion of that very sermon I walked to my home a block away and climbed up to my little attic room in the top of the house and lighted a little coal-oil lamp that was on the little table, and I read the first chapters of Genesis. A year later I closed the Bible, having read every chapter in that big and glorious book.

I found that this Bible that I was reading had in it 66 books, and then I was nearly dissuaded when I found that it had in it 1,189 chapters, and then I also found that it had 1,519 pages. It was formidable, but I knew that if others did it, I could do it.

I found that there were certain parts that were hard for a fourteen-year-old boy to understand. There were some pages that were not especially interesting to me, but when I had read the 66 books and 1,189 chapters and 1,519 pages, I had the glowing satisfaction that I had made a goal and that I had achieved it.

Now I am not telling you this story to boast; I am merely using this as an example to say that if I could do it by coal-oil light, you can do it by electric light. I have always been glad I read the Bible from cover to cover.

Ensign, May 1974, 88.

"DOCTOR, WON'T YOU PRAY FOR ME?"

GEORGE ALBERT SMITH

A little boy was upon the operating table, ready to undergo an operation for appendicitis—an orphan boy, about eight years of age. It was a rather unusual case, and by the way a charity case. As the boy lay there he looked up at the surgeons—there were several of them present—and addressing the surgeon in charge he said: "Doctor, before you begin to operate, won't you pray for me?" The surgeon looked at the boy amazed and said, "Why, I can't pray for you." Then the little fellow turned his eyes from one to the other, asking each if they would pray for him. Each in turn declined. Then the little man said: "If you won't pray for me, won't you please wait while I pray for myself?" The little fellow got up on the operating table on his knees, folded his hands, and uttered a prayer. He said to the Lord: "Heavenly Father, I am only a little orphan boy, but I am awful sick, and these doctors are going to operate. Will you please help them that they will do it right? And now, Heavenly Father, if you will make me well I will be a good boy. Thank you for making me well." He then turned over and laid on his back and looked up at the doctors and nurses who were all standing around, but he was the only one in the room who could see because the others had tears in their eyes. He said: "Now I am ready."

A few days after that a man went into the office of the chief surgeon and asked him to tell him the story of the little boy he had operated on a few days before. The surgeon said: "I have operated on a good many little boys."

"Yes, I know, but this was an unusual case—tell me about it."

Then the doctor looked at him for some time and said, "I don't know whether I will tell you or not. I am not sure but what it is too sacred to talk about."

"Please tell me," he replied; "I will treat it as sacred, too." Then the doctor told the story as I have related it, and when he got through the visitor said, "My, that was a remarkable experience, wasn't it?"

The doctor said, "Remarkable? That was the most remarkable experience of my whole life. I have operated on hundreds of men, women, and children, and I have known some of them to pray, but never until I stood in the presence of that little boy, have I heard anyone talk to their Heavenly Father face to face."

George Albert Smith, *Sharing the Gospel with Others,* 144–45.

"Aunty! The Wind Has Gone Down!"

SOPHY H. VALENTINE

I often think of an incident that occurred in my childhood [in the 1860s and early 1870s] and gave me great comfort to dwell upon.

I was then living with my aunt in Wisconsin on a big farm

three or four miles from Racine. I had no playmates of my own age. I received private instruction three times a week by the Danish clergyman, so I did not even have the pleasure and exhilaration of school life. I was far away from my dear home and was often very lonely. I had, however, one friend, a girl of my own age, who lived four miles farther out in the country. To her I was very much attached, and at her home I spent my happiest days.

It was on my birthday, the 12th of February. I had been promised that I should be allowed to spend two days at my friend's and I had looked forward to this for weeks; I had drowned many a little grief in the hope of this pleasure.

Well, the day dawned at last and I awoke by hearing the limbs of the apple tree beat violently against the window shutters. My heart sank within me, for I knew that with this terrific windstorm and the thermometer ten degrees below zero, I would not be permitted to go.

All morning I went about with a tearful face, looking despairingly out of the window for a sign of some encouragement in the look of the weather, but the wind kept up its terrible howl and shook the trees till many of them broke. Aunty scolded me for my despondent looks and told me to give it up, as there was no hope of the wind going down from the looks of things.

I went up in the front room and stood shivering with cold, chewing my apron in deepest despair and trying to check the deep sobbing that shook me. Then in my sorrow I dropped on my knees and cried imploringly to the Lord to have pity on me and my loneliness; to let the wind go down that I might go. I ended my prayer by reminding him how Jesus had promised that we should receive whatsoever we asked in his name. Full of faith and courage, I arose and went to the window. The trees shook as if some mighty hand had hold of them, and then suddenly let go. I stood and stared, not daring to breathe. The trees swayed softly to and fro and finally made not a move. I knelt again and whispered a hurried, excited, thanks dear Lord, and then flew into the sitting room. "Aunty! The wind has gone down!"

"No?"

"It has!"

Aunty went to the door and looked out and then exclaimed, "Well, I declare, so it has—I never saw anything like it." I went to my friend's house, of course.

Now, call it childishness if you like, or chance or anything, but it will not rob me of the pleasure I find in putting my own interpretation on it.

If I live to be an old, old woman I shall never forget it. I always thank the Lord, who remembered the poor lonely child though she was not then a member of The Church of Jesus Christ of Latter-day Saints. It shows to me that God is interested in the everyday affairs of his children.

Young Woman's Journal, March 1897, 313–14.

Faithfulness

The Sabbath in a Mining Camp

O. H. SNOW

From my earliest childhood days, I had been taught that the Sabbath day was a day of rest. It had been the custom in my mother's childhood home to complete all preparations Saturday for the sacred observance of the Sabbath day. Shoes were shined, clothing made ready, and even much of the cooking essential for the Sunday meal was prepared.

With this background, I had always felt there was a sacredness about Sunday observance that could not be set aside without bringing down the displeasure of the Lord. Because of the early impressions Mother's example and teachings made upon me, I could never bring myself to play baseball or go swimming on the Sabbath with the other boys of my age.

I returned from my mission when I was about twenty-three years of age. Naturally, among the teachings held up to the Saints, as well as those not of our faith, was strict Sabbath observance.

It so happened that my mission ended when Grover Cleveland was President of the United States. The country was passing through one of its worst depressions of the time. Work was hard to find. I came back home in debt. My mother had been a widow since I was ten years of age. It was very necessary that I find some kind of work to assist her. I also desired to get a little something to begin making a home for myself. Father had left Mother with but very little property, and it was not possible for Mother to give further aid after my mission expenses were met.

It was about this time that the new mining camp of DeLamar, Nevada, was opened up. Some of the boys went out to find work, and were able to get contracts to haul wood to a smelter that was being built.

In company with [some friends] I went out to the new camp, and we soon took a contract to deliver five hundred cords of wood. We procured choppers, and began work. When the week ended and Sunday morning rolled around, I arose early, watered and fed my team, and turned them loose on the hillside to graze. . . .

When [our foreman] saw what I had done, he asked what it meant. I said, "It is Sunday." He asked, "Don't you intend to haul wood?" I replied, "No." He then said, "We are going to get our loads." I said, "That's all right, but I'm not." He argued, and the other boys joined in, saying that we were in a mining camp. I told them that I had been out teaching others who lived outside of Mormon communities Sabbath observance along with other gospel truths, and that I could not conscientiously work on Sunday. I felt the Lord meant the Sabbath as much for a mining camp as for any other place.

Our foreman then gave the ultimatum that if I would not work on Sunday, we should have to pile our wood separately. I said that that was all right; that we could measure up what was already in, and I would begin next day to pile my wood in a different place.

The next day I moved camp about a quarter of a mile away, went to town with my load of wood, and found two acquaintances hunting work. I hired them to chop my wood for me, and assist me in loading and cleaning up the timber.

We continued to work for about four months to complete our contract. I lost only two half days during the summer, one for resetting my wagon tires, and the other when I changed camps and found my new wood choppers. I rested each Sunday, spending the time reading good books. I made twelve trips each week, with two exceptions, after I left the other boys, while they made but ten trips, and made more misses than I did by reason of some accidents. My team was fatter; I was much less worn;

and, when we settled up, my average monthly earnings were approximately twenty-five dollars a month in excess of those of my partners.

Improvement Era, June 1946, 360.

"HE RAISED A GLASS OF MILK"

N. ELDON TANNER

I should like to tell you the experience of one of our young men we will call John, who went east to an officer's training school. A new commanding officer came into the school, and they put on a banquet to honor him. There, by every plate, was a cocktail glass. When the proper time came, every one of those potential officers stood up with his cocktail glass to toast that incoming officer—that is, all but one boy, and he raised a glass of milk. It would take a lot of courage, wouldn't it, to stand there with all those officers and see all of those cocktail glasses come up, and stand and raise a glass of milk!

Well, the officer saw it, and he made a beeline for that boy after the entertainment was over and said, "Why did you toast me with a glass of milk?"

"Well, sir," he said, "I've never touched alcohol in my life. I don't want to touch it; my parents wouldn't want me to touch it; and I didn't think you would want me to either. I wanted to toast you, so I thought you would be satisfied if I toasted you with what I am accustomed to drinking."

The officer said, "Report to my headquarters in the morning."

I suppose that boy spent a sleepless night, but when he went to the officer's quarters the next morning, do you know what happened? The officer assigned him a place on his staff with this explanation: "I want to surround myself with men who have the courage to do what they think is right regardless of what anybody else thinks about it."

Conference Report, April 1976, 65.

A WIDOW'S MITE

LLEWELYN R. McKAY

After the dedication of the temple site at Bern, Switzerland, the spectators gathered around father [David O. McKay] to shake his hand and to ask for his autograph.

One sweet, old lady came up to him and placed a small purse in his hand. Father beckoned to me to act as interpreter. With tears in her eyes, she said: "President McKay, ever since I learned that a temple was to be built in my land, I have saved a ten-centime piece each week. I am quite ill and very old, so I shall never be able to do work in the temple when it is built, but I wish to do my part in helping the great cause."

The actual amount in the purse, figured in dollars and cents, was not much, but each week's savings meant less food for that dear, old soul. She was giving all she could with a deeper sincerity than is perhaps felt by many others who offer more—and even when she knew that no return in the use of the temple would ever come to her, she was happy in the thought that she was helping her fellow men.

This is why, I am sure, that father put his arm around her, and with tears in his eyes, thanked her in behalf of all her fellow Church members throughout the world, and added: "You are true gold; I am sure God is pleased with your sincere heart and worthy soul; and in behalf of the Church I accept this gift in the spirit in which it is given!"

The old sister hobbled away, lame and decrepit in body, but with a smile which reflected the happy sparkle in her eyes and of her beautiful soul!

Llewelyn R. McKay, comp., *Home Memories of President David O. McKay,* 158–59.

Family

"Close to Those Beyond"

HAROLD B. LEE

One day a beautiful, flaxen-haired girl—about ten years of age—came with her mother to the home of her grandparents. The Primary song "I Am a Child of God" had just been sent out through the Church. As the mother sat at the piano and accompanied, this little flaxen-haired beauty sang "I am a child of God. . . . Lead me, guide me, walk beside me, help me find the way. Teach me all that I must do to live with Him some day." (*Sing with Me,* no. B-76.)

The grandparents sat with tears in their eyes as this beautiful little child sang that glorious song. Little did they know that in a few short years, suddenly and without warning, that young mother would be snatched away in just a moment. The pleadings of the grandfather over in the Hawaiian Islands and the piteous cries for the mercies of the Almighty to spare her were unavailing. In the hospital, surrounded by doctors with all the medical skill they could summon, she slipped away.

The children, including this little flaxen-haired girl, were called, and around the lonely table in the family room they sat with bowed heads, sobbing their hearts out. The grandfather was summoned to come home, and that night all the family were at the airport to meet him. Then, with arms surrounding that little family, the grandfather said, "I do not know how you can be so brave. Grandfather is crying his heart out, and you stand here with your arms around each other, seemingly with no tears." One of them said, "Grandfather, we have no more tears to shed. We have cried our tears away all day long."

That night this little girl had a dream, one so vivid that, as she slept in bed by her aunt, she awakened and gripped her aunt and said, "I have had a visit from Mother. We were in the family room and she came and I said to her, 'Mother, you are not dead; you are still here.' And Mother said, 'Yes, my darling, I am not gone. You won't be able to see me, but all through your life, Mother will be very close by you. Mother will not always be seen, but you can know that she won't be far away.'"

Address given at Brigham Young University Sixth Stake quarterly conference, 27 April 1969. See also Harold B. Lee, *Stand Ye in Holy Places,* 13–14.

THE FAITH OF A MOTHER

HAROLD B. LEE

As just a high school boy, I went away on a high school debating team trip. We won the debate. I came back and called Mother on the telephone only to have her say, "Never mind, son. I know all about it. I will tell you when you get home at the end of the week."

When I came home she took me aside and said, "When I knew it was just time for this performance to start, I went out among the willows by the creekside, and there, all by myself, I remembered you and prayed God you would not fail."

I have come to know that that kind of love is necessary for every son and daughter who seek to achieve in this world.

Harold B. Lee, *Ye Are the Light of the World,* 327–28.

"WHY DON'T YOU ASK HIM TO GIVE YOU YOUR BLESSING?"

SPENCER W. KIMBALL

I was down in Toquepala, Peru. We were dedicating a chapel. Many of the men who were employed in that mining town were Americans. After the dedication they had a dinner at one of the homes. As we moved around in the home, a young boy came to me and said, "Brother Kimball, I'm thinking about a mission. Would you give me a blessing?"

I said, "Why, of course. I'd be very happy to give you a blessing, but isn't that your father I met in the other room?"

He said, "Yes, that's Dad."

I said, "Well, why don't you ask him to give you your blessing?"

"Oh," he said, "Dad wouldn't want to give a blessing to me."

So I excused myself. I went out and found the father, and I said, "You have a wonderful boy there. I think he would like to have a blessing from his father. Wouldn't you like to give him a blessing?"

He said, "Oh, I don't think my boy would want me to give him a blessing."

But as I mingled among these people and saw the father and the son a little later, close together, I could understand that they had come together in their thoughts and that the boy was proud to have his father bless him, and the father was delighted to be asked.

I hope you boys in this audience will keep that in mind. You have the best dad in the world, you know. He holds the priesthood; he would be delighted to give you a blessing. He would like you to indicate it, and we would like you fathers to remember that your boys are maybe a little timid. They know you are the best man in the world, but probably if you just made the advance, there would be some glorious moments for you.

Ensign, May 1974, 89.

"I GUESS THAT MAN OVER THERE LOVES YOU"

EMMA RAY RIGGS McKAY

Last summer on reaching Los Angeles, we decided to have our car washed by one of those "Quickies" on Wilshire Boulevard.

As I was watching the last part of the operation from a bench, to my surprise a tiny voice at my elbow said, "I guess that man over there loves you."

I turned and saw a beautiful little curly-haired child with great brown eyes who looked to be about seven years of age.

"What did you say?" I asked.

"I said, I guess that man over there loves you."

"Oh, yes, he loves me; he is my husband. But why do you ask?"

A tender smile lighted up his face, and his voice softened as he said, "'Cuz, the way he smiled at you. Do you know I'd give anything in this world if my pop would smile at my mom that way."

"Oh, I'm sorry if he doesn't!"

"I guess you're not going to get a divorce," he questioningly remarked.

"No, of course not; we've been married over fifty years. Why do you ask that?"

"'Cuz everybody gets a divorce around here. My pop is getting a divorce from my mom, and I love my pop and I love my mom . . . "

His voice broke, and tears welled up in his eyes, but he was too much of a little man to let them fall.

"Oh, I'm sorry to hear that!"

And then he came very close and whispered confidentially into my ear, "You'd better hurry out of this place or you'll get a divorce, too!"

Then he picked up his papers and walked disconsolately down the street.

Llewelyn R. McKay, comp., *Home Memories of President David O. McKay,* 189.

Healing

Miracles in New Zealand

HENRY A. SMITH

In no other way more than through the blessings he gave and the miracles that followed these blessings did Matthew Cowley demonstrate he was truly a man of faith. There can be no doubt but that his was the inspired touch of hands and prayer of faith that healed the sick. In the isles of the Pacific and the stakes of Zion there are many who can attest to the healing power of his blessings. . . .

Matthew Cowley felt that man "was at his greatest when he was on his knees." He learned the real power of prayer as a youth on his first mission to the Maoris, and he never lost sight of this lesson. He said, "I was called to faraway New Zealand, and in that mission I was assigned, without a companion, to one of the most humble places I have ever seen in my life, one of the most poverty-stricken places, and in that little village I had to pray."

He had been in that country but a few days when he was summoned by a native woman to the side of her husband. He found the man lying on the ground being consumed by the fire of typhoid fever. "All I could do was pray," he said, "and I knelt down beside that suffering native, and I prayed to God, and opened up my heart to him; and I believe the channel was open; and then I placed my hands upon that good brother; and with the authority of the priesthood which I as a young boy held, I blessed him to be restored to health."

The next morning the native wife informed the seventeen-year-old missionary he was now free to go where he wanted, for her husband was up and well again. It was his first miracle of healing.

* * *

He kept the channel open, and there were many other miraculous healings during his two missions in New Zealand and his subsequent trips to other missions of the Pacific and the stakes of Zion. Not only were individuals blessed and healed but a whole native village also felt the power of his priesthood. Of his experience he said:

"I remember that on one occasion I rode horseback all day long and far into the night to arrive at a native village on the seacoast of New Zealand, and when I arrived at a bay dividing the place where I had to stop at that little village, I made a fire so that the people across in the village would send a rowboat to get me, and when that boat arrived, I was taken across the bay, and walked through that village, and in every home there were cases of typhoid fever. I walked fearlessly, with my head erect, impelled by the priesthood of God which I held, and in each of these homes I left the blessings of heaven, and I laid my hands upon the sick. And then I had to go across the bay again and get on my horse and ride all night long to arrive at another native village where there was sickness." . . .

* * *

"I was called to see a young lady in the hospital. She was a native. She was about to deliver a child. The doctor had told her she shouldn't have the child. She was shot through with TB. The people were there giving her a farewell party. They don't just let you die. They say, 'When you go over there, see so-and-so and tell him I'm not doing so good, but will do better and fix a place for me.' . . . We administered to that girl. The next morning we went back. . . . The farewell was still on. We blessed her and administered to her again. I was there about a year ago, and she was having her fifth child." . . .

* * *

"Thirty-six natives came to the mission home one time. They were all relatives and said they all wanted a blessing. I said, 'That is quite a job—the hardest thing I do in this Church.' They answered, 'We don't want you to put your hands on us—just stand up in front of us.' The spokesman said, 'Many years and generations ago one of the chiefs put a curse on our family, and every generation since someone would produce a leper, and the last one in the last few days has been taken off to the leper colony. We want you to stand up and rebuke that curse and take away that leprosy.' There was no doubt in my mind when those people spoke. I blessed them and commanded the power of God to cleanse that family of that curse; and I know as well as I am standing here there will never be another leper in that family." . . .

* * *

"A lady came to me in the mission home suffering from what the Samoans call *mu mu*—or elephantiasis—her legs swollen all out of proportion. She said, 'Brother Cowley, bless me and remove from me this dread disease.' A month ago in Samoa she came to the mission home, and she said: 'Do you remember me?' I said, 'Yes, you are Sister Purcell who was suffering from *mu mu* when I was here before.' She showed me her ankles, and they were entirely normal. Then she said, 'Now, I want the cataracts to drop from my eyes. Bless me now, that I may receive this blessing through the priesthood of God, from God who has all power to heal.'" . . .

* * *

The whole Church thrilled at general conference in April, 1953, with his recitation of the story of Little Joe, the boy afflicted with polio and pneumonia, who came running to meet him two weeks after the blessing had been pronounced upon him while in an unconscious condition by this man of faith. Many such incidents can be related. . . .

* * *

He [Matthew Cowley] told of standing in line shaking hands with the people when a missionary standing next to him said, "The next lady you shake hands with, take a good look at her face." Elder Cowley did, but couldn't see anything wrong. When the line had passed by, he asked the missionary the purpose of his request. This was his answer:

"Two weeks ago she was a leper, confined behind barbed wire fence. Her nose was being eaten away. They fed her through barbed wire—no one could go in. They had sent tissue to a lab in Los Angeles; it was sent back labeled 'positive leprosy.' The same report came back from other samples. One day two of us missionaries went down to visit her. She said, 'I want you to go up and see the doctor and get permission to come in here. I want to go home.' We knew what she wanted. So we went to the doctor and finally got permission. We put on white clothing and masks and went in with a bottle of oil. This was two weeks ago, and she doesn't even have a scar on her nose.

* * *

"We have to have the faith of a child in order to believe in these things," he said. Such was the faith of this man of miracles.

Henry A. Smith, *Matthew Cowley: Man of Faith,* 136–43.

"WE DON'T NEED A DOCTOR"

MATTHEW COWLEY

When I went over to New Zealand on my first mission, I had only been there a day or two when a nice sister came running to me. And she said, "Come over, please." I was all alone. I didn't have a companion. I went over to the home, and there was a little boy, ten or eleven, I guess. He had fallen from a tree. She said, "Fix him up." I said, "You ought to have a doctor." I had never administered to anybody in my life, never. She said, "The doctor isn't home. He is away from town. We don't need a doctor. You fix him."

Well, I got down. He lay on the floor. I anointed him, and I sealed the anointing. You know, I guess God wanted to humble me. The next day he was climbing trees again. Every bone had knit. It was only a few days after that that her husband was stricken with typhoid fever. I was scared to death. The water was bad. I was all alone, just a youngster. She called me in to her husband. I got down and anointed and blessed him, and the next morning he came over to my house and visited with me. And he said, "If you are going anywhere now, you can go. I am well."

Matthew Cowley, *Matthew Cowley Speaks,* 411.

The Gift of Healing

AUTHOR UNKNOWN

Many anecdotes are related of Elder Abel Evans, formerly of Lehi. . . . He was a man of wonderful faith, and possessed the gift of healing in a remarkable degree. . . .

On one occasion Brother Evans was sailing from Liverpool to Bangor, at which place he had an appointment to preach, when a terrible storm arose, which threatened the destruction of the vessel. When the officers and crew were all ready to give up hope, Elder Evans retired to a secluded part of the vessel, called upon the Lord in prayer, reminding Him of the appointment to be filled and that he was upon His business, and, in mighty faith, rebuked the storm, when it calmed so suddenly that all hands onboard were as much surprised as delighted, and quite at a loss to account for the sudden change in their prospects.

In the year 1846, a man living in Merthyr Tydvil, who was a member of the Church, happened accidentally to break his leg between the knee and ankle. A surgeon was called in, who set the broken bones, bound the limb up with bandages and splints and cautioned the patient to keep perfectly quiet until the fracture could have time to knit. Three days afterwards Elders Abel Evans and Thomas D. Giles called to see him, and the former questioned him as to his faith. "Do you believe," said he, "that the Lord has power to heal your broken limb?"

The man acknowledged that he did.

"Do you believe," he again asked, "that we, as the servants of God, holding the Priesthood, have authority to call upon the Almighty and claim a blessing for you at His hands?"

The man assured him that he did.

"Then," said he, "if you wish it we will take the bandages off your broken leg and anoint it."

The man consented, the bandages and splints were removed and his leg was anointed with consecrated oil. The brethren then placed their hands upon his head, and Elder Evans rebuked the power of the evil one, commanded the bones to come together and knit, and, finally, that the man should arise from his bed and walk. He got out of bed immediately and walked about the house, and from that time had no occasion to use a bandage on the injured limb or even walk with a stick.

While crossing the sea in 1850, emigrating to Utah, a number of remarkable cases of healing occurred under his administration. One was that of a young girl who was terribly afflicted with evil spirits, and who was entirely relieved when he placed his hands upon her head. Another was that of a little boy who fell through the hatchway of the vessel, alighting upon his head on the ring and bolt of the lower hatchway. When he was picked up it was found that the force of the fall had driven the iron upon which he struck into his head, and within a minute afterwards the injured place puffed up like a distended bladder. Of course, he was knocked insensible and apparently lifeless, but Brother Evans and one or two other elders immediately administered to him, and while their hands were upon his head the swelling entirely disappeared and he was restored to consciousness and to health. This was witnessed and marveled at by a number of persons who were not in the Church as well as a great many of the Saints who were onboard.

Early Scenes in Church History, 38–40.

"The Epidemic Ceased Its Ravages"

Author Unknown

When Elder [Abel] Evans was crossing the Atlantic in charge of a company of Saints emigrating to Utah, a terrible epidemic in the nature of a fever broke out on the ship, and threatened the destruction of all onboard. He felt that their only hope lay in securing the favor of the Almighty, and determined to muster all the faith he could in appealing to the Lord.

He called together four elders of experience who were onboard, and asked them to retire with him to the hold of the vessel and unite in prayer. They did so again and again without any apparent good result, and Brother Evans marveled at the cause. It was such an unusual thing for him to fail to have his prayers answered, that he was surprised that it should be so in that instance, and he could only account for it by lack of union or worthiness on the part of the elders.

He therefore called the four elders again to retire with him to the hold of the ship, and took with him a basin of clean water. When they had reached a secluded place where they were not likely to be overheard or disturbed by others, he talked to the elders about the necessity of their being united in faith and clear of sin before God if they desired to call upon Him and receive a blessing.

"Now," he said, "I want each of you elders, who feels that his conscience is clear before God, who has committed no sin to debar him from the enjoyment of the Holy Spirit, and who has faith in the Lord Jesus Christ sufficient to call upon the Almighty in His name and claim the desired blessing, to wash his hands in that basin!"

Three of the elders stepped forward and did so; the fourth could not—his conscience smote him. He was therefore asked kindly to retire, and the four others joined in earnest prayer before the Lord and rebuked the disease by which the people were afflicted. The result was that the epidemic ceased its ravages and the sick recovered from that very hour, much to the surprise of the ship's officers and others onboard who knew nothing of the power by which such a happy result was accomplished.

Early Scenes in Church History, 40.

"SHE WAS HEALED INSTANTLY"

AUTHOR UNKNOWN

A sister in the Church, named Morgan, was taken very sick. Her friends did all they could for her, but she continued growing worse. When she had grown so bad that the persons waiting upon her expected her to die almost hourly, she fell asleep and dreamed that Elder [John T.] Evans came and laid his hands upon her and she recovered immediately. On relating the dream to her friends, they tried to find out where Brother Evans was, and sent to different parts of the country in search of him, without finding him, however; but during the day Elder Evans happened to call at the house where the sick woman was. She saw him as he passed the window before he entered the door and she declared afterwards that the sight of him caused her pain to vanish, and when he laid his hands upon her head she was healed instantly, and arose and ate her supper.

Early Scenes in Church History, 60.

"BROTHER COWLEY, WOULD YOU GIVE ME A BLESSING?"

LOUISE LAKE

Jane [my daughter], who was then about fifteen years old, became ill and was feeling too miserable to get out of bed. After a couple of days of the illness, the doorbell rang with a familiar ring. When I opened the door, Matthew Cowley stood there. He said, "I haven't seen you folks lately. How are you?"

"Well," said I, "Jane is sick and I have no idea why. Would you like to step inside and see her?" He came in and put his head around the doorway of the bedroom to speak to her. After his cheerful greeting she asked, "Brother Cowley, would you please give me a blessing?"

"You bet," came the answer. After pausing a few seconds and

moving back down the hallway to the front door, he said, "I will be back in a little while."

A short time later the doorbell rang again. Upon opening the door I saw two men—Elder Cowley and a Polynesian friend by his side. He had often told us of the simple but powerful faith of those great Pacific Island folks. He had gone to find Elder Wi Peri Amaru to assist in giving the blessing my teenager had requested. I took them into the bedroom.

There were twin beds in the room. Jane was in the bed nearest the wall, and it was therefore necessary for them to cross over the room to her. I sat silently a little way inside of the door. After introducing his fine-looking companion, Elder Cowley dropped to his knees by the bedside. His friend followed. They placed their hands on Jane's head, and Brother Cowley's friend gave a wonderful spiritual blessing.

The tears coursed down my face at that sight and the witness that I sat near the presence of angels. The man spoke fluently in the Maori tongue as he uttered the blessing. It was indeed a spiritual experience to behold this choice apostle of the Lord and his worthy friend as they knelt and petitioned our Heavenly Father in Jane's behalf in our humble home.

I thought, No wonder Brother Cowley says, "No man is greater than when he is on his knees praying!"

Immediately following the blessing, they departed. As he was about to close the door, Brother Cowley (knowing I did not understand the Maori language) said, "Someday I will tell you something about that blessing."

The next day the doctor told me that Jane must go to the hospital because she had pneumonia. She made a speedy recovery there.

After she returned home and was well, one day Brother Cowley said, "Now that's what was told her that day in the blessing—that she would be sicker and it was necessary for her to go to the hospital. But she was also blessed with a quick recovery. I didn't tell you at that time because I didn't want you to worry about it."

Louise Lake, *Each Day a Bonus,* 86–87.

HEALING OF BODY AND SOUL

HAROLD B. LEE

There is a power beyond the sight of man that heals not only sick bodies but sick souls.

I met a young man in Tokyo, where we were holding a servicemen's conference. He had his right arm in a sling, and as he was introduced, he put out his left hand to acknowledge the introduction. "I am not a member of the Church," he said, "but I understand you are going to be in Manila in a few weeks. We will be there with the U.S. Seventh Fleet, and I hope to be able to tell you when you get there that I have become a member of the Church."

The weeks went by and I had almost forgotten the incident until, as we held a conference at Clark Field in Manila, I spotted the same man whom I had met in Tokyo. In an interview we had with him later he said, "You noticed when we met in Tokyo that I had my arm in a sling. It was hurting me terribly all through that service, but after we had shaken hands on the stand, suddenly the throbbing pain seemed to stop. I took my arm out of the sling and began to flex it, and there was no more pain. When I went back to the ship, I didn't need any treatment; the infection seemed to have gone. I sensed the fact that I had been in the presence of a power that had taken away the pain from my body, even healed my sick body. I am going back home now to prove that I am worthy of the love of my sweet wife."

A few years later I was with a companion in Norfolk, Virginia, where we were organizing a new stake, and right down in the front seat sat this same man with a beautiful woman by his side, his wife. We sustained him as a member of the elders presidency in that stake. Yes, the Lord can heal sick bodies, but the greatest miracle we see is the healing of sick souls.

Harold B. Lee, Baccalaureate Address, Ricks College, Rexburg, Idaho, 6 May 1970.

A MIRACULOUS HEALING

AUTHOR UNKNOWN

While journeying to Missouri with the "Kirtland Camp," Brother Peck's son, Edwin, had his leg accidentally run over by a heavily loaded wagon, on a very hard road. When he was picked up, the limb appeared to be flattened as if almost crushed to a pulp, and the flesh was laid open. Brother Peck had seen the power of God manifested in so many instances then, and he had such confidence in the Almighty hearing and answering his prayers, that he never thought of summoning a surgeon, but immediately administered to the boy and then placed him in the wagon. In an hour afterwards he examined his leg and found that it was entirely well, the only sign of the injury left being a slight scar which had the dry and scaly appearance of an old sore, long since healed up. The place was not even discolored. There were numbers of witnesses to this miracle, many of whom are living today.

Early Scenes in Church History, 73–74.

"I REBUKED THE PAIN"

NEWEL KNIGHT

On the 2nd of January, 1831, the third conference of the Church assembled. . . . It was at this conference that we were instructed, as a people, to begin the gathering of Israel. . . . In the early part of April [we] started for our destination [Kirtland, Ohio]. . . . We had proceeded but a few days on our journey when I was subpoenaed as a witness and had to go to Colesville. . . . The whole company declined traveling until I should return. . . .

After I left, my aunt, Electa Peck, fell and broke her shoulder in a most shocking manner; a surgeon was called upon to relieve her sufferings, which were very great. My aunt dreamed that I returned and laid my hands upon her, prayed for her, and she was made whole and pursued her journey with the company. She related this dream to the surgeon, who replied, "If you are able to travel in many weeks, it will be a miracle, and I will be a Mormon, too."

I arrived at the place where the company had stopped, late in the evening; but on learning of the accident, I went to see my aunt, and immediately upon entering the room, she said, "O, Brother Newel, if you will lay your hands upon me, I shall be well and able to go on the journey with you." I stepped up to the bed and, in the name of the Lord Jesus Christ, rebuked the pain with which she was suffering and commanded her to be made whole; and it was done, for the next morning, she arose, dressed herself, and pursued the journey with us to Kirtland.

Newel Knight, in *Scraps of Biography,* 19.

"I Was Directed as by a Voice"

AMANDA SMITH

During the Haun's Mill Massacre] the entire hip joint of my wounded boy had been shot away. Flesh, hip bone, joint, and all had been ploughed out from the muzzle of the gun, which the ruffian placed to the child's hip through the logs of the shop and deliberately fired. We laid little Alma on a bed in our tent and I examined the wound. It was a ghastly sight. I knew not what to do. . . .

Yet was I there, all that long, dreadful night, with my dead and my wounded, and none but God as our physician and help. "Oh my Heavenly Father," I cried, "what shall I do? Thou seest my poor wounded boy and knowest my inexperience. Oh, Heavenly Father, direct me what to do!"

And then I was directed as by a voice speaking to me. The ashes of our fire was still smouldering. We had been burning the bark of the shag-bark hickory. I was directed to take those ashes and make a lye and put a cloth saturated with it right into the wound. It hurt, but little Alma was too near dead to heed it much. Again and again I saturated the cloth and put it into the hole from which the hip joint had been ploughed, and each time mashed flesh and splinters of bone came away with the cloth; and the wound became as white as chicken's flesh.

Having done as directed I again prayed to the Lord and was again instructed as distinctly as though a physician had been standing by speaking to me. Nearby was a slippery-elm tree. From this I was told to make a slippery-elm poultice and fill the wound with it. My eldest boy was sent to get the slippery-elm from the roots, the poultice was made, and the wound, which took fully a quarter of a yard of linen to cover, so large was it, was properly dressed. . . .

I removed the wounded boy to a house, some distance off, the next day, and dressed his hip; the Lord directing me as before. I was reminded that in my husband's trunk there was a bottle of balsam. This I poured into the wound, greatly soothing Alma's pain. "Alma, my child," I said, "you believe that the Lord made your hip?"

"Yes, mother."

"Well, the Lord can make something there in the place of your hip, don't you believe he can, Alma?"

"Do you think that the Lord can, mother?" inquired the child, in his simplicity.

"Yes, my son," I replied, "he has showed it all to me in a vision."

Then I laid him comfortably on his face and said: "Now you lay like that, and don't move, and the Lord will make you another hip."

So Alma laid on his face for five weeks, until he was entirely recovered—a flexible gristle having grown in place of the missing joint and socket, which remains to this day a marvel to physicians.

On the day that he walked again I was out of the house fetching a bucket of water, when I heard screams from the children. Running back, in affright, I entered, and there was Alma on the floor, dancing around, and the children screaming in astonishment and joy. It is now nearly forty years ago, but Alma has never been the least crippled during his life, and he has traveled quite a long period of the time as a missionary of the gospel and a living miracle of the power of God.

Andrew Jenson, *LDS Biographical Encyclopedia,* 2:793–96.

"I Was Healed in an Instant"

Joseph Smith

On the sixth of May I gave the parting hand to the brethren in Independence and, in company with Brothers Rigdon and Whitney, commenced a return to Kirtland, by stage to St. Louis, from thence to Vincennes, Indiana, and from thence to New Albany, near the falls of the Ohio River. Before we arrived at the latter place, the horses became frightened, and while going at full speed Bishop Whitney attempted to jump out of the coach, but having his coat fast, caught his foot in the wheel, and had his leg and foot broken in several places; at the same time I jumped out unhurt.

We put up at Mr. Porter's public house, in Greenville, for four weeks, while Elder Rigdon went directly forward to Kirtland. During all this time, Brother Whitney lost not a meal of victuals or a night's sleep, and Dr. Porter, our landlord's brother, who attended him, said it was a pity we had not got some "Mormon" there, as they could set broken bones or do anything else. I tarried with Brother Whitney and administered to him till he was able to be moved.

While at this place I frequently walked out in the woods, where I saw several fresh graves, and one day when I rose from the dinner table, I walked directly to the door and commenced vomiting most profusely. I raised large quantities of blood and poisonous matter, and so great were the muscular contortions of my system, that my jaw in a few moments was dislocated. This I succeeded in replacing with my own hands and made my way to Brother Whitney (who was on the bed), as speedily as possible; he laid his hands on me and administered to me in the name of the Lord, and I was healed in an instant, although the effect of the poison was so powerful as to cause much of the hair to become loosened from my head. Thanks be to my Heavenly Father for his interference in my behalf at this critical moment, in the name of Jesus Christ. Amen.

Joseph Smith, *History of the Church,* 1:271.

"I REBUKED THE DEVIL"

JOSEPH SMITH

During this month of April, I went on a visit to the residence of Mr. Joseph Knight, of Colesville, Broome County, New York, with whom and his family I had been previously acquainted, and of whose name I have above mentioned as having been so kind and thoughtful towards us, while translating the Book of Mormon. Mr. Knight and his family were Universalists, but were willing to reason with me upon my religious views and were as usual friendly and hospitable. We held several meetings in the neighborhood; we had many friends and some enemies. Our meetings were well attended, and many began to pray fervently to Almighty God that he would give them wisdom to understand the truth.

Amongst those who attended our meetings regularly was

Newel Knight, son to Joseph Knight. He and I had many serious conversations on the important subject of man's eternal salvation. We had got into the habit of praying much at our meetings, and Newel had said that he would try and take up his cross and pray vocally during meeting; but when we again met together, he rather excused himself; I tried to prevail upon him making use of the figure, supposing that he should get into a mud hole would he not try to help himself out? And [I said] that we were willing now to help him out of the mud hole. He replied that provided he had got into a mud hole through carelessness, he would rather wait and get out himself than have others help him; and so he would wait until he should get into the woods by himself, and there he would pray.

Accordingly, he deferred praying until next morning, when he retired into the woods; where (according to his own account afterwards) he made several attempts to pray but could scarcely do so, feeling that he had not done his duty, but that he should have prayed in the presence of others. He began to feel uneasy, and continued to feel worse both in mind and body, until, upon reaching his own house, his appearance was such as to alarm his wife very much. He requested her to go and bring me to him.

I went and found him suffering very much in his mind, and his body acted upon in a very strange manner. His visage and limbs distorted and twisted in every shape and appearance possible to imagine; and finally he was caught up off the floor of the apartment and tossed about most fearfully.

His situation was soon made known to his neighbors and relatives, and in a short time as many as eight or nine grown persons had got together to witness the scene. After he had thus suffered for a time, I succeeded in getting hold of him by the hand, when almost immediately he spoke to me, and, with great earnestness, requested of me that I should cast the devil out of him, saying that he knew he was in him and that he also knew that I could cast him out. I replied, "If you know that I can, it shall be done"; and then almost unconsciously I rebuked the devil and commanded him in the name of Jesus Christ to depart from him; when immediately Newel spoke out and said that he saw the devil leave him and vanish from his sight.

This was the first miracle which was done in this Church, or by any member of it, and it was done not by man nor by the power of man, but it was done by God, and by the power of godliness; therefore, let the honor and the praise, the dominion and the glory be ascribed to the Father, Son, and Holy Spirit for ever and ever. Amen. . . .

The scene was now entirely changed, for as soon as the devil had departed from our friend, his countenance became natural, his distortions of body ceased, and almost immediately the spirit of the Lord descended upon him, and the visions of eternity were opened to his view. . . .

All this was witnessed by many, to their great astonishment and satisfaction, when they saw the devil thus cast out, and the power of God and his Holy Spirit thus made manifest. So soon as consciousness returned, his bodily weakness was such that we were obliged to lay him upon his bed and wait upon him for some time. As may be expected, such a scene as this contributed much to make believers of those who witnessed it, and finally the greater part of them became members of the Church.

Times and Seasons, 15 November 1842, 12–13, 22.

"The Lord Was Able to Make Him an Instrument"

PHILO DIBBLE

When Joseph came to Kirtland his fame spread far and wide. There was a woman living in the town of Hiram, forty miles from Kirtland, who had a crooked arm, which she had not been able to use for a long period. She persuaded her husband, whose name was Johnson, to take her to Kirtland to get her arm healed.

I saw them as they passed my house on their way. She went to Joseph and requested him to heal her. Joseph asked her if she believed the Lord was able to make him an instrument in healing her arm. She said she believed the Lord was able to heal her arm.

Joseph put her off till the next morning, when he met her at Brother Whitney's house. There were eight persons present, one a Methodist preacher, and one a doctor. Joseph took her by the hand, prayed in silence a moment, pronounced her arm whole, in the name of Jesus Christ, and turned and left the room.

The preacher asked her if her arm was whole, and she straightened it out and replied: "It is as good as the other." The question was then asked if it would remain whole. Joseph hearing this, answered and said: "It is as good as the other, and as liable to accident as the other."

The doctor who witnessed this miracle came to my house the next morning and related the circumstance to me. He attempted to account for it by his false philosophy, saying that Joseph took her by the hand, and seemed to be in prayer, and pronounced her arm whole in the name of Jesus Christ, which excited her and started perspiration, and that relaxed the cords of her arm.

Early Scenes in Church History, 79.

"I Have Witnessed the Power of God"

ABRAHAM O. SMOOT

I have witnessed the power of God displayed in the healing of persons who were sick in hundreds of instances, in some cases that would probably be considered by the world as very wonderful, but to which the Saints, whose experience has been similar to my own, had become accustomed. I think Elder David W. Patten possessed the gift of healing to a greater degree than any man I ever associated with. I remember on one occasion when I was laboring with him as a missionary in Tennessee, he was sent for to administer to a woman who had been sick for five years and bedridden for one year and not able to help herself. Brother Patten stepped to her bedside and asked her if she believed in the Lord Jesus Christ. She replied that she did. He then took her by the hand and said, "In the name of Jesus Christ, arise!"

She immediately sat up in bed, when he placed his hands upon her head and rebuked her disease, pronounced blessings upon her head and promised that she should bear children. She had been married for seven years and had never had any children, and this promise seemed very unlikely ever to be fulfilled. But she arose from her bed immediately, walked half a mile to be baptized and back again in her wet clothes. She was healed from that time, and within one year became a mother, and afterwards bore several children.

Early Scenes in Church History, 29.

"I'LL DIE AND GO TO HELL YET"

ABRAHAM O. SMOOT

During the winter of 1846–7 while the Saints were encamped on the banks of the Missouri there was a great deal of sickness among them, and many died. Among others who were afflicted was a man by the name of Collins, who had followed up the Church for some time on account of his wife being a member, but who never felt quite satisfied to embrace the gospel, although he never opposed the work. When he was taken sick it was not thought by his friends that he could recover, as he had appeared to be sinking rapidly under the effects of the disease, and for some time he lay in a semi-unconscious state, from which it was feared he would never rally.

However, he finally regained consciousness and looked around, when I asked him if he had any message to leave before he died. He immediately replied that it would not do for him to die then, as he had not been baptized, and urged very strongly to be taken right down to the river to receive this ordinance.

Yielding to his solicitations, some of the brethren brought the running gear of a wagon with a few boards on it, up to the door of the cabin in which he was living, and his bed, with him lying upon it, was carried out and placed on the wagon. When we had proceeded part way down to the river the wagon tire commenced running off one of the wheels and a halt was made to hammer it on again. On noticing the wagon stop and hearing the hammering, he inquired what was the matter, and when he was informed that the tire was running off, he replied impatiently, "Oh, never mind the tire; go on, or I'll die and go to hell yet before I'm baptized!"

We proceeded on with him till we reached the river, which at that time was frozen over, but the ice had been cut away near the shore in order that our animals might drink. There he was lifted from his bed, carried into the water and I baptized him for the remission of his sins and his restoration to health. After being taken out of the water a blanket was wrapped around him and he was seated for a moment to rest upon a block of ice upon the shore. Seeing the brethren turning the wagon around, he inquired what they were going to do. They replied that they were going to put him on the bed and haul him back home, when he arose to his feet and assured them that they need not go to that trouble, for he could walk back, and he did so, and from that time became a healthy man.

Early Scenes in Church History, 30–31.

The Wagon Passed over His Arm

Oliver B. Huntington

Tuesday, Dec 27th, 1881: Sister Eliza R. Snow related the circumstances of a miracle that was performed in some of the extreme northern out-of-the-way settlements of the Saints.

It was this: A certain brother was hauling wood and was thrown from the load by the roughness of the road. The wagon passed over his left arm between the shoulder and elbow, crushing his arm bone to many pieces.

Assistance accidentally came along, by which came along an elder of the Church with oil and anointed the crushed arm and laid his hands upon it and prayed, during which the elder shook and trembled under the power of God.

When the ceremony was over, he asked the man if he felt anything strange while being administered to? He replied, as he raised the crushed arm above his head, "I should think I did." His arm was healed and the bone went "bone to bone" knit and grew together sound while the ordinance was being performed.

Oliver B. Huntington, "History of the Life of Oliver B. Huntington, 1878–1900," 12.

"HE IS BREATHING HIS LAST!"

ELIZA R. SNOW

The following incident took place as Lorenzo Snow returned from a mission to England aboard the ship *Swanton.*]

The steward, a German by birth, was a young man, very affable in manner and gentlemanly in deportment—a general favorite and respected by all. During the latter part of the voyage he took sick and continued growing worse and worse, until death seemed inevitable. All means proved unavailing, and the captain, by whom he was much beloved, gave up all hope of his recovery and requested the officers and crew to go in, one by one, and take a farewell look of their dying friend, which they did silently and solemnly, as he lay unconscious and almost breathless on his dying couch.

Immediately after this sad ceremony closed, one of our sisters, by the name of Martin, without my brother [Lorenzo Snow]'s knowledge went to the captain and requested him to allow my brother to lay hands on the steward, according to our faith and practice under such circumstances, saying that she believed that the steward would be restored. The captain shook his head and told her that the steward was now breathing his last, and it would be useless to trouble Mr. Snow. But Sister Martin was not to be defeated; she not only importuned, but earnestly declared her faith in the result of the proposed administration, and he finally yielded and gave consent.

As soon as the foregoing circumstance was communicated to my brother, he started toward the cabin where the steward lay, and in passing through the door met the captain, who was in tears. He said, "Mr. Snow, it is too late; he is expiring; he is breathing his last!" My brother made no reply, but took a seat beside the dying man. After devoting a few moments to secret prayer, he laid his hands on the head of the young man, prayed, and in the name of Jesus Christ rebuked the disease and commanded him to be made whole. Very soon after, to the joy and astonishment of all, [the young man] was seen walking the deck, praising and glorifying God for his restoration. The officers and sailors acknowledged the miraculous power of God, and on landing at New Orleans several of them were baptized, also the first mate, February 26, 1843.

Eliza R. Snow, *Biography and Family Record of Lorenzo Snow,* 65–66.

"There Is No Use Doing Anything for a Dead Man"

ANDREW MAY

I was born February 22, 1871, at Call's Fort, north of Brigham City, in Box Elder County, Utah, and I was living there in 1894. I was twenty-three years of age. During June of this year, I was stacking hay for Thad Wight. It was about eleven A.M. in the forenoon, and Conrad Nelson was running the Jackson fork. The hay was green. A load came up, and I called for Nelson to trip it. And I thought the fork had gone over me. As I raised up the long fork tine struck me in the back and went right through my body. The tine broke my ribs and pushed the bones through my breast.

Hyrum G. Smith (late Patriarch of the Church) was working across the fence and was one of the first to reach me. He helped carry me on a sheet into Brother Wight's house. They sent to Brigham City for Dr. Carrington, who arrived about five P.M. He just looked over me, probed the wound, took some blood out of my lungs through my breast and said, "Tom Yates, there is no use doing anything for a dead man. . . . He will not need anything more. I cannot do anything for him."

They carried me over to my own home, then my mother-in-law came; she put her hand on my breast. I became semiconscious and everything seemed like a dream. I could not remember anything during the night. Dr. Carrington said, "If he should live he will not amount to anything because he will never get well and will be subject to all kinds of diseases and will have a weak lung and system." He said he could do nothing for me and then went back to Brigham City.

President Lorenzo Snow was in Brigham City, and the next morning he heard of my accident . . . and came to our house to see me. He and my father were very close friends. He came in, looked me over, and my wife asked him to administer to me. Instead of doing so he stood by the bedside and asked if I had been anointed. He was told that I had. He then put his hands on my head and gave me a wonderful blessing. The doctor said I was going to die, but President Snow said to me I would not die, but that I would live just as long as life was desirable unto me.

Thomas C. Romney, *The Life of Lorenzo Snow,* 395–97.

"You Shall Return in Safety"

DANIEL TYLER

After the meeting was opened, Sister More arose and began to speak in tongues. She addressed her remarks to me, and I understood her as well as though she had spoken the English language.

She said: "Your leg will be healed, and you will go on a foreign mission and preach the gospel in foreign lands. No harm shall befall you, and you shall return in safety, having great joy in your labors."

This was the substance of the prophecy. It was so different from my own belief and the fears of many others that I was tempted not to give the interpretation, lest it should fail to come to pass. The Spirit, however, impressed me and I arose, leaning upon my crutches, and gave the interpretation.

Not long afterwards I was told in a dream what to do to strengthen my fractured limb, and it began to receive strength immediately, and in the short space of about one week I dispensed with my crutches and walked with a cane.

Daniel Tyler, in *Classic Experiences and Adventures,* 41–42.

"PAIN WENT THROUGH ME LIKE AN ARROW"

WILFORD WOODRUFF

On the fifteenth day of October, 1846, while with the Camp of Israel building up Winter Quarters, on the west side of the Missouri River (then Indian Country), I passed through one of the most painful and serious misfortunes of my life. I took my ax and went two and one-half miles upon the bluff to cut some shingle timbers to cover my cabin. I was accompanied by two men. While felling the third tree, I stepped back of it some eight feet, where I thought I was entirely out of danger. There was, however, a crook in the tree, which, when the tree fell, struck a knoll and caused the tree to bound endwise back of the stump. As it bounded backwards, the butt end of the tree hit me in the breast, and knocked me back and above the ground several feet, against a standing oak. The falling tree followed me in its bounds and severely crushed me against the standing tree. I fell to the ground, alighting upon my feet. My left thigh and hip were badly bruised, also my left arm; my breastbone and three ribs on my left side were broken. I was bruised about my lungs, vitals, and left side in a serious manner.

After the accident I sat upon a log while Mr. John Garrison went a quarter of a mile and got my horse. Notwithstanding I was so badly hurt, I had to mount my horse and ride two and one-half miles over an exceedingly rough road. On account of severe pain I had to dismount twice on my way home. My breast and vitals were so badly injured that at each step of the horse pain went through me like an arrow. I continued on horseback until I arrived at Turkey Creek, on the north side of Winter Quarters. I was then exhausted, and was taken off the horse and carried in a chair to my wagon.

I was met in the street by Presidents Brigham Young, Heber C. Kimball, Willard Richards, and others, who assisted in carrying me to the wagon. Before placing me upon my bed they laid hands upon me, and in the name of the Lord rebuked the pain and distress, and said that I should live, and not die.

I was then laid upon my bed in the wagon, as my cabin was not yet done. As the apostles prophesied upon my head, so it came to pass; I did not die. I . . . was administered to by the elders of Israel, and nursed by my wife. I lay upon my bed, unable to move, until my breastbone began to knit together on the ninth day. In about twenty days I began to walk, and in thirty days from the time I was hurt, I returned to my laborious employment.

I have not now a lame limb about me, notwithstanding it all. I have been able to endure the hardest kind of manual labor, exposures, hardships, and journeys. I have walked forty, fifty, and, on one occasion, sixty miles in a single day.

Matthias F. Cowley, *Wilford Woodruff: His Life and Labors,* 10–12.

"He Was Full of Blessing and Prophecy"

LORENZO DOW YOUNG

When the temple was enclosed, in a meeting of the brethren, called to consult about its completion, the Prophet desired that a hard finish be put on its outside walls. None of the masons who had worked on the building knew how to do it. Looking around on the brethren, his eyes rested upon me; he said, "Brother Lorenzo. I want you to take hold and get this finish on the walls. Will you do it?"

"Yes," I replied; "I will try." The following day, with horse and buggy I went to Cleveland, twenty-two miles, determined, if possible, to find a man who understood the business of putting a hard finish on the walls. I had been there but a short time, inquiring after such a man, when I met a young man who said he understood the business, had just completed a job, and wanted another. I employed him at once, put him and his tools into the buggy, and returned to Kirtland.

We soon had the materials and fixtures on hand to make the mortar. In a short time the finish was being put upon the walls.

I made a suitable tool and, before the mortar was dry, I marked off the walls into blocks in imitation of regular stone work. When the finish was on I commenced penciling.

It was then the last of November, and the weather daily grew colder. A Brother Stillman assisted me a day or two, but said that he could not stand the cold, and quit the work.

I continued, day after day, determined, if possible, to complete the job. When I got badly chilled I went into my house, warmed myself and returned again to the work.

I completed the task in the fore part of December, but was sick the last two days. I had caught a bad cold, had a very severe cough, and in a few days was confined to my bed.

My disease was pronounced to be the quick consumption. I sank rapidly for six or seven weeks. For two weeks I was unable to talk. Dr. Williams, one of the brethren, came to see me, and, considering my case a bad one, came the next day and brought with him Dr. Seely, an old practicing physician, and another doctor whose name I have forgotten. They passed me through an examination. Dr. Seely asserted that I had not as much lungs left as would fill a tea saucer. He appeared a somewhat rough, irreligious man. Probably, with what he considered a good-natured fling at our belief in miracles, he said to my father, as he left the house:

"Mr. Young, unless the Lord makes your son a new pair of lungs, there is no hope for him!"

At this time I was so low and nervous that I could scarcely bear any noise in the room. The next morning after the visit of the doctors, my father came to the door of the room to see how I was. I recollect his gazing earnestly at me with tears in his eyes. As I afterwards learned, he went from there to the Prophet Joseph, and said to him: "My son Lorenzo is dying; can there not be something done for him?"

The Prophet studied a little while, and replied, "Yes! Of necessity, I must go away to fill an appointment, which I cannot put off. But you go and get my brother Hyrum, and, with him, get together twelve or fifteen good faithful brethren; go to the house of Brother Lorenzo, and all join in prayer. . . . After prayer, divide into quorums of three. Let the first quorum who administer, anoint Brother Young with oil; then lay hands on him, one being mouth. When all the quorums have, in succession, laid their hands on Brother Young and prayed for him, begin again with the first quorum, by anointing with oil as before, continuing the administration in this way until you receive a testimony that he will be restored."

My father came with the brethren, and these instructions were strictly followed. The administrations were continued until it came the turn of the first quorum the third time. Brother Hyrum Smith led. The Spirit rested mightily upon him. He was full of blessing and prophecy. Among other things, he said that I should live to go with the Saints into the bosom of the Rocky Mountains, to build up a place there, and that my cellar should overflow with wine and fatness.

At that time, I had not heard about the Saints going to the Rocky Mountains; possibly Brother Smith had. After he had finished he seemed surprised at some things he had said, and wondered at the manifestations of the Spirit. I coughed no more after that administration, and rapidly recovered.

I had been pronounced by the best physicians in the country past all human aid, and I am a living witness of the power of God manifested in my behalf through the administration of the elders.

Fragments of Experience, 43–45.

The Faith of a Uruguayan Woman

MARK E. PETERSEN

At the close of the morning general session in the new meetinghouse at Montevideo on Sunday, December 12, 1954, I was approached by a middle-aged Italian woman by the name of Sister Beathgen. After shaking hands with me and exchanging some pleasantries, she showed me her right hand and asked if I could see the small scar just about an inch below the first finger in the palm of her hand. I told her that I could see it. Then she told me this story:

More than a year ago she was suffering with bone cancer in that hand. A swelling had developed there which made a lump nearly as big as a golf ball. She went to several of the principal doctors of the city and also to the clinics and hospitals of the city, seeking every type of relief. All of the doctors diagnosed it as cancer of the bone. There was no question about the diagnosis as the doctors agreed with each other. The examinations and charts from hospitals indicated the same thing, so she told me. May I say that all of this was confirmed by the mission president and other missionaries who knew this sister during the past couple of years. They also tell me that this is a woman of good reputation, honest and firm and true.

The doctors told her that there was no cure for this cancerous condition. The only thing would be amputation of the arm. She did not wish to have an operation of that kind. When she heard that President McKay was coming, the thought occurred to her that if she could just shake hands with him, her hand would be healed.

With this in mind she stood in line when President McKay was shaking hands with the people following the meetings he attended there in Montevideo. When it came her turn to shake hands, she merely did so and expressed her pleasure at his coming to the conference. She said nothing about her sore hand and said nothing about her hope that she would be healed by shaking the President's hand. She merely shook hands, expressed a few pleasantries, and went on her way.

She told me there in Montevideo that within three days the cancer was gone from her hand. She said further that there had been no recurrence in the past year. I examined her hand again, and it was perfectly free from any kind of sores but merely had a well-healed scar in the palm as I have described.

I talked about this whole situation with the missionaries and President Shreeve, and they confirm this entire story and say that not only do they know that the diagnosis was true but that they themselves also saw this large lump on her hand and knew of this affliction for a fact. They also knew that immediately after the visit of President McKay, Sister Beathgen showed them her hand which was healed.

Mark E. Petersen, as quoted in David O. McKay, *Cherished Experiences,* 159–60.

"FIX ME UP, I WANT TO GO HOME"

MATTHEW COWLEY

One of our dearest friends in New Zealand . . . owned a taxicab company out there in one of the cities; every cab in the town he owned. One day he was stricken and started to have a hemorrhage from the nose, which couldn't be stopped. So they took him to the hospital, and the doctors couldn't stop it. So they sent for his family, and they came to be there when he passed on. When the family was standing around and the nurses were still working on him, he said to one of the nurses, "You go to the phone, and call my switchboard at the taxi office, and tell the girl to send a couple of my drivers out here quick." Every driver of every cab he owned was an elder in the Church.

The nurse went to the switchboard and called her and said, "The big man wants you to send a couple of his drivers out here to the hospital fast." She knew what it meant, so out went two drivers. "Fix me up, I want to go home." Just like that you know. One anointed him, the other sealed the anointing, and he got up out of bed and went home. The hemorrhage had ceased immediately. It was the simplest thing in the world, wasn't it? He didn't have any doubt at all about the power of God to heal. Medicine had failed, medical science had failed, so with simple faith he had his taxi drivers bless him.

Matthew Cowley, *Matthew Cowley Speaks,* 148.

"YOU DO WHAT I SAW IN MY DREAM"

MELVIN S. TAGG

A native, crawling on his hands and knees to show respect, approached Elders Wood and Dean. Through an interpreter, the native told of a lady on another island who wanted the missionaries to come and heal her sick child. He said the lady had seen these two elders in a dream, and he asked them to follow him quickly. . . . The native Saints warned the elders that harm would come of it, that it was only a trap to ensnare the servants of the Lord.

The elders tried to anticipate the result of a successful healing and an unsuccessful healing. In their dilemma, they went to a secluded spot under a banyan tree and there inquired of the Lord as to whether it would be right to undertake this mission of mercy. [Elder Wood] said that while they were in the attitude of prayer, he heard a voice telling him "it was alright to go to the other island." This was the assurance the elders needed, and they were soon on their way across the three-mile stretch of ocean that separated the two islands. Despite a stormy sea, they reached their destination in safety.

The mother, who had been waiting on the beach for them, greeted them respectfully and motioned for them to follow her to her house. Addressing the elders, the woman remarked, "I am glad that you have come. It is alright. Here is my child." Thereupon, she lifted a white sheet from off the body of the child who was lying on the floor of the hut.

The elders declared the child to be dead, but the mother insisted otherwise and added, "You do what I saw you do last night in my dream, and she will be well." The faith of the elders was at a low ebb, and knowing the natives to be extremely superstitious, they feared the consequences "should they administer to the afflicted one without the desired results." While the elders were thus meditating, the mother submitted this question to them: "Have you the authority to do what I saw you do in my dream? You anointed that child with oil; you laid your hands upon her head." No longer could they hesitate. They were convinced they had the authority, so they administered to the child. After completing the ordinance they covered the child with the cloth and took their departure.

Nothing more was heard of the child or its mother until about two years later when Elder Wood was called to labor on yet another island. Much to his surprise he was greeted on the beach by half-clad natives running back and forth and swinging long knives. He was soon entirely surrounded by them, but before long he was greeted kindly by a woman who called him by name. "I do not know you," he replied as he stepped back from her.

Reminding Mr. Wood that he did know her, she called to her side a young child about nine years old and, addressing the crowd, she said: "This is a living testimony of the great power of the gospel, and the power and authority held by Mr. Wood and his associates. They administered to this child over two years ago. I have never seen them since, but I know they have the power of God with them, and all of you must listen to their message."

Then addressing Mr. Wood, she said that she was the daughter of the high chief of the island and that he could stay at her home and his needs would be supplied. The group then proceeded to her father's house, where Elder Wood spent nearly all night preaching to them with great power. The good woman, daughter of the chief, told him that she had been praying earnestly for Mormon missionaries to be sent to her home, where, she felt, there would be great good accomplished in the spreading of the gospel.

Melvin S. Tagg, "The Life of Edward James Wood, Church Patriot," 22–24.

SHE TURNED LOOSE ON HIM

MATTHEW COWLEY

We have a . . . friend down in Honolulu, . . . a man who is a young bishop down there, very wealthy, and yet a young man with a lot of humility. He was called one day from the Queen's Hospital to come and bless a boy who had polio. A native sister had called him. He was her bishop, and she said, "Bishop, come up here, my boy is stricken with polio, and I want you to come up here and administer to him and bless him."

All day she waited for him, and the bishop never showed up. All night he never showed up. The next morning he never showed up, but early in the afternoon here he came.

She turned loose on him. She called him everything she could think of. "You, my bishop, I call you and tell you my boy is here stricken with polio. And you your own boss. You have your cars, you have a beautiful yacht, you have everything you want; and your time is your own; and you don't show up. You just come now after a whole day."

After she had finished and couldn't think of anything more to call him, he smiled and said, "Well, after I hung up the receiver yesterday, I started to fast, and I've been fasting and praying for twenty-four hours. I'm ready now to bless your boy." At five o'clock that evening the boy was released from the hospital, entirely cured of his polio. ". . . This kind goeth not out but by prayer and fasting."

Matthew Cowley, *Matthew Cowley Speaks,* 149–50.

ATTACKED WITH A VIOLENT FEVER

BRIGHAM YOUNG

I was suddenly . . . attacked with the most violent fever I ever experienced. The Prophet Joseph and Elder Willard Richards visited and administered unto me; the Prophet prophesied that I should live and recover from my sickness. He sat by me for six hours, and directed my attendants what to do for me. In about thirty hours from the time of my being attacked by the fever, the skin began to peel from my body, and I was skinned all over. . . . It was not until the fourteenth day that Brother Joseph would give his consent for me to be showered with cold water, when my fever began to break, and it left me on the 18th day. I laid upon my back, and was not turned upon my side for eighteen days.

I laid in a log house, which was rather open; it was so very cold during my sickness, that Brother Isaac Decker, my attendant, froze his fingers and toes while fanning me, with boots, great coat and mittens on, and with a fire in the house, from which I was shielded by a blanket.

When the fever left me on the 18th day, I was bolstered up in my chair, but was so near gone that I could not close my eyes, which were set in my head—my chin dropped down and my breath stopped. My wife, seeing my situation, threw some cold water in my face; that having no effect, she dashed a handful of strong camphor into my face and eyes, which I did not feel in the least, neither did I move a muscle. She then held my nostrils between her thumb and finger, placing her mouth directly over mine, blew into my lungs until she filled them with air. This set my lungs in motion, and I again began to breathe. While this was going on I was perfectly conscious of all that was passing around me; my spirit was as vivid as it ever was in my life, but I had no feeling in my body.

Millennial Star, 12 March 1864, 167.

"I SAW MY WIFE AT THE POINT OF DEATH"

JOHN TAYLOR

When I was in Paris, France, about thirty years ago, I had a dream that troubled me very much, in which I saw my first wife . . . lying sick at the point of death. And it so affected me that I awoke, being troubled in my feelings. I fell asleep again, and again the same scene presented itself to me when I again awoke and experienced the same feeling of sorrow, and after some time slept again, and it was repeated a third time. I knew then that my wife was very sick, lying at the point of death.

I got up and fervently prayed the Lord to spare her life until, at least, I should have another opportunity of meeting her in the flesh. He heard my prayer. I took a note of the circumstance at the time, and learned afterward that such had been the case, exactly as it had been shown to me.

On the following morning I remember meeting a gentleman who was a Protestant minister, and he observed that my countenance looked sorrowful, and then inquired the cause. I told him that my wife was lying at the point of death, and he asked me if I had received a letter. I told him how it had been shown to me. But, I said, I got up and prayed the Lord to spare her life, and I feel consoled in knowing that she will be healed.

Journal of Discourses, 22:354.

"I CRIED UNTO THE LORD FOR STRENGTH AND WISDOM"

NEWEL KNIGHT

After the close of the meeting Brother Hyrum [Smith] and myself intended going to spend the night with one of the brethren who lived a short distance from my uncle's, but as we were ready to start, the Spirit whispered to me that I should tarry there at my uncle's all night. I did so, and retired to bed, where I rested till midnight when my uncle came to my room and desired me to get up, saying he feared his wife [Electa Peck] was about to die. This surprised me, as she was quite well when I went to bed.

I dressed myself, and having asked my Heavenly Father to give me wisdom and power to rebuke the destroyer from the habitation, I went to the room where my aunt lay. She was in a most fearful condition; her eyes were closed, and she appeared to be in the last agonies of death. Presently she opened her eyes, and bade her husband and children farewell, telling them she must die for the redemption of this generation, as Jesus Christ had died for the generation in His day. Her whole frame shook, and she appeared to be racked with the most exquisite pain and torment; her hands and feet were cold, and the blood settled in her fingers; while her husband and children stood weeping around her bed.

This was a scene new to me, and I felt she was suffering under the power of Satan—that was the same spirit that had bound and overpowered me at the time Joseph cast him out.* I now cried unto

*For the story of Joseph Smith healing Newel Knight, see page 129.

the Lord for strength and wisdom that we might prevail over this wicked and delusive power. Just at this time my uncle cried aloud to me saying: "O, Brother Newel, cannot something be done?"

I felt the Holy Spirit of the Lord rest upon me as he said this, and I immediately stepped forward, took her by the hand, and commanded Satan, in the name of the Lord Jesus Christ, to depart. I told my aunt she would not die, but that she should live to see her children grown up; that Satan had deceived her, and put a lying spirit in her mouth; that Christ had made the only and last atonement for all who would believe on His name; and that there should be no more shedding of blood for sin. She believed and stretched forth her hand, and cried unto me, and Satan departed from her.

Newel Knight, in *Scraps of Biography,* 66–67.

"You Must Do Something for Her"

NEWEL KNIGHT

Brother Joseph from time to time sent copies of revelations to me for the benefit of the branch over which I presided in common with all the Saints in Zion. On reading one of these revelations to the branch, my aunt [Electa Peck] of whom mention has been made, arose and contradicted the revelation, saying it must be taken in a spiritual light. She went to such a length that I felt constrained to rebuke her by the authority of the priesthood. At this she was angry, and from that time sought to influence all who would listen to her.

The result was a division of feeling in the branch, and her husband partook of her spirit until he became so enthusiastic, that he went from branch to branch crying, "Hosanna, glory to God! Zion is redeemed! and blessed is he that bringeth good tidings to the people!" Sister Peck at length began to feel the weight of what she had done, but she could not recall it. She seemed racked with great torment, her mind found no rest, until a burning fever brought her to a sick bed. She sent for several of the elders to administer to her, but found no relief.

At last she sent for P. P. Pratt, Lyman Wight, and myself; we laid our hands upon her and administered to her, after which she looked up in despair and said she hoped I would deliver her from the awful state she was in. Her whole frame was racked with intense anguish while her mind seemed almost in despair. Brother Parley said to me: "Brother Newel, you must do something for her." My soul was drawn out in pity for her, yet I knew not what to do. I felt impressed to call the branch together that evening.

When the meeting had been opened as usual, I arose, not knowing what to do or what to say. After requesting the prayers and united faith of all present, the Spirit of the Lord came upon me, so that I was able to make plain the cause of Sister Peck's illness—that she had risen up in opposition to the priesthood which had been placed over that branch of the Church, and contradicted the revelations of God, and that by the sympathies shown her, a division of feeling had gained advantage over them, until Sister Peck had fallen completely under the power of Satan, and could not extricate herself. I told the brethren and sisters, if they would repent of what they had done, and renew their covenants one with another and with the Lord, and uphold the authorities placed over them, and also the revelations which the Lord had given unto us, it would be all right with Sister Peck, for this would break the bands of Satan and make us free.

I had no sooner closed my remarks than with one united voice, all came forward and agreed to do so. I then went to Sister Peck, and in the name of Jesus Christ, and by virtue of the Holy Priesthood, commanded the evil powers to depart from her, and blessed her with peace and strength, both of body and mind. I then dismissed the meeting and told the family to go to bed, and rest as usual, and all would be well.

Early the next morning I called to see her, she stretched out her hand as soon as she saw me, and said, "O, Brother Newel, forgive me! I did not believe one word you said last night, but when I awoke this morning I found I was not in hell." Her rejoicings were very great, and union again prevailed with us, and we all felt we had learned a lesson that would be of lasting benefit to us.

Newel Knight, in *Classic Experiences,* 73–75.

Humor

"Another Story"

From Barbara Neff Autograph Book

Twenty-two-year-old Barbara Matilda Neff traveled with her parents in 1844 to meet the Prophet Joseph Smith in Nauvoo, where they stayed in the Mansion House between May 8 and 13. While there, Barbara collected autographs from prominent citizens, and she collected other autographs many years later in Salt Lake City. Among those who wrote in her book were William W. Phelps, Joseph Smith, and Brigham Young.

William W. Phelps wrote:

> Two things will beautify a youth
> That is: Let *virtue* decorate the *truth*
> and so you know; every little helps
> yours—W. W. Phelps

Joseph Smith continued his clerk's train of thought with these lines:

> The truth and virtue both are good
> When rightly understood
> But Charity is better Miss
> That takes us home to bliss
> and so forthwith
> remember Joseph Smith

On a later page Brigham Young added this verse:

> To live with Saints in Heaven is bliss and glory
> To live with Saints on Earth is another story.

Barbara Neff Autograph Book, Church Historical Department, Salt Lake City, Utah.

"YOU'VE BEEN AWFULLY SICK, HAVEN'T YOU?"

DAVID O. McKAY

Brother Hugh J. [Cannon] was in prime condition, I thought, when we boarded the *Empress of Japan,* a Canadian Pacific Ocean Steamer in the Royal Mail Service, on the evening of December 7, 1920. Kind friends had showered us with good wishes and blessings, had feasted and dined us for weeks previous, and had sent along with us boxes of the choicest cream chocolates to make our journey sweet and delightsome.

No voyage, therefore, was ever entered upon with more appreciation in one's heart for farewells given or more hopeful anticipations for a delightful trip.

It was storming when we went to bed, and the movement of the boat was keenly perceptible even when we went to sleep.

The pitching of the vessel in the night awoke me. The roar of the wind and the dashing, splashing sound of water told me that we were in a gale at sea. Sleep from then until morning was only intermittent. Every nerve and muscle in my body responded to every movement of the boat. As this movement became more pronounced and intense, the contents of my digestive organs joined in unison with nerves and muscles. Twenty-one years ago, one morning on the Atlantic, I had experienced a similar feeling, so I knew I had better dress carefully, and get up on deck.

At that moment Brother Cannon jumped out of bed as bright and pert as a ten-year-old boy. He could steady himself as though he were anchored. With no apparent difficulty, he dressed himself, and even shaved—an operation, which though ordinarily simple enough, seemed to me under the circumstances, almost marvelous. I concluded to take his advice when he said:

"If you aren't feeling well, I suggest that you don't look in this mirror."

He invited me to breakfast, but I couldn't think of anything that this ship could put on a table that was worth eating, so begged to be excused. It was a dismal sounding gong that called us to breakfast anyhow—a fitting accompaniment to the gloom of the weather. However, before attempting to dress, I ate an apple Brother Hugh J. handed me.

Without hurried exertion, I put on my clothes and started for the deck; but the swaying staircase and the madly moving world of water stirred my feelings with a yearning desire for solitude. Yielding, I hurried to my room, where in less time and seemingly with less effort than it takes to tell you, the apple and I parted company forever. I threw myself on the berth, and wondered what there was in common between a Jonathan apple and Jonah that could produce such like effects. Though I arrived at no definite conclusions about the matter, one thing was most certain: My sympathy was wholly with the whale. I understood, too, how Jonah escaped being thrown into the sea. If I could entirely have followed the whale's example, I, too would have swum for land.

Hugh J. returned from breakfast looking as robust and rosy as an athlete, and smacking his lips in appreciation of an excellent meal. What a blessing health is! I was feeling pretty miserable, and I hated myself for getting sick so early in the game. As he looked at me, I fancied I saw spreading over his countenance indications of a laugh he was trying hard to suppress. I said something which enabled him to lift the lid and let off his mirthful steam. Limp and dejected, I looked at him, healthy and happy, and began, right then and there, to doubt the wisdom of the Revolutionary statesmen who declared that "all men are created equal." However, he gave me the comforting assurance that only a few passengers were at breakfast.

Feeling somewhat better, I started again for the deck and was not a little consoled when I passed a poor Chinaman with perspiration standing in beads on his jaundiced-looking face, and sitting holding his knees, looking, as I'm sure he felt, the most forsaken, limpy lump of humanity in existence.

At any rate, I had company in furnishing gratuitous amusement for the "chosen few." This time I reached only the top of the stairs, when that intense yearning to be alone drove me back to my cabin. Good-bye last night's dinner! Good-bye yesterday's Rotary luncheon! And during the next sixty hours, Good-bye everything I had ever eaten since I was a babe on Mother's knee. I am not sure I didn't even cross the threshold into the pre-existent state.

In the tossing and heaving of the ship, as well as of internal conditions, there was no respite. She would mount the crest of a huge wave and then plunge head-on; but before hitting the bottom of the trough, she would take a plunge to "port," then instantly veer to "starboard"; hesitating a moment, she would give a "shimmy"-like shiver and plunge again—turning, veering, "shimmying" in endless repetition, until it seemed that life was made of nothing else.

And all this rough sea was on the placid Pacific! Truly, Balboa was not in a ship but on the sunny side of a California hill when he named these waters the Pacific Ocean. Heaven be merciful to me if we sail a tempestuous sea!

In the afternoon (December 18th) another blizzard swept down from the north. I believe it is the worst yet. The waves on the port side look like the hills on our Huntsville range, and rolling almost as high. The foam, the billows, and the wind-driven spray give the ocean today the coldest, bleakest aspect I have ever beheld. Every once in awhile a tremendous wave strikes the ship with a boom, breaks over the top, and pours down in a torrent on the colored glass skylight in the center of the roof of the library where I am writing. The old boat is strongly built, but she quivers when she gets a real body blow.

One woman talking to another, said, "You've been awfully sick, haven't you?"

"No," replied the other in all seriousness, "I haven't been sick, but I couldn't keep anything on my stomach."

Llewelyn R. McKay, comp., *Home Memories of President David O. McKay,* 39–41.

A JOURNEY THROUGH ECHO CANYON

B. H. ROBERTS

It is of general repute that the governor [non-Mormon Easterner Alfred Cumming] was a little imposed upon in his night journey through Echo Canyon. In order to make as impressive an appearance of their forces as possible, as also, doubtless, to keep concealed the location and the nature of their "fortifications" in the canyon, the journey of the governor's party was made in the night. After the militia at the first campfire halt had been drawn up in form and solemnly addressed by his excellency, they were dismissed and hurried down to the second encampment to again solemnly receive the governor in military array, and again hear his speech; again to cheer what he had to say about returning peace; and so again at the third encampment this performance was repeated. Stenhouse, who makes too much of the incident, states that when the governor discovered the trick played upon him, "he was ever afterwards unpleasantly reticent when the affair was mentioned." He also says that Cumming held Brigham responsible for the mortifying joke; but that is not likely, since Brigham Young did not know of the governor's advent into the "Mormon" camps in time to plan it. Stenhouse makes the following attempt at description of the illuminations:

"From one end of the canyon to the other, great fires could be seen at night on the hillsides and on the mountain tops, representing the works and bivouacks of a great army, while the lurid flames of the pinetree fires rendered the darkness still more impressive, and conveyed to the bewildered governor the idea that near at hand there was a mighty host under arms. The military chieftains managed to keep his excellency in a continued strain of feverish expectation. At every important bend of the road the governor and his escort would be suddenly challenged by the pickets, and the countersign demanded. On one occasion there was a call to arms, and a mock effort at hostility, but some of the principal officers arrived just in time to save his excellency's life, and to call off the pugnacious militia, and hinder them from taking him prisoner!"

At the mouth of Echo Canyon Colonel Kane detained the governor by a day's shooting; and further down the Weber, at the camp of Ben Simons, the Cherokee Indian trader and interpreter, another day was spent in shooting. By express, Colonel Kane sent word to President Young that he expected to arrive in Salt Lake City with the governor on Monday, the 12th of April. Undoubtedly the delay en route was meant to kill time in order to give opportunity for the church leaders and the people to adjust themselves to the new situation created by Governor Cumming consenting to come among them without a military escort, to assume the duties of his office.

The snow was still so deep on Big Mountain, over which the road usually traveled passed into Salt Lake Valley, that it was decided to bring the governor through Weber Canyon via Farmington to Salt Lake City. "At the mouth of Weber Canyon the Farmington guards, mounted and in uniform, met him. On his reaching the courthouse (in Farmington) the band played 'The Star-Spangled Banner.' Sunday evening he stopped at Judson Stoddards at Farmington. Monday morning he was visited by the Farmington band in carriages: they played 'Hail Columbia,' 'Yankee Doodle,' 'The Star-Spangled Banner,' and other popular airs. Cumming made a speech, remarking that he was astonished at such attachment for national airs; he believed it could not be feigned."

B. H. Roberts, *Comprehensive History of the Church,* 4:378–80.

A Cart Full of Apples

BRIGHAM YOUNG

A man was going to market, a pretty wicked swearing man, with his cart full of apples. He was going uphill, and the hindboard, as the Yankees call it—the Westerners call it the hindgate, slipped out of his cart, and his apples rolled down the hill. He stopped his team and looked at the apples as they rolled down the hill, and said he, "I would swear if I could do justice to the case, but as I cannot I will not swear a word."

Journal of Discourses, 15:19–20.

"I WAS IN HOPES YOU WOULDN'T RECOGNIZE ME"

FRANCIS M. GIBBONS

President Kimball's sense of humor . . . was reflected in an encounter he had with a highway patrolman. The officer saw a car driving without lights on State Street in Salt Lake City. He pulled the car over and on approaching saw that President Kimball was the driver.

"Sir," he said, "did you know you were driving with your lights off?"

"Yes," he answered, "I just noticed it."

"President Kimball," he said, "please let me see your driver's license."

"I was in hopes you wouldn't recognize me," President Kimball said.

"I was in hopes it wouldn't be you," the officer said.

Writing out only a warning ticket, he handed it to President

Kimball, who said, "Now, young man, do not fail, merely because of my position in the Church, to give me a ticket if I deserve one."

Said the officer, "All right, President Kimball, if you insist."

"I don't insist," President Kimball said.

All the while this was going on, Sister Kimball sat chuckling on the passenger side of the front seat.

Francis Gibbons, *Spencer W. Kimball: Resolute Disciple, Prophet of God,* 290–91.

JAPANESE COURTESY

DAVID O. McKAY

We have observed that no man (in Japan) ever gives up his seat in a street car to a woman, unless it be an old woman, or a woman with a baby on her back or carrying bundles. No aged person is ever permitted to stand.

The first time Brother Cannon and I were given seats, we were carrying satchels, and the kindness of the gentlemen who stood up for us made us deeply grateful. The next time, we concluded it was because we were foreigners, and were even more grateful; but about the fifth or sixth time, it suddenly dawned on me that these people were giving us seats because they thought us two old men! It seems that Brother Cannon had surmised as much before, because when I said, "Do you know, I believe I understand why these men give us their seats in the car?" Brother Cannon smiled and said,

"Has it just dawned on you?" And then for his personal comfort only, he added:

"And I've noticed that you've always been the first to be given consideration."

Well, though this realization somewhat lowered my appreciation of the kindness, I still maintain that the Japanese are second to none in true courtesy and hospitality.

Llewelyn R. McKay, comp., *Home Memories of President David O. McKay,* 45–46.

"DON'T BE AFRAID TO LAUGH"

LLEWELYN R. McKAY

Don't be afraid to laugh," father [David O. McKay] has said. "A person without a sense of humor misses much of the joy of living!" Perhaps this is one of the main reasons why people delighted in being with him, for he was always a cheerful and entertaining companion. His charm which awakened friendship included a sparkling wit, and he was always ready to tell and to hear a good story.

One example occurred in Scotland when we arrived on an early morning at the railway station at Glasgow. Here we had to change trains which necessitated our taking a taxi to the Bucannon Street station.

"So you're going to Aberdeen?" said our taxi driver. "You'll find the town absolutely deserted, because it's Flag Day today in Aberdeen." I bit at that—after all, it was only six in the morning, and I was still sleepy. "Why," I inquired, "will the streets be deserted on Flag Day?" "Because," he answered with a twinkle, "the flags sell for thrupence!"

Father laughed for several minutes—probably more at me than at the joke.

A good laugh is a panacea for many ills. Father has often said: "Every time a man laughs he takes a kink out of the chain of life."

Llewelyn R. McKay, comp., *Home Memories of President David O. McKay,* 165.

"THAT'S IT, THAT'S IT, YOU ARE, YOU ARE"

DAVID O. McKAY

When speaking of his Welsh lineage on his mother's side, David O. McKay liked to relate the following incident:]

I visited Malad soon after I was called to the Council of the Twelve. The grandfather of Brother Ralph Richards, one of our secretaries who drove us down, was president of the Malad Stake and just before the Saturday morning session of that quarterly conference began, I whispered to President Richards that I had Welsh blood in my veins. He, of course, was a pureblood Welshman. With a toss of his head or an expression on his face, I don't remember just which, he implied that I was making that claim simply because I was in Malad, a town principally of Welsh people.

When I arose to speak to the congregation, I told them, "Just before this service began I whispered to President Richards that I have Welsh blood in my veins, but by the shake of his head or the expression on his face, he implied that I made the claim merely because I am here with you Welsh people. But I wish to say to President Richards and to you that my mother was born in Plasagon House, Cleydyfagwyr Cefn Eved Cwmer, near Merthyr-Tydfil, South Wales, and her name was Evans."

An old lady sitting in the front seat rose and said, "That's it, that's it, you are, you are."

Llewelyn R. McKay, comp., *Home Memories of President David O. McKay,* 24–25.

THE UNWELCOME SUBSTITUTE

FRANCIS M. GIBBONS

Occasionally Joseph Fielding [Smith] was . . . sent to fill speaking assignments for his father [Joseph F. Smith]. One notable example occurred when the prophet, unable to fill a commitment to dedicate a chapel in Brigham City, Utah, sent Joseph Fielding as a substitute without telling the stake president, Oleen H. Stohl, of the change. There are differing versions of President Stohl's reaction and comments when he met the train to find that the Joseph Fielding Smith who had arrived was not the Joseph Fielding Smith whom he expected and wanted. The version most often told, and certainly the funniest, has President Stohl saying, "I could bawl. We were expecting the President of the Church and we get a boy instead." Flashing his wry sense of humor, Joseph, in another version, is reported to have answered, "I could bawl too."

Francis M. Gibbons, *Joseph Fielding Smith,* 113.

Doomed for Sure

FRANKIE JANE TAYLOR

Faith and prayer are two great and important instruments in our Church. If you were in trouble or needed help in any way, you most likely would call upon God through prayer. To get an answer to this prayer, you must exercise faith.

I would like to tell you a story told by my grandfather in church recently. A man was wandering in the forest one day and it began to rain. Looking around for shelter, he spied a hollow log and crawled in. As he crawled, he became stuck fast in the log. He felt he was doomed for sure so he decided to pray and thank God for all his blessings. In appreciation for all these things, he felt so small he crawled out of the log.

Improvement Era, November 1951, 793.

UNCLE J. GOLDEN AND THE BILL COLLECTORS

SPENCER W. KIMBALL

I want to mention a story I have told about Uncle Golden. You have heard about my Uncle J. Golden Kimball, who was a rather interesting person. I don't think it is true, but it was told of him that his creditors kept coming and bothering him all the time and they wanted payments on their accounts. And he began to get a little tired of it, and he said, "Now listen here, fellows. You know the way I handle my accounts. I take all of the bills at the end of the month and I put them in the wastebasket. Then I stir them around and if I see one that looks good and I can I'll pay it. But," he said, "if you don't quit bothering me I won't even put yours in the wastebasket."

Conference Report, April 1975, 168.

THE MISCHIEVOUS MONKEY

J. GOLDEN KIMBALL

When I was in California I was very low spirited and broken down in body; and I tried to die, but I made a miserable failure of it. . . . One day when I was laying on the sand, near the ocean, I happened to pick up a paper, and it gave me new life and new energy. It was a funny picture; it was a picture of a great big monkey, it represented, "Fate—The Old Monkey." It was an editorial. I haven't it with me, but I have read it a good many times, and I desire to make a comparison.

There was a very prominent citizen that had an intelligent monkey. [The monkey] was a mischievous fellow, and he just went around the house knocking everything down that he could get hold of. He knocked over everything that he came to; he discovered that the things he knocked over did not get up again. He was just as mischievous as fate seems to be with us.

Finally, this good citizen took the image of a little man, made of some kind of material, and placed it on a very strong base. It was so arranged that when you knocked it over it would come up again. So he set this little man in the room. The monkey came around, took his right hand and cuffed it over. To his surprise it wobbled a little and staggered, and then rose up and seemingly looked at him. Then he took his other hand and cuffed it again, and it came up again. Then he took the hand of his right leg and knocked it again, and then with his left hind leg; then he got on it with all four hands and took one hand up at a time. To his surprise, the little man rose up.

The intelligent monkey almost became a monkey maniac. He

kept at it and kept at it until he hated and despised the little man; and whenever they would move the little man near the monkey, he would get off in the corner and chatter and become angry. He wouldn't have anything to do with the little man.

The Church of Jesus Christ of Latter-day Saints is similar, or like that little man. You can knock it down one hundred times; you can knock it down one thousand times; it may wobble, but it will rise up again, and it will keep rising up until God has accomplished His work.

This is God's work, and I look in sympathy upon men who oppose it. I stood on the street last night—something I hardly ever do—and listened to a man abuse the Church; and I had to laugh. I was a good deal like father was once when he was praying. In the midst of his prayer, he burst out in a loud laugh, and he said, "O Lord, forgive me; it makes me laugh to pray about some men"; it always amuses me when I see a man or a coterie of men try to break down this Church. I would say to these kind of men: You had better let the Church alone; you had better let the people alone; because you can't destroy the Church.

Conference Report, October 1910, 34.

Integrity

"We Want a Man of Character"

HUGH B. BROWN

While I was in training [for the military], a young Mormon boy came into the camp. He was awkward. He was not educated very well, but he was a young Mormon boy who had been taught to live the gospel. After one parade, when he had gone through everything backwards, he was called by the captain to come into his office. The captain said, "I have noticed you, young fellow. You are from Cardston, aren't you?"

He said, "Yes, sir."

"You are a Mormon, I suppose."

"Yes, sir."

"Well, I just wanted to make friends with you. Will you have a glass of beer?"

"Sir, I do not drink liquor."

The captain said, "The ——— you don't. Maybe you will have a cigar then."

He said, "Thank you, sir, but I do not smoke."

The captain seemed much annoyed by this, and he dismissed the boy from the room.

When the young man went back to his quarters, some of the lesser officers accosted him angrily and said, "You fool, don't you realize the captain was trying to make a friend of you, and you insulted him to his face?"

The young Mormon boy answered, "Gentlemen, if I must be untrue to my ideals and my people and do things that I have been instructed all my life I should not do, I'll quit the army."

When the time came for the final examinations in that camp, the captain sent this young man down to Calgary from Sarcee Camp to do some work for him, and they were having examinations while he was gone. When he returned the captain said, "Now you go in the other room there, and I will give you the list of questions, and you can write your examination."

He went in and returned and said, "Sir, all the books we have studied are there on that desk. Surely you don't want me to write my examination there where I can turn to those books."

The captain said, "That is just what I do want. I know from my knowledge of you that you will not open a one of those books. You will be honorable, you will be honest, and I trust you."

Well, that young man, while overseas later on in the war, was sent for by his captain, who had then become a lieutenant colonel, in response to a call from general headquarters for the best man he had in his battalion. They had a special mission for him to perform. They said, "We don't care anything about his education or his training. We want a man who can't be broken when put under test. We want a man of character." The lieutenant colonel, his former captain, selected and assigned this young man who had the courage to stand before him and say, "I do not smoke. I do not drink."

Conference Report, April 1969, 112.

RESPONDING TO THE BELL

HUGH B. BROWN

May I tell a story to illustrate the point that a man must respond to his better self if he is going to be a worthy holder of the priesthood. The story is told that the Arabians, when they are training their horses, put them to a final test of character and stamina. It is said that the finest of the Arabian horses which are kept for breeding stock are trained from the time they are colts to respond to a bell which rings intermittently at the tent of the master. Wherever they are and whatever they are doing, they must run to the tent of the master when the bell rings. Their mothers were taught it before them, and they respond, and the colt, running beside the mother, habitually as time goes on responds to the bell and knows that it is the call of duty.

When the colts are three years old, they are placed in a corral, a pole corral that they can see through. They are left there three days and nights without food or water. At the end of the third day, hay and grain and water are placed just outside the corral. You can imagine the eagerness of the young colts as they look through the bars at the food and water. When the gate is opened the young colts rush out, and just as they are about to reach the food and water, the bell rings. Only those of them that have stamina enough to respond to the bell and resist the urge of appetite are kept for the breeding stock of the future.

Brethren, as we go forward, we become increasingly aware of the fact that there is a bell which rings very frequently throughout life. Sometimes men become unresponsive or hard of hearing and disregard the bell to their own sorrow. You young men are going to hear it many times between now and the time you are our age. We plead with you to resist the call of appetite and passion and hearken to the bell which is your conscience. If you are tempted to do wrong, there will always be something within you saying, "Don't do it." Hearken and respond to that bell, and you will be worthy of the confidence that the President of the Church has in you, worthy to take over the responsibilities now held by your fathers, your brothers, your leaders.

Conference Report, April 1963, 91.

"IT GIVES ME PLEASURE TO SIGN YOUR BONDS"

HEBER J. GRANT

In 1890–91, earnest efforts were being made to establish the beet-sugar industry in our territory. Because of the financial panic of 1891, many who had subscribed for stock were unable to pay their subscriptions, and I was sent east to secure the funds needed to establish the industry. Having failed in New York and Hartford to obtain all of the money required, I was subsequently sent to San Francisco where one hundred thousand dollars was secured from Mr. Henry Wadsworth, cashier of Wells, Fargo & Co.'s bank in that city. I am confident that my having been faithful when a boy in his employ, at the time he was agent of Wells Fargo & Co., in Salt Lake City, had some influence in causing him to loan to my associates such a large sum, at a time when there was a great demand for money.

One of the parties who signed bonds with me when I engaged in the insurance business was Brother Horace S. Eldredge, and as each bond required two signatures, he suggested that I ask Captain William H. Hooper to sign with him. I explained that I knew the Captain only slightly, and feared he would not care to become one of my sureties. Brother Eldredge thought otherwise, so I solicited the Captain's signature, but he promptly declined.

I walked direct to my office and had been there but one or two minutes when a messenger from the Deseret National Bank, where I had just left the Captain, called and said that Mr. Hooper desired to see me. My answer was that I had just seen the Captain and our conversation had been of such a character that I had no particular desire for another interview. The messenger insisted that he had seen the Captain since I had, and I finally concluded, therefore, to call again.

On reaching the bank, the Captain said: "Young man, give me those bonds." He signed them, and then said, "When you were here a few moments ago, I did not know you. I have met you on the street now and then for a number of years, and have spoken to you, but really did not know you. After you went out, I asked who you were, and learning that you were a son of Jedediah M. Grant, at once sent for you. It gives me pleasure to sign your bonds. I would almost be willing to sign a bond for a son of Brother Jedediah if I knew I would have to pay it. In this case, however, I have no fears of having to do that." He related a number of incidents about my father, which showed the Captain's love for, and confidence in, him.

What the Captain told me filled my heart with gratitude to God for having given to me such a father, and Captain Hooper's remarks have never been forgotten. They impressed me with a strong desire to so live and labor that my children would be benefited, even after I have passed away from this life, by the record which I shall have made. The action of Captain Hooper profoundly impressed me with the benefits derived from having a good father. Although my father died when I was a babe nine days old, twenty years after his death I was reaping the benefits of his honesty and faithful labors.

The incident referred to above happened twenty-three years ago. Many, many blessings have since come to me because of the honesty and integrity of my father.

Improvement Era, January 1900, 190–91.

Love

"We Want Another Meeting"

EZRA TAFT BENSON

I know that the Lord can touch the hearts of men behind the iron curtain. I have seen it happen. I have been very close to it. I remember very well our efforts to get to Warsaw, Poland, in 1946 and my desire to get up to Selbongen in East Prussia where we had one congregation, the only congregation in Poland and the only Church-owned building in Germany at that time. There was one plane going, taking supplies to the American Embassy, but no passenger service.

We had to get permission from the Russians and the Poles to get into Warsaw. Brother Fred Babbel, who was with me, had tried to make arrangements without success, and then I had tried, and we still weren't successful. But our plane was to leave in two days, and so we did some fasting and praying.

At last I went to see the Russian general who was in charge of the Poles and finally, after about two hours in his office with him, he signed the document to permit us to go. Then we made arrangements to ride on the plane with the Americans who were carrying supplies to the American Embassy. I learned later that this general lost his commission because he had given permission for an American to go into Poland, and I always felt that the Spirit worked on this man, because he had previously turned us down.

In Warsaw there was only one hotel that was even partially intact, and that was the Polonia Hotel. I shared one room with seven other men, most of them members of the press. We got the Americans to loan us a jeep, and we drove up to Selbongen. It took us all day to drive there on Sunday, through two rainstorms and with no cover on the jeep. When we drove into the little town of Selbongen we found the name had been changed to Zelback, because the Poles had changed all the names throughout the area. There was no one on the street because it was Sunday, and as we approached our little chapel, we saw a woman running away from us. She had seen this military vehicle and had thought it meant more trouble, because the people had been persecuted and their homes had been ransacked.

Well, we stopped the jeep and I jumped out. When the woman saw we were civilians, she turned around and came walking toward us. Then she recognized us—I guess from a picture, I don't see how else—and she screamed, "Oh, it's the brethren! They have come at last!" She ran to us with tears in her eyes and then guided us to the home of the branch president. I think I never saw so many tears shed by a small group as we saw that day, as the word spread and the people came into the branch president's home. Then we held a meeting. I said, "Haven't you had your meetings today, yet?" They said, "Yes, we have had our meetings—priesthood, Sunday School, and sacrament meeting—but now that you are here we want another meeting." It was five o'clock, just starting to get dusk, and so we set the meeting for six and sent the members out to notify the Saints. At six o'clock the little chapel was filled.

During the service, as I was speaking near the time of closing, two Polish soldiers came in the front door and took a few steps into the building. I motioned for them to come forward. There were only two vacant seats, on the front row. Then, through the interpreter, I told them why I was there and on what authority and something about our work. I went ahead speaking to the people after the soldiers had taken seats at my invitation. I could tell the people were frightened of them, because as they came down the aisle the women would push away from the aisle. As we came to the end of the service and were starting to sing the closing song, they left the meeting place.

We had planned to close the meeting, but three or four people stood up immediately and asked, "Couldn't we have another meeting? This was not like a real meeting with soldiers here." One lady said, "I have a candle at home I have been saving for a special occasion [there were no lights in the building]." She said, "I will go get it if you want to read from the scriptures." And so we held another meeting for an hour and a quarter with these wonderful people.

Ezra Taft Benson, *God, Family, Country,* 71–73.

"HE BROKE DOWN AND CRIED"

SHERI L. DEW

As Elder [Ezra Taft] Benson and his associates drove toward Keil, Germany [after World War II], they saw dozens of people combing the ditch banks. He described the scene in a letter home: "Some take ordinary grass and weeds and cut it up to mix with a little chicken feed and water which is their meal. I noticed between meetings some would take out of their pocket a little cup partly filled with chicken feed or cereal and water which they would eat cold. . . . I didn't intend to write all this sad picture. I have tried to spare you at home most of the heart-rending scenes in Europe today. But somehow I just couldn't hold it this morning. It's terrible to contemplate. . . ."

When the first shipment of welfare supplies arrived in Berlin, Elder Benson took acting mission president Richard Ranglack to the battered warehouse that, under armed guard, housed the precious goods stacked nearly to the ceiling. "Do you mean to tell me those boxes are full of food?" President Ranglack asked. "Yes," Ezra replied, "food, clothing, bedding, and a few medical supplies." To prove his point, he pulled down a box of dried beans. As Ranglack ran his fingers through the contents, he broke down and cried. Ezra opened another box, this one filled with cracked wheat. Ranglack touched a pinch of it to his mouth. When he could finally speak, he said, "Brother Benson, it is hard for me to believe that people who have never seen us could do so much for us."

Sheri L. Dew, *Ezra Taft Benson: A Biography,* 218–19.

"The Mortgage Is Paid Off"

Matthew Cowley

Over in Colorado once, I was at stake conference, and I asked one of the elders quorum presidents how his elders were getting along as a quorum. I said, "Do you do anything to help one another?"

"Oh, yes, we don't do bad."

I said, "Well, what are you doing?"

He said, "Well, I can tell you this: we've got a member of our quorum in the hospital down in Santa Fe, New Mexico. He was a strong, vigorous young man, buying a beautiful farm—a hard worker with a lovely little family. He was going ahead, paying off his bills and his mortgage, when all of a sudden he was stricken." Ordinarily that would have been the end of the farm, the end of security of the family. The elders quorum president said to me, "That was our loss as much as it was a loss for his wife and children. So we took over, and we've gone out and operated that farm. It doesn't take much time with all of our tractors and all our equipment. The mortgage is paid off, and the family has a good income from the farm. All the man has to worry about is getting well, down there in that hospital."

Matthew Cowley, *Matthew Cowley Speaks,* 308–9.

"That Young Man Will Amount to Something"

EMMA RAE McKAY ASHTON

Ray [Emma Ray Riggs] was about eighteen when her mother called to her one day to look out of the front room window. Joining her mother, she was impressed by what she saw. Two tall, handsome young men, each holding an arm to help their mother up the walk, were accompanied by their two younger sisters.

"See, Ray, how attentive the boys are to their mother. They will make fine husbands for some fortunate girls someday." While attending the University of Deseret, these young people were to be tenants of her mother's home for the next two years and were to be numbered among Ray's best friends. Little did she realize then that six years hence, the dear friends would be her brother and sisters, and David O. McKay, the dearest one of all, her beloved, lifelong companion.

Ray, too, was attending the University of Deseret. One day as she was walking down a corridor she heard someone speaking. Noticing the door of the room ajar, she stood in the hallway and listened to a talk given by young David O. McKay before the Normal Society.

That young man will amount to something someday, she thought to herself.

In June 1897, David O. McKay, president of his class, was graduated from the Normal School and was chosen to be the valedictorian. During the commencement exercise, Ray, thrilled by his words, wondered whether she would ever see him again. She was overjoyed when, in July of that same year, his sisters, Jeannette and Ann McKay, invited her to Huntsville to attend David O.'s missionary farewell, and she willingly accepted. That evening after the program David O. walked Ray from the chapel to the McKay home, holding her hand all the way. They agreed to correspond while he was away.

Just before he was released from his mission, David O. received an appointment by mail to teach at the Weber Stake Academy in Ogden, which he readily accepted. The courtship that had begun at his missionary farewell blossomed through correspondence and was continued in earnest for a year and a half after he returned from Scotland in August 1899.

One colorful autumn afternoon under a graceful umbrella

tree, he proposed to her in Lester Park in Ogden. She was thrilled but answered, "Are you sure you want me?"

"Yes. I am very sure," smiled her sweetheart.

They became engaged. It was some months later, January 2, 1901, when David O. called for Ray in his horse-drawn hack to drive her three blocks to the Salt Lake Temple. Here they were married by Elder John Henry Smith to be companions for eternity.

Relief Society Magazine, June 1967, 409–11.

"A Six-Shooter in His Hip Pocket"

Alma Burton

In the southern part of Utah there lived a poor widow and her son, the latter a wild, impudent, intractable youth, whose transgressions often brought his mother into sore distress. He was known as the terror of the town. He had almost reached the period of manhood without having curbed this insubordination. One evening the bishopric of the ward in which he lived proposed to him that he attend the Brigham Young Academy. In this proposition they had two purposes: one was that they might rid themselves of him, and the other that he might improve himself. They were willing to furnish the money if he would but go.

When the proposition was placed before him he accepted; his mother agreed to it; and in a very short time he was enrolled as a student in the above-mentioned school. One glance was sufficient to convince his associates that he was not to be trifled with. He came to school with his books under his arm and a six-shooter in his hip pocket. It was difficult for him to accustom himself to his new surroundings; he felt like a young bronco, newly saddled.

Before the end of the first week he had a difficulty with his teacher, to whom he manifested such a degree of insubordination that his instructors appealed to President Maeser of the Academy to have him suspended. With bowed head the principal listened without uttering a word. Finally he broke the silence and said, "Try him once more; he is the son of a widow whose entire hope is centered in him. She knows her boy better than we do. She hopes and prays that some day he will see the foolishness of his ways and change them. She has written me several letters in which she has pleaded with me to try and save him. I have promised that I would do my best, and I will keep my promise. Give him one more chance."

The instructors returned to their classrooms in compliance with the master's wishes. Try as they would, all their efforts were in vain, and the young man remained wholly uncontrollable. At the end of another week the instructors returned to the office of the principal and placed two propositions before him. The one was that this young man should be dismissed from the school forthwith; the other, that in the event the principal could not see his way clear to dismiss him, they would hand in their resignations to take effect immediately. "That young man is a terror," said one of the instructors; "we have done our best, but have failed absolutely." "Send him to me," said Brother Maeser.

In a few minutes the young man entered the principal's room. "Did you send for me?" he said in a low but defiant voice.

"Yes, sir," replied the genial principal. "I sent for you because I have to inform you that you must leave this institution tomorrow morning."

"Good," answered the yet unsubdued youth; he then turned about and left the room.

In the middle of the following night, Brother Maeser awoke from his slumber and thought of the wild youth whom no one seemed able to tame, who was to be expelled from the school on the following morning. He also thought of the anxious widow and how she had pleaded with him that he might save her son. He arose from his bed, knelt by the side of it, and laid the matter before the Lord; and this was the purport of his supplication: "Dear Father, there is at this time a young man in our school whom we are unable to control. We have tried to do our best, but, sad to say, we have failed. If there is a way whereby we may reach him, I pray thee in our Redeemer's name to make it known unto us; and thy name shall have the praise, the honor, and the glory."

"I received no satisfaction from my supplication," said Doctor Maeser; "and therefore thought it possible that the Lord himself had given him up."

The next morning, about ten o'clock, as the principal was sitting in his office, there came a knock at the door. . . .

"Well," said the principal, "what can I do for you?" The young man, with downcast eyes, replied: "May I speak with you for a few moments, Professor Maeser?"

"Certainly," was the reply.

The young man's lips quivered; and with trembling voice, he said: "You will not dismiss me, Brother Maeser, will you? Will you not please give me one more chance?"

Brother Maeser sprang to his feet, extended his arms toward

this once obstinate youth and exclaimed: "Come to my arms, my son, God bless you! I will not give you up; not one chance, but a thousand chances shall we be glad to give you." The master and the student fell into each other's arms and wept.

This was the turning point in the life of this young man. He studied energetically and worked so industriously that upon various occasions the principal had to caution him against over-exertion.

You ask, "Whatever became of the boy?" The last we heard of him he was a counselor to the bishop who had sent him to Provo to school partly that the ward might be relieved of his presence.

Alma Burton, *Karl G. Maeser, Mormon Educator,* 47–49.

CAESAR

LLEWELYN R. McKAY

Caesar was a full-blooded boar. We children were a little apprehensive of him because he was large and had ferocious-looking tusks. He responded to father's [David O. McKay's] kindness and took every opportunity to stay by him in hope of having his back scratched with a stick.

On a Sunday morning, just as father was leaving for Ogden to catch a train, Caesar broke out of his enclosure. There was no time to repair the fence, and not wanting him to run loose, father put him in the chicken coop with the intention of writing a note of instructions to one of us boys.

That night at two A.M. the telephone rang incessantly, waking up the whole household. Uncle Tommy answered the phone and was told that a telegram had arrived for Lawrence, my older brother. Lawrence was called out of bed. By this time everyone was alerted to the fact that a telegram was to be read over the phone. Naturally all were concerned, wondering what had happened: sickness? an accident? a death? All members gathered around the phone as Lawrence wrote down the following message:

"Caesar in chicken coop. Water him!"

Even though we lost a lot of sleep, we had a good laugh.

This is what had occurred: As father sat on the train he began worrying that his note of instructions would not be read, and he couldn't go peacefully on his way worrying that Caesar might suffer from thirst. Needless to say, Caesar was well cared for by his boys the next morning.

Llewelyn R. McKay, comp., *Home Memories of President David O. McKay,* 127–28.

"LET US GO BACK"

LLEWELYN R. McKAY

The strain of shaking hands with hundreds of people on a tour of missions and branches is tremendous. With the purpose in mind of saving father [David O. McKay] from overexertion, the mission authorities suggested to the people of Frankfurt, Germany, that handshaking be withheld. After the meeting, the people lined up on both sides of the sidewalk to greet father and mother as they walked from the meeting hall. True to their instructions, not one person put out his hand, but only smiled and nodded as the visitors walked by. The disappointment on their faces, however, was evident, and father had the impression that they were very unhappy to miss the opportunity of shaking his hand. When he got to the end of the line, he said, "I'm going back to the beginning of the line, and even if it takes more than an hour, I am going to shake hands with every one of these good people." His guess of an hour was correct. He was tired after strenuous travel, and the hottest day recorded for many a year had descended upon Frankfurt, but he left all members happy in the realization that they had shaken the hand of their President.

Llewelyn R. McKay, comp., *Home Memories of President David O. McKay,* 145–46.

MISSIONARY WORK

“Why Had I Come?”

REED H. BRADFORD

Have you ever had an experience with such meaning to you that it changed the course of your whole life? I had such an experience, and the memory of it is as clear to me now as it was that day twenty-five years ago when it happened.

I was walking along the streets of a beautiful little town in Germany [just before World War II]. It was Maytime and the fragrance of lilacs was everywhere. It seemed so good to be alive.

Oh, I admit there were some things troubling me. Take that first meeting in the office of the mission president in which he asked us all why we had come on a mission. Someone said it was because his parents had always wanted him to come. Another replied that he had always admired the German people and wanted to learn their language and absorb some of their culture. A humble farm boy was of the opinion that it was his duty to come since his bishop and President Heber J. Grant had personally called him.

The thing that kept bothering me was the look on the face of the mission president after each person had finished speaking. For some reason it seemed to me that he was disappointed and, yes, even a little hurt. But I did not know why.

Then there was the tracting problem. My companion, as part of my orientation, had shown me the mission statistics. “We have to average at least three hours a day tracting or we’ll be getting a letter from the mission office,” he said. I did not want any such letter, but it was not easy to spend those hours, what with most people slamming doors in your face and you unable to speak German very well.

But this morning I shoved such problems into the back of my mind. It was spring and I felt good.

Suddenly, I heard a loud voice coming from somewhere in the near vicinity. At first I could not tell whence it came, but, looking more closely, I saw a huge crowd of people standing in formation. I surmised that they were listening to a special broadcast over the radio. Approaching the crowd, I asked a man what this was all about. "Don't you know," he said, "that this is Labor Day and everyone who works gathers to listen to the Fuehrer's instructions?" I was about to reply that I had not known about this when suddenly the voice from the loudspeaker shouted, "Heil Hitler," and everyone directed his gaze to a swastika flying from a flagpole and gave the Nazi salute.

I realized immediately that I was in an embarrassing position. To salute or not to salute, that was the question. I only had a couple of seconds to make this decision, but for my own reasons, I decided against it.

The events of the next few minutes happened quickly and violently. To begin with, two men asked me why I had failed to raise my hand. In my best German, I explained that I was not a citizen but was representing an organization whose principles and aims were in some respects quite different from those espoused by Adolf Hitler. I was about to say something more when the next thing I knew I was trying to pick myself up off the ground. Someone had struck me and, as I looked up, I saw some of the most hateful human beings I had ever seen, all staring down at me. They were about to renew the attack when someone shouted: "He's no German; he's an American."

For some reason they ceased beating me but dragged me away from the crowd. After finding out where I lived, they took me home and everyone left except one man in plain clothes, who I later discovered was the district leader of the Gestapo, or secret police. "You stupid moron," he shouted, "how dare you insult the greatest man living, the Fuehrer of the German people, one who will one day conquer the world! Why have you come here anyway?"

He told me many other things, but they are unimportant. What was important was that ringing question: Why have you come here anyway? It was the same question our mission president had asked in that first meeting. My soul was in a turmoil and no amount of lilacs or brightness of the sunshine could calm it. Why had I come?

Over and over again I sought the answer and gradually, like a fog lifting from the marshes, things began to clear. I discovered that those reasons we had given the mission president were not good enough. The great reason, the one that should have been central to everything we did, was to bring souls to an understanding of God's way of life. But how was one to be sure that his way was as good or better than some other ways? We had always assumed that his way was better, but how was one to know? Somehow I would have to find out.

I remember reading that verse in John in which he said: "If any man will do his will, he shall know of the doctrine, whether it be of God, or whether I speak of myself" (John 7:17). It came to me clearly that if one wanted to do his will, he would have to discover what his will was. I now began to read the scriptures with the same zeal and desire I had read *David Copperfield* as a child. And as I began to understand them, I tried to make them part of my life. It was no perfect performance, but something important was taking place from within.

For example: I must have listened to the prayer on the sacrament hundreds of times, but now it had a new meaning for me. Certain parts of it even bothered me because I knew I had not been worthy to take upon me the name of his Son. But I realized that in a sense, since I was a member of his church, I did represent him, and I ought to represent him honestly and well.

In a way I suppose you could say I had been born again. So many things were taking on new meanings. I no longer tracted those many hours in order to have my name high on the list in the mission office. I had found a better reason to tract. Gerhardt, a wonderful young friend whose life characterized His principles as well as any I know and who was killed in a tank going through the Maginot line, said it was the "personal commitment" to God, his principles, and his church, that brought this new understanding and the peace that "surpasseth all understanding." He was right. I discovered that His way of life brought not just temporary satisfactions, but the most intensive, extensive, and permanent satisfactions I had ever known.

As I went to say good-bye to our mission president before sailing for America, there came a wonderful radiance into his face as he listened to my story. "Your mission is just beginning," he said. This time I knew what he meant.

Instructor, March 1959, 76–77.

"HE WAS SPEAKING WORDS WHICH HE DID NOT UNDERSTAND"

ANTHON H. LUND

The writer recollects hearing the late Elder George G. Bywater relate an incident in his experience while upon his first mission.

He was laboring in Wales in company with another elder of more experience than himself. The senior [missionary] generally did most of the preaching. Upon one occasion the latter took a severe cold on his lungs and became so hoarse that he could scarcely whisper. An appointment had been made for him to preach at a certain place where the congregation would be mostly composed of Welsh-speaking people. The experienced missionary was unable to speak on account of his hoarseness, so he informed his young companion that he would have to do the speaking.

Elder Bywater felt his weakness and inability to satisfy the people's expectations, as he did not understand the Welsh language; but, on being requested to do so, he arose to address the audience as best he could, depending upon the Spirit of the Lord to assist him in his utterances. He began by speaking in the English tongue—the only one he understood—but soon he found that he was speaking words which he did not understand, and the fluency with which they came from his lips astonished him.

After he had finished preaching, his companion, who understood the Welsh tongue, told him that he had delivered an excellent sermon in that language, and that if he lived to the age of Methuselah he would not be able to preach a better one. He had been blessed with the gift of tongues that his hearers might understand the message he had to declare to them.

Edwin F. Parry, *Sketches of Missionary Life,* 59–61.

"WHERE IS THE FROG THAT CROAKED HERE A DAY OR TWO AGO?"

AUTHOR UNKNOWN

In the year 1845, I was appointed on a mission from Nauvoo, to labor about Cass County, Illinois, in company with Theodore Curtis.

After traveling together we concluded to separate, and I continued alone, preaching wherever an opportunity presented itself.

One evening I was approaching a little town called Virginia, foot-sore and weary, having been frequently denied food.

I retired, as was my wont particularly when so impressed, for prayer, and for God to soften the hearts of those I might meet, to give me shelter, food and rest, and finally to open up my way.

Towards evening I found a number of persons congregated at the country store. I saluted them with "Good-evening," and inquired the opportunity of getting a chance to preach in that place.

I carried the badge of a "Mormon" preacher in my hand,

namely, a small round valise, containing a shirt, change of socks, Bible and hymn book. I was soon assured by one or two that there was no earthly show for a "Mormon" preacher to be heard in that place.

I replied, "I would like to preach in that nice, newly-finished meetinghouse just opposite." A man spoke up quite authoritatively, and said that no "Mormon" should preach in that house, which had just been dedicated—I think for Presbyterian worship.

They termed this man the deacon. This produced considerable talk, for many of the crowd were of what is termed the liberal or infidel persuasion, so much so that the deacon was overwhelmed by argument, shame and reproach, for refusing a boy like me a chance to preach.

To cover his shame and to nonplus me, he remarked, "I have heard say that your preachers are pretty apt with the scriptures, and can produce almost any doctrine you like from the Bible." I replied that the men were, but that I was but a boy; yet I thought I knew a little of the scriptures.

He remarked, "Your people believe in laying hands on the sick; don't you?"

I answered that we did, and because Christ had said in His remarkable commission to His apostles, that this was one of the signs following, quoting Mark 16:15–18. I also quoted James 5:14.

"Yes, yes;" says he, "that is all very good, but that says only once, and your elders sometimes lay hands twice in succession on the same person. Whoever heard of Jesus or the apostles doing anything like that?" He then cited an instance where, as he said, Joseph Smith had done this in administering to a sick woman.

The good-natured excitement was intense. The deacon thought I was overwhelmed, and proposed that if I could prove a similar transaction from the scriptures, I might preach in that house that very night.

Eagerness now seized the men, and the deacon chuckled over his presumed victory, and boasted of his acquaintance with the "Blessed Word."

I unbuckled my valise, drew forth my little Bible, and opened it intuitively to this passage in Mark 8:22–25: "And he cometh to Bethsaida; and they bring a blind man unto him, and besought him to touch him. And he took the blind man by the hand, . . . and put his hands upon him, and asked him if he saw aught. And he looked up, and said, I see men as trees, walking. After that he put his hands again upon his eyes, and made him look up: and he was restored, and saw every man clearly."

The reading of this scripture; the sudden finding of it, for I was led to it as clearly as a man leads his horse to the water; its aptness and conclusiveness, accompanied by the jeers of the infidel portion of the crowd, mortified the deacon—he was discomfited.

I remarked that I would, according to the deacon's terms, preach in the church that evening, provided some one would find candles. The candles were instantly offered, and accordingly, I preached with power and the demonstration of the Spirit.

After the close of the services, I found a resting place with one of the most avowed infidels of the neighborhood, who had listened to the talk between the deacon and myself, and who particularly enjoyed the good man's discomfiture. By his persuasion I stayed some time in the neighborhood, occupying occasionally the schoolhouse.

He even proffered me some land to build me a house if I would stay, preach and teach school; but my mind was bent on returning to Nauvoo.

But one evening, when I had been preaching my intended farewell sermon in the closely-packed schoolhouse, and just at its close, a person arose and said that, God willing, he would deliver a discourse there the next Sunday, and expose the "Mormon" delusion, giving his announcement all the force and emphasis possible.

My friends gathered at my place of stopping, and, joining with my host, prevailed upon me to stay. The word was given out that I had gone to Nauvoo.

At the time appointed a great crowd had convened—time, early candlelight.

I arrived late, purposely. My friend and I took seats near the door.

The preacher, after preliminaries, opened the Bible, and, for his text, read the 13th and 14th verses of the 16th chapter of Revelation.

After dilating upon the swampy nature of the soil contiguous to Nauvoo, styling it a good place for frogs, and facetiously comparing it to the "mouth of the dragon," he came down heavily on the "false prophet," the miracles, etc. It was a most scathing rebuke on "Mormonism."

His final peroration was on the habits of the frogs, which, while no footsteps were heard, croaked and croaked, but at the first sound of an approaching footstep, dodged their heads beneath the water. "So," said he, at the same time rising to the sublime height of his oratory, "where, oh where is the frog that croaked here a day or two ago? Gone to that slough of iniquity, Nauvoo, the seat of the dragon and the false prophet. Why has he fled? Because he heard the footsteps of your true shepherd." After much interlarding, he dismissed by prayer.

I immediately arose and said that the frog was there yet, and would croak once more, naming the time.

Shouts from the audience named that same evening as the time, and the reverend preacher, amid jeers, cheers and cries of, "Give the boy a chance!" made for the one door.

My friend was alive to the emergency, and I, nothing loth, opened a fusilade from First Timothy, 4th chapter, while the preacher was hemmed in by the crowd, and my friend with his back to the door.

After an exhaustive testimony of the work, we all departed, some pleased, some chagrined.

In both of the instances here narrated, the opening of the Bible to the apt and confirmatory passages, were then to my mind clearly the answer to prayer, for if ever previously read they had escaped my memory.

How much good I did on that mission, I cannot guess. One thing I do know, as a general rule not many are truly converted by the clamor of crowds, or the frenzy of debates.

My object in giving these two instances is to incite my young brethren to a study of the scriptures, the necessity of earnest secret prayer, and confidence in the promise that at the hour and time God will help them, and bring them off victoriously.

Great care must be taken to give God the glory in your after prayer, "for no flesh can glory in his sight."

Encomiums should produce humility, lest we be puffed up, and, in an after time, display our complete nothingness.

Fragments of Experience, 9–13.

"I FELT A PECULIAR SENSATION IN MY EARS"

GEORGE Q. CANNON

In the fall of 1850, George Q. Cannon, then twenty-three years old, was called on a mission to the Sandwich Islands.]

My desire to learn to speak was very strong; it was present with me night and day, and I never permitted an opportunity of talking with the natives to pass without improving it. I also tried to exercise faith before the Lord to obtain the gift of talking and understanding the language. One evening, while sitting on the mats visiting with some neighbors who had dropped in, I felt an uncommonly great desire to understand what they said. All at once I felt a peculiar sensation in my ears; I jumped to my feet, with my hands at the sides of my head, and exclaimed . . . that I believed I had received the gift of interpretation! And it was so.

From that time forward I had but little, if any, difficulty in understanding what the people said. I might not be able at once to separate every word which they spoke from every other word in the sentencc; but I could tell the general meaning of the whole. This was a great aid to me in learning to speak the language, and I felt very thankful for this gift from the Lord.

I mention this that my readers may know how willing God is to bestow gifts upon his children. If they should be called to go as missionaries to a foreign nation . . . , it is their privilege to exercise faith for the gifts of speaking and interpreting that language, and also for every other gift which they may need.

George Q. Cannon, *My First Mission,* 23.

"SHE RECOGNIZED ME"

FREDERICK SCHOLES

In June 1894, as a traveling elder in the British Mission], I had just left a Primitive Methodist minister after a prolonged conversation, and called at the next house, at which a lady answered the door and asked me to step inside.

I commenced to talk of the gospel message I had been sent to proclaim, and found her an attentive listener. She informed me that she had been praying to know which of the different religions was true, believing that the Bible is true, and that there is but "one Lord, one faith, one baptism." In answer to her prayers she had a manifestation, or a vision, and was carried away to a large hall; here she saw a man preaching the gospel to her; after preaching to her for some time, he left her, saying: "I will see you again and preach the gospel to you."

During her recital of this manifestation she shed tears of joy, for her heart was full. She had desired to hear further of this person whom she had seen. Now she had that privilege, for she informed me that I was that person; she recognized me when she opened the door, and the words I had addressed to her were similar to the words spoken to her in the vision.

I felt thankful to learn that I was chosen to bring "glad tidings of great joy" to one who was searching after truth. I gave her some of our literature, with the admonition to read and learn further of the doctrine of which I had spoken. She has told me since then that she believes and will be baptized.

Edwin F. Parry, *Sketches of Missionary Life,* 86–88.

"HOW IS THIS WAR COMING OUT?"

GEORGE ALBERT SMITH

During World War I, I was in Washington, D.C., and wrote New York's Governor Charles Seaman Whitman telling him that on my way home I would like to stop and pay my respects to him. I received a telegram: "Come right along. I will receive you here."

But I found myself in Albany a day early. The governor was out of town. I left the telephone number of my hotel with the governor's secretary and then contacted the missionaries. They were going to visit the home of one of the families of Saints that evening, and I was invited to go along. I left that telephone number with the hotel clerk.

About nine o'clock that evening the telephone rang. The sister answered it and reported, "Brother Smith, the governor of New York wants to talk to you."

"You are certainly coming to see me, aren't you?" the voice on the telephone asked.

"I stopped here for that purpose," I said. "What time shall I come?"

"Ten o'clock."

"Ten o'clock tomorrow morning?"

"Ten o'clock tonight—at the Governor's mansion, not at the office."

I went back to the missionaries, saying that one of them would have to come and help me find the Governor's mansion. One of them offered to come, and we said good-bye to those Saints who had entertained us in their home.

The mansion was surrounded by guards as a wartime precaution. We had a little difficulty convincing them that we had an appointment at that hour, but finally were past the gate and introduced to the governor, who said: "Come with me and we will go up to my den, and we will have a good time together; no one will bother us up there."

Surrounded by the governor's library, the three of us talked. Finally, the conversation turned to the war, and the governor was happily surprised at the number of LDS boys that I told him were in the services. And of how we had supported the bond drives.

"You have done better than we have done. But, how is this war coming out?"

"Don't you know, Governor?" I asked.

"No, I don't know who is going to win it."

"Well," I said, "where is your Book of Mormon?"

He turned around in his swivel chair and reached into the book cupboard behind him, and laid a copy of the Book of Mormon on the table in front of me. And the young missionary's eyes fairly popped out of his head. Here we were in the home of the governor of the state of New York, and he had a Book of Mormon.

"Governor," I said, "I am not going to take a lot of time, but you can find out right in here how this war is coming out. We are going to win the war." I read to him what is found in the Book of Mormon with reference to this people and this nation, in which the Lord told us: "There shall be no kings upon this land which shall rise up unto the Gentiles. . . . I, the Lord, the God of heaven, will be their king," and then he refers to the fact that if we keep his commandments we have the promise from him of his preservation and his watchcare.

"I had not seen that," the governor said.

I replied, "You are not doing a very good job reading your Book of Mormon."

I laid the book down, and our visit continued. Out of the corner of my eye I saw the young missionary pick up that book. I knew what he was wondering—just how the governor had a copy. The missionary turned to the first page, and there he read the inscription: "To the Honorable Charles Seaman Whitman, Governor of New York, with compliments and best wishes of George Albert Smith."

Albert L. Zobell, *Story Gems,* 23–26.

"GIVE THE LORD A CHANCE"

GEORGE ALBERT SMITH

I remember one day I was impressed to say to a missionary who was going to a certain town in England where they would not let us hold street meetings:

"Now remember, give the Lord a chance. You are going to ask a favor. Give the Lord a chance. Ask him to open the way."

The young man went to that city, went into the office of the mayor, and asked if he could see him. He was going to ask if they might change the rule.

When he got there, he found that the mayor was out of town. The young man came out of the office, looked down the hall and saw on a door at the end of the hall, "Chief Constable's Office." He hesitated a moment, and something said to him: "Give the Lord a chance." He walked into the chief constable's office and told him what he had come for. When he finished, the man said:

"Well, what street corner would you like?"

He said: "I don't know this city as well as you do. I would not ask for a corner that would be undesirable, or where we would block the traffic. Would you mind going with me to select a corner?"

Just think of a missionary asking the chief constable to pick a corner on which to preach the gospel!

The constable said:

"Surely, I will go with you."

In fifteen minutes they had one of the best corners in town, with permission to preach the gospel of Jesus Christ where it had not been preached on the streets since before the war [World War I].

George Albert Smith, *Sharing the Gospel with Others,* 14–15.

"I HAD NEVER PREACHED IN MY LIFE"

CLAUDIUS V. SPENCER

I went aboard a New York steamer and applied for a ticket for passage and state room to that city [en route to my mission in England]. . . . On this same day I had the "blues" as I hope never to have them again. I had nearly concluded that there could not be either sense or inspiration in the authorities of the Church sending me to England on a mission, and, that when I got to New York City I would go over to my native town where I had some property and quietly settle among friends and relatives. So great was the power that the devil had over me that when I first stepped on the boat I drew a chair into the niche by the "figure head" to avoid having conversation with anyone. I had sat there but a few moments when a person came up behind me and remarked that it was a pleasant evening. I made no reply.

"Boat making fine time," said he.

Still I did not answer. Soon he spoke again: "Are you traveling far, young man?"

I jerked my chair around and answered very spitefully, "I have *come* a long way and I am *going* a long way, all the way from Salt Lake to England. Is there anything else you want?" My abruptness had sent him back several feet, and he was looking at me with about as much curiosity as if he were viewing a wild animal.

Very soon he smiled and said, "Yes, if you come from Salt Lake there is a good deal more I want."

He commenced asking questions, and soon several more persons gathered around; but just then the dinner bell rang, and they invited me to go to dine, which I did not do, as it seemed to me that I could not have eaten at that time even if it were to save my life. After finishing their repast I was waited upon by three gentlemen, who stated they had engaged the cabin from the captain and wished me to preach. I told them I had never preached in my life. They wanted to know for what I was going to England. I told them to preach. They then wanted to know why I would not preach in the cabin, my answer being that it was because I was not sent here to preach. We finally compromised the matter by my consenting to go to the cabin and answer questions. The room was so crowded that they could not sit down, but stood around in circles, and took turns in asking me questions.

When I first sat down I noticed a large, black-eyed, black-haired man, and said to myself, "When he comes I will have the devil." After some time he pushed forward and literally covered me with compliments. He then remarked, "You must excuse me, young friend, after your testimony of the goodness of your people, for asking why *such* men as George J. Adams, John C. Bennett, Dr. Foster, Charles Foster and others could not live peaceably in your community?"

My answer followed like lightning: "It was because they were such gamblers, whore-masters, black-legs and rascals as you are."

He made a bound for me; six men caught him, pulled him to the outside of the circle, and slapping him on the back told him with an oath, that if God Almighty had come down out of heaven He could not have told his character any better than the little "Mormon" had.

I answered questions until about eleven o'clock at night, when I sprang from my chair and said, "Gentlemen, you have had 'Mormonism' enough for one night," and I started for my room. I was stopped and led back to my chair, when I received a unanimous vote of thanks and the proffer to raise me three hundred dollars if I would accept the amount. I told the gentlemen that we preached the gospel without purse or scrip, and that I had already received enough to take me to England. I selected, however, three reliable men, who promised me to see that the three hundred dollars were given to the poor in their neighborhoods during the next winter.

I went into my room and prostrated myself with my face on the floor, and thanked God for the gift of the Holy Ghost, for I had most surely talked by inspiration. I asked forgiveness for my unbelief, and from that time I was wholly contented to go to England.

Labors in the Vineyard, 13–15.

"AFRAID MY FEELINGS WOULD BE HURT"

CLAUDIUS V. SPENCER

Brother Neslen . . . was president of the Lowestolt branch during my presidency of the Norwich conference. He was in good circumstances and had a nice house, but, during my first visits to the branch he never invited me to his house, and after late meetings used to take me away quite a distance to sleep. On one of my visits . . . I turned to him and said, "Brother Neslen, you may think it rather strange manners, but I feel impressed to ask you the reason why you never invite me to your house?" He replied that none of his family belonged to the Church and he was afraid if he did my feelings would be hurt. (His family consisted of a wife and nine children.)

I turned to him and said, "Brother Neslen, you are president of this branch, and as foreign as it may be to Gentile manners I must do my duty. I want you to invite me to your house; if you do so I promise you in the name of the Lord that every one of your family shall embrace the gospel, and everyone shall live to go to Zion; if you do not, and have not faith to stand up in your place as the head of your own family you are not fit to stand as president of the branch; and more than that, you will apostatize and none of you be saved in the kingdom of God."

The next time I visited Lowestolt he took me to his home: his wife was kind as a mother in her treatment and in a few months the ten souls were baptized and all lived to reach Zion in safety.

Labors in the Vineyard, 26–27.

A Beautiful Personage Appeared

"Maha"

Elder John W. Taylor, while on a mission to the Southern States, was once traveling in Kentucky. When going through some woods he was met by two men, who were delegates sent by a mass meeting to notify Elder Taylor to leave the state. The reason for this announcement was asked, and the answer was that the doctrines he was teaching were arousing the people and ruining the neighborhood.

"Why," said the elder, "Paul, the ancient apostle, was similarly accused, and the people were angered at his ministry and success."

"Well, now," replied one of the men, "we don't care a d——— about Paul the apostle, but you have got to leave the state."

"Gentlemen," was the reply, "I will not leave the state until I am ready, and that time has not yet come. I am an American citizen and claim the right to remain where I please so long as I interfere with no one's business and attend to my own affairs. I am a minister of the gospel and am here to preach in Union Church tomorrow at 2 o'clock and I will be glad to see them at meeting."

With this the two men took their departure, and the next day Elder Taylor appeared at Union Church to fill his appointment, but he found that influence had been used with those in charge so that he was not permitted to occupy the building. Subsequently, however, he met a man who pointed to a frame building in a clearing in the woods with the remark, "There is a building and an acre of ground which I own and will give you to preach the gospel in."

Announcements for meeting were consequently made, and at the appointed time Elder Taylor made his way towards the building, which he had christened "Liberty Church." On emerging from the woods he beheld a crowd of men whom he soon recognized as friends working away at his church, and he hastened forward to inquire the cause of the commotion. He soon learned that someone in the neighborhood was suddenly filled with the desire, as soon as they were informed that a Mormon meeting was to be held in the house, to have all the land surveyed, and either intentionally or otherwise the surveyor had run the dividing line directly through the house. As a result, the party on whose land a part of the house stood had forbidden the holding of meetings on his land.

When the men who came to listen heard of this prohibition, they immediately placed logs and rollers under the frame building and moved it over to the acre of land which had been donated for the use of Elder Taylor. The chimney, however, which had been built up from the ground, was left standing on the other party's property.

The house was crowded and the audience extended out beyond the end where a hole had been left by the removal from the chimney. Elder Taylor spoke with great freedom on the principles of the gospel, and hesitated not to proclaim against the numerous sins which many of his congregation had committed. After he had spoken some time one man arose and said, "What this man has said is true, and as for me and my family, we wish to be baptized if he will administer the ordinance."

Elder Taylor consented to act and then said, "If I have not told the truth I would like anyone in this congregation to tell me so," but no person responded.

The company then repaired to a pond of water that was near

by, and the converted man and his family were baptized. As this ordinance and that of the laying on of hands were administered, they were successively explained to those assembled, and thus a profound impression was made on their minds. When almost ready to separate, Brother Taylor said he would prophesy that many more people would shortly be baptized in that pond of water.

At this time Brother Taylor had been in the mission what was thought to be a sufficient length of time, and his release to return home had therefore been sent and he had it in his pocket. After making the above prediction, however, he desired to see it fulfilled, and consequently he and Elder Bigler, who now became his traveling companion, started out to visit through the country.

One night when weary and hungry they came to a house and Elder Taylor stepped up to the door and knocked. The proprietor appeared and was told, "We are ministers of Christ sent out to preach the gospel; we desire something to eat and a place to sleep, and if you will give us these, the angels of God will visit you this night and inform you as to who we are."

They were invited to enter and, after supper, bore their testimony of the gospel to their host and his family. A comfortable bed was provided and they rested well. Early next morning the lady of the house arose and prepared breakfast, eating which the elders started again on their journey. As they were passing out of the gate Elder Taylor remarked to a little girl who had followed them, "It will storm here today," though at that time the sky was perfectly clear and there was not the slightest indication of a change in the weather. In that country a storm means a hurricane or very severe change, and not merely a little rain or snow.

The child ran and told her parents what had been said, when the father immediately began to board up his windows and fasten his doors. It was well he did so, for within an hour a cyclone swept over the place, utterly demolishing his orchard and barely leaving his house, which was only saved through its having been closed up.

When the storm passed he hitched up his team and sought the elders, but did not succeed in finding them. They, however, before many days had elapsed, felt impressed to return to this gentleman's home, and when they did so were joyfully entertained. The brethren were now reminded of their promise to these people concerning the visitation of angels, and the parents and even the children testified that the night of the elders' sojourn in their house was filled with pleasant visitations by angelic messengers.

The lady was so full of joy that she could scarcely contain herself. She said she had but retired when she fell into a peaceful slumber and the vision of her mind was opened up. A beautiful personage appeared and by some unseen power wafted her to the face of a high cliff, where she was located on a projecting ledge of rock about six feet below the top. Here she stood endeavoring to reach the top where her minister stood. He was pretending to try and help her, but was merely extending to her pieces of dry weeds and straw which broke in her hand when she attempted therewith to draw herself to the summit of the rock. She had worked some time at this discouraging labor and was about to give up, when she saw Elders Taylor and Bigler approaching. As they came to the edge of the cliff they extended their hands to her and quickly raised her to the place she desired to stand.

Just at this moment her guide appeared and inquired if she was satisfied, to which she replied, "No."

She was next taken to her home. As she stood there looking into the street she saw approaching a long procession of ministers of every denomination. Every preacher she had ever heard, and these were not a few, was in the concourse. After passing before her, they marched down into a field where they gathered in a great crowd, when there was a humming noise as if all were talking at once. As she watched this motley crowd, all suddenly vanished, and there were left standing alone only Elders Taylor and Bigler.

As her guide again inquired if she was satisfied she answered in the affirmative. She awoke with a contented spirit and felt assured that her guests were servants of the Most High.

This whole family received baptism at the hands of the elders, and many more accepted the gospel. The pond was used for the administration of the ordinance, and thus Elder Taylor's prediction at the water's edge was fulfilled.

Juvenile Instructor, 1 March 1890, 152–54.

"You Have Not Come Here to Listen to the Gospel"

J. GOLDEN KIMBALL

When I was president of the Southern States Mission, after a year's time I concluded that I would try to hold a conference in a city. Up to that time we had always kept out of cities. So I made my arrangements with the president of the conference to hold such a meeting and to secure some place where we could hold it. We had no money. The only place they could secure was the court house. I told the elders: "I will do the preaching, and if they kill me you need not bother any further." The people were very prejudiced.

When the time came I met those elders, a fine body of men, wonderful, courageous men, men of faith—they had to be in the

South. We went to the court house—all those present were men; there wasn't a woman among them, and we all knew what that meant. When there are no women there is a great deal of danger. It is dangerous enough when they are present.

At any rate, I made up my mind to deliver my message as fervently and humbly as ever a president of a mission preached. I intended to do all the talking. I went there determined to preach the gospel. I had my Bible, and I am well acquainted with my Bible. I cannot find anything in anybody else's Bible. I have owned this Bible for forty years and it is well marked and every subject traced in my own penmanship. I would not take money for this Bible. I went there believing that the Spirit of God was on me as the president of the mission. I was humble as a child. It was the only time in my life that I have ever been far enough away that I could do as I pleased. Ever since that time I have been close in.

I got up to preach the gospel, faith and repentance, etc. All at once something came over me and I opened my mouth and said to that body of men (the building was crowded; among them were some of the leading men): "Gentlemen, you have not come here to listen to the gospel of Jesus Christ. I know what you have come for. You have come to find out about the Mountain Meadows Massacre and polygamy, and God being my helper I will tell you the truth."

And I did. I talked to them for one hour. When the meeting was out you could hear a pin drop. There was no comment; there was no noise or confusion, and we went to the hotel. We had arranged for lodgings at a cheap hotel.

After a short time a brass band played. Elder Willard Bean was the president of the conference. I sent him out to find what it all meant. I thought it meant trouble. So he inquired and they told him: "We are serenading that big long fellow." That is the only brass band I have ever had dispense music after one of my talks.

What I want to ask you good people is this: Was I moved upon by the right spirit? The next day when we went to the woods to hold our priesthood meeting, which we always held in the woods—we had no other place—I said to those elders: "Don't one of you dare preach that sermon; it will cost you your life." And I have never preached it since.

What I am beating around in the brush to put over is this: Does the Lord God direct his servants? He certainly does. If he doesn't we are a failure and we are no better than others. We do not know just what to say. I don't. I don't know just how to say it, but the Lord being my helper as long as I live I am going to try to be natural and I am going to try to have my mind open with the hope that God will give me his Holy Spirit when I open my mouth and use the talent which the Lord has given me.

Now, brethren and sisters, I know what that feeling is. I have not had it very often, but I know that there is such a thing as "the still small voice." I have heard it.

Conference Report, April 1932, 78–79.

An Interesting Conversation

David O. McKay

The other day aboard this ship [en route to Syria, Alexandria, Egypt], a very clever and fairly charming Scotch woman with whom [Sister McKay] and I had had several conversations, approached me with the startling news that the young woman who shared her cabin believed that "Mrs. Booth is a Mormon agent, and the young girl believes Mrs. Booth has marked the young woman for a Mormon victim."

"Dreadful," said I.

Then seeing my interest, the garrulous Scotch woman launched out into an extended narration of "facts" about Mormon elders "infesting" a particular district in Edinburgh, and ferreting out women whom they shipped to Salt Lake City never to be heard of again.

I listened as long as I could with propriety, then said:

"Now Mrs. MacClellan, do you really believe what you say? Have you ever stopped to think how foolish those Mormon elders must be to come way over to England to get girls when they could get all they wanted in any large city in America? They go to Japan as well; and to the South Sea Islands, to Australia, New Zealand, and to India. How foolish to spend all that money to travel so far if they want only girls!"

"Well," she answered, "it does seem strange that they would do such a thing, doesn't it?"

Then, I told her the facts—as gently as I could, because when she learned that I was one of those very Mormon elders, she began to sizzle in her embarrassment.

Llewelyn R. McKay, comp., *Home Memories of President David O. McKay*, 164.

A NEW HAT FOR ELDER PHILLIPS

THOMAS PHILLIPS

I was traveling in the towns and villages in a part of the County of Surrey, England, preaching the gospel as revealed from the heavens through the ministry of holy beings. Under these circumstances, food and raiment were sometimes hard to obtain; consequently, at one time I had a hat that was very much the worse for wear.

In a village called Hersham, in that county, lived a brother by the name of William Hobbs, at whose house I sometimes visited, and received food and lodgings.

One night Brother Hobbs dreamed that a personage came to him and told him that Brother Phillips would be at his house on a certain day, naming the time, which I think was four or five days from the time he dreamed. He was further told that he must get a new hat for Brother Phillips; for the one he wore was very shabby.

This dream was very much impressed on the mind of Brother Hobbs, and troubled him sorely, for it found him without money and some miles from any town where he could buy a hat.

Brother Hobbs was the overseer of a small number of men, whose work was to keep some miles of railroad in repair for the safety of the trains.

When the day came that I was to be at his house in the evening, he went to his work very low-spirited, not having obtained the hat. While at work on the track, a long train of cars came along, and when passing the place where Brother Hobbs and his hands were at work, a hat, suitable for the finest gentleman in the land, flew out of one of the windows.

Brother Hobbs shouted, "That's the hat for Brother Phillips! Thank God!"

When Brother Hobbs came home in the evening, I was there, it being the time specified in the dream.

He walked up to me and said:

"Brother Phillips, I was to give you a hat, and here it is." To our surprise, it fitted me well.

As a matter of course, I was anxious to know who was so thoughtful for an elder of The Church of Jesus Christ of Latter-day Saints; and, in answer to my questions, Brother Hobbs told me the dream.

Then I knew, and still know, that the providences of our Heavenly Father were, and are, working in favor of the servants and Saints of the Most High.

George Q. Cannon, *A String of Pearls*, 72–73.

KARL MAESER'S CONVERSION TO THE GOSPEL

HEBER J. GRANT

Karl G. Maeser read a vicious attack upon the "Mormons"—about the "Danites" and the "Destroying Angels," and so on, and so forth. Then he found in the same article that the "Mormons" were industrious, that they were frugal, that there was not a poor-house in all the territory of Utah, that the fifteen percent of Gentile population among them then furnished eighty-five percent of the criminals, according to United States statistics, compiled by the Gentiles themselves.

He found that there was not one saloon in the entire territory of Utah, and that the only place where whiskey was sold was in Salt Lake City; and, to the disgrace of the city government, they were selling it. That is what he found on the temperance question. He found that there was not a single house of ill fame in the whole of Utah. He found that the people went to bed at night with their front and back doors open.

After reading all this he said to himself: "The man who wrote this illustrated article for the magazine is a liar. The fruits of honesty, industry, sobriety, and brotherly love do not grow among immoral and wicked people," so he sent for some tracts, investigated the gospel and embraced it.

On the night of his baptism, which occurred at midnight, he looked up to heaven and said, in substance: "O, God, if what I have done tonight meets with your approval, and you will give to me the witness of the Spirit that this gospel, that I believe, is in very deed the truth, that I may know it, I pledge my life, if need be, to its promulgation and its advancement."

From Canada on the north to Mexico on the south there are thousands, yes, tens of thousands, who can bear witness that this pledge, made at Dresden, Germany, at midnight, was fulfilled by one of the most devoted, unselfish, and self-sacrificing mortals who ever embraced the gospel of Christ. For if any man ever gave his life, his heart, and his soul for the advancement of this cause, Karl G. Maeser did so. God heard and answered that prayer.

Walking from the river in which he was baptized, Karl G. Maeser was conversing upon the principles of the gospel with the late Apostle Franklin D. Richards, and Brother William Budge was acting as interpreter, Brother Richards talking in English and

Brother Maeser in German. They began their walk of several miles to return home. After walking a short distance Brother Maeser announced to Brother Budge that he need not interpret the answers, that he understood them. Immediately thereafter, Brother Franklin said, "You need not interpret those questions; I understand them." They walked for miles, Franklin D. Richards answering questions in English, Karl G. Maeser asking them in German, neither knowing the other's language, yet by the inspiration of the Spirit of God, both understanding each other.

Do you tell me that I don't know that we have the gift of tongues in The Church of Jesus Christ of Latter-day Saints? As well tell me that I do not know that I am standing here before you today. I have this testimony from the lips of a man, than whom no more honest, no more upright, no truer man ever drew the breath of life.

When these two men reached the bridge that spans the river Elbe, on their way into the city of Dresden, they were separated, and when they reached the other side of the bridge Brother Maeser again began asking questions, but Brother Richards could not then understand him, nor could Brother Maeser understand anything further that was said in reply; and they were obliged to revert to Brother Budge's interpretation. Then Brother Maeser turned to Brother Richards and said, "What does this mean, we could understand each other for miles, and now we can't understand?"

"Brother Maeser," said Apostle Richards, "the Lord has given to you a portion of the fruit of the gospel of Jesus Christ, as restored in our day. For some wise reason he has allowed you to enjoy one of the manifestations of the Spirit accompanying the true gospel of Christ."

Brother Maeser told me, with tears rolling down his cheeks, although it had been nearly fifty years since he had that manifestation, that he realized that God had heard and answered his prayers. At the close of the incident I have related, Brother Maeser looked up again into heaven, and he said, "O God, my Father in heaven, I will fulfill my promise to give my life to this cause"; and he did it.

George C. Lambert, comp., *Gems of Reminiscence,* 104–7.

"A MORMON TRACT WAS STUFFED INTO EACH SHOE"

JOHN A. WIDTSOE

One day [Anna Widtsoe] asked a neighbor, a ship's captain living in the same house, an older resident, to recommend a shoemaker to whom she might take her son's shoes for repair. One Olaus Johnsen, a very competent, honest workman, was recommended. In fact, the shoemaker's son Arnt brought to the house a pair of the captain's shoes, and took with him, for repair, a pair of John's shoes. When the boy's shoes were returned, a Mormon tract was stuffed into each shoe.

A little later with a parcel containing another pair of old shoes, the widow set forth in the warm sunshine of the spring of 1879 for the half-hour walk to Johnsen's shoemaker shop. It certainly did not occur to her that she was making the most fateful visit of her life. . . .

Olaus Johnsen was a wholesome, well-spoken man in his

forties, a workman who knew his craft. His wife was of the sturdy Norwegian type. Anna Widtsoe first met the wife, and made inquiry about the meaning of the tracts found in her son's shoes that had been returned, repaired. Mrs. Johnsen declared that they told the truth, but that Mr. Johnsen would explain the whole matter.

The shoemaker agreed to put soles on the shoes, strong enough to last a good while even under the wear of a lively, active lad, who was always moving about. The details of business were soon agreed upon; the commonplaces of courteous people were exchanged; the widow was about to leave the shop, yet a little curious about the tracts which she had found in the first pair of shoes when they were returned, but unwilling to ask too many questions.

Anna Widtsoe's hand was on the door latch, when the shoemaker said, somewhat hesitatingly, for the business was concluded and the lady was a stranger, "You may be surprised to hear me say that I can give you something of more value than soles for your child's shoes." She was surprised. She looked into the eyes of the man, who stood straight and courageous in his shop.

"What can you, a shoemaker, give me better than soles for my son's shoes? You speak in riddles," she answered.

The shoemaker did not hesitate. "If you will but listen, I can teach you the Lord's true plan of salvation for his children. I can teach you how to find happiness in this life, and to prepare for eternal joy in the life to come. I can tell you whence you came, why you are upon earth, and where you will go after death. I can teach you, as you have never known it before, the love of God for his children on earth."

Understanding, happiness, joy, love—the words with which she was wrestling! But, this was a shoemaker shop. This man was clearly a humble man who knew little of the wisdom of schools and churches. She felt confused. She simply asked, "Who are you?"

"I am a member of the Church of Christ—we are called Mormons. We have the truth of God."

Mormons! It was terrible. She had innocently walked into a dangerous place. Hurriedly she thanked the shoemaker, left the shop, and climbed the hill.

Yet, as she walked homeward, the words of the shoemaker rang in her ears; and she remembered a certain power in his voice and majesty in his bearing when he delivered his message and bore his testimony. He was a shoemaker, but no ordinary man. Could it really be that the Mormons had the truth of the Lord? No, it was absurd! But, it made her thoughtful and restless. When the repaired shoes were brought to the house a day or two later by the shoemaker's young son, Arnt Johnsen, Anna Widtsoe found, carefully tucked into each shoe, other Mormon tracts. . . .

Then began two years of struggle.

The tracts in the shoes aroused her curiosity to the extent that one Sunday she went to a Mormon meeting. The meeting room was on the second floor of the shoemaker's home, a sturdy log house. A small group of people were there; and a fiery speaker, a missionary, raised all manner of questions in her mind. The main effect of that meeting was a resentment against the primitive environment of the meeting, and the quality of the people who were present. Very humble people constituted the membership of the Trondhjem Branch. Class distinctions were sharply drawn in the land. Anna Widtsoe, though a fishermaiden, had been well born, in the economic as well as in the moral sense; and she had moved upward with the years. She was now of the professional class. To join such a group as she saw there that Sunday seemed to her tradition-bound mind to be a step downward.

One day, some months later, when the truth was forcing itself upon her, she came home, stood quietly in the middle of the floor, and said aloud, to herself, "Must I step down to that? Yes, if it is the truth, I must do so."

Soon, however, all else was forgotten in her battles with the shoemaker and the missionaries upon points of doctrine. She knew her Bible. Time upon time she came prepared to vanquish the elders, only to meet defeat herself. She had not read the Bible as these men did. Gradually she began to comprehend that her reading had been colored and overshadowed by the teachings of the church of her childhood; and that these men, these Mormon missionaries, accepted the Bible in a truer, more literal manner. She liked it. Nevertheless she fought fearlessly. It was no use. At length she had to admit that the Bible was all on the side of the Mormons.

Even then she was not ready. There were other matters to be settled. Questions of authority, revelation, life within the Church, and a hundred others that her quick mind formulated, were presented to the missionaries, debated, discussed and taken up again. She had a worthy teacher in the missionary then in Trondhjem, Elder Anthon L. Skanchy, whose knowledge of the gospel was extensive and sound, and whose wisdom in leading inquirers to truth was unusually fine. This well-informed, intelligent widow tested his powers. Upon her he directed the full battery of gospel evidence. Unwillingly, yet prayerfully, she became convinced that she was in the presence of eternal truth.

At length, on April 1, 1881, a little more than two years after she first heard the gospel, she was baptized into the Church by Elder Anthon L. Skanchy. Thin ice still lay over the edges of the fjord, which had to be broken to permit the ordinance to be performed. The water was icy cold. Yet, she declared to her dying day that never before in all her life had she felt warmer or more comfortable than when she came out of the baptismal waters of old Trondhjem's fjord. The fire within was kindled, never to be extinguished. The humble people of the branch became her brethren and sisters. She loved them, and rejoiced in their company.

John A. Widtsoe, *In the Gospel Net,* 53–57.

"Awakened with a Terrible Shouting"

George Albert Smith

We were in a wooded rural area [during my mission in the southern states]. During the day we had held meetings with the people in the neighborhood who were very friendly and very receptive to our message. One of the local Saints had invited us to accept the hospitality of his home for the night. It was a humble home, built of split logs. It consisted of two rooms and a small log lean-to. There were six missionaries in the group, so it strained the capacity of the little house to be there.

About midnight we were awakened with a terrible shouting and yelling from the outside. Foul language greeted our ears as we sat up in bed to acquaint ourselves with the circumstances. It was a bright moonlit night and we could see many people on the outside.

President [J. Golden] Kimball jumped up and started to dress. The men pounded on the door and used filthy language, ordering the Mormons to come out, that they were going to shoot them. President Kimball asked me if I was going to get up and dress and I told him, "No, I was going to stay in bed, that I was sure the Lord would take care of us."

In just a few seconds the room was filled with shots. Apparently the mob had divided itself into four groups and they were shooting into the corners of the house. Splinters were flying over our heads in every direction. There were a few moments of quiet, then another volley of shots was fired and more splinters flew.

I felt absolutely no terror. I was very calm as I lay there, experiencing one of the most horrible events of my life; but I was sure that as long as I was preaching the word of God and following his teachings that the Lord would protect me. And he did.

A Story to Tell, 155–56.

"THE GREATEST THING IN LIFE"

WALLACE F. TORONTO

I should like to relate a story . . . which to me is an evidence of the truthfulness of the gospel of Jesus Christ, and of the protecting power and goodness of God.

A young Ukrainian, Tarnawskyj by name, who had been studying for the ministry in the Greek Catholic Church, was on his way from Warsaw, Poland, to New York City, there to attend a graduate school for the ministry of that church. He came by the way of the city of Prague. As he was going down the street he saw the sign, "Church of Jesus Christ of Latter-day Saints." He noticed that we were holding a meeting at that time. He thought to himself: "I have learned of those people in my studies. I am curious. I think I will go in and see what they have to say."

He entered, dressed in his black robe and white collar, and sat in the back. He was a young man about twenty-eight or thirty years of age. Two of our missionaries stood up and explained some of the principles of the gospel. They bore their testimonies. Since he spoke Ukrainian, which is kindred to Czech, he understood them. After the meeting he came up and asked: "When do you hold the rest of your services?" We enumerated the meetings of the week and he came to all of them, even including the Relief Society. In a few weeks he made this request: "Brother Toronto, I would like to be baptized into this Church."

"Now, Brother Tarnawskyj, you know you can't make your living in this Church. Our missionaries sustain themselves, either from their own savings or through the sustenance which their folks send them."

"Oh, Brother Toronto," he replied, "I know all about that. Your missionaries have been teaching me the gospel." Continuing, he said: "I have found the most priceless thing in all the world. I want the gospel of Jesus Christ. I have been seeking it for years in the universities and the divinity schools of many lands, and I have never found anything that can equal this."

I said: "All right. As soon as we instruct you a little more fully in the gospel we shall be happy to have you as a member of the Church." He was subsequently baptized. Upon accepting baptism a great characteristic of truth took hold of him, that of wanting to tell somebody else about it. Of course, those he thought of first were his loved ones back in Poland. He wrote them a long letter, in which he declared: "I have found the greatest thing in life. I want to tell you something of the gospel of Jesus Christ, that you, too, might enjoy the blessings which flow from it."

I met him a few days later. He wore a long face and was very dejected. "What on earth has happened to you, Brother Tarnawskyj?"

"I just received a letter from my folks in Poland. They tell me here: 'Dear Son and Brother: If you do not immediately renounce this thing you call Mormonism we shall cease to send you one penny of support, which you know is your only means of livelihood; and furthermore, we shall disown you as a son and a brother!'"

"What is your answer, Brother Tarnawskyj? You are at the crossroads. You have a grave decision to make."

"Oh, Brother Toronto, you know what my answer is: 'Dear loved ones, I cannot renounce the thing I hold dearest in life, the gospel of Jesus Christ. I pray God that you, too, at some future time, through my efforts or the efforts of others, might also come into this church.'"

From that day until this, so far as I know, he has not received one penny or one word from his people. He found himself in Czechoslovakia, a foreigner, unable to secure employment.

During these troublesome times the subtle political forces in Central Europe had operated to break down the Czecho-Slovakian Republic, so that Slovakia gained its freedom, as well as the little province of Ruthenia or Sub-Carpathian Russia, far to the east, hardly larger than the county of Salt Lake. Brother Tarnawskyj finally proposed: "Brother Toronto, many of my countrymen are out there in Ruthenia, a large group of Ukrainians among whom I could work. Since I am an educated man, I think I could get a position as an inspector in the Ministry of Education. Can you help me get there? I want to become a self-sustaining citizen."

"All right. We will help you get to Ruthenia, if you think you can succeed."

Upon his arrival in this new autonomous state, he filed his application for a position in the ministry. It went through the various hands and much red tape through which such things have to pass, and finally reached the Minister himself. Up to this point all went well. When it reached the Minister there was great delay. Finally our brother wrote me a letter and said: "Brother Toronto, I don't know what the trouble down here is. I am qualified for the position, and I have pulled every string I know. And I have prayed.

The Lord God knows I am hungry. He knows I need a place to rest my head. I have tried to live the gospel since I joined the Church. From the earnings on little jobs I have secured here and there I have set aside my tithing, and as soon as the mails go through I will send it on to you. Why, oh why does the Lord persecute me like this?" But in conclusion he added (I wish I had the letter here to read to you): "Perhaps it is all for the best."

A card came a few days later: "I am going to take a job out in the little town of Perecyn as a humble school teacher, where I can make enough to at least buy me a few crusts of bread."

He was employed there for three days, when that tiny state of Central Europe, Sub-Carpathian Russia, was drenched in blood by the Hungarian hordes which swept over it. Men, women and children by the hundreds were left dying in the streets. He and nine of his Ukrainian companions were routed out of bed at five o'clock one morning and thrown into prison. After twenty-four hours of intense suffering they were called before a military court consisting of one man in the uniform of a Hungarian officer. He had the sole right to say, "You live," or "You die." The ten men came before him. They were asked two questions: "How long have you been in this country?" and "What is your religious affiliation?"

Our brother led the others. To the first question he replied that he had been there so and so many weeks. "What is your religious affiliation?"

"I am a member of The Church of Jesus Christ of Latter-day Saints. Sometimes they call us 'Mormons.'"

"Mormons? Mormons? I have heard of you folks. I have read of you in the newspapers of Budapest. I hear your people have done some good in this world." A tense moment of hesitation and then, "You go free."

His nine companions came up after him. They were asked the identical questions. Being no more guilty than he himself, they were nevertheless condemned to death, and shot down in cold blood before the sun went down that day.

This brother finally got out of the country, and wrote me another letter. "Brother Toronto," he said, "I know the Lord does move in a mysterious way His wonders to perform. The gospel is the most priceless thing I have in the world. I know the Lord has preserved my life, that I may be a beacon light to my fellow men. He has not only preserved my life, in the way I have described to you, but He has also protected me, for had I received the position of inspector in the Ministry of Education I today would have been sitting in the concentration camps of Hungary, subjected to some of the most terrible torture known to humankind. I owe all I have to the gospel of Jesus Christ."

Conference Report, April 1940, 53–56.

"IS THAT ALL YOU KNOW?"

EDWARD J. WOOD

A tribe of Indians came to our country [Canada], called the Kree Indians. They were headed by a man named "Yellow Face." He said that he was a member of a council of five who lived in the eastern part of Saskatchewan, the province to the east of Alberta. They spend their time in winter in hunting and fishing. They roam around the country for that purpose and then go back again in the spring. They are the wards of the British Government and are a superior tribe. This man and his one hundred twenty-eight families came into our country, and camped in the woods by a river, right where the road led from two of our wards. We did not know anything of their business. They went about hunting and fishing.

One day this man, "Yellow Face," sent to a ward for the "high chief" of that ward, as he called him (we call them bishops), and wanted him to come to his tent and have a visit with him. Their people visited us; we had asked them into our meetings. They had come to our entertainments and we had become interested in them. They are a very well educated people, are the Kree nation. . . . They dress as we do and are educated. They have a written language of their own, not made by white men, according to signs and sounds, but composed of hieroglyphics, which appear to be a scientific alphabet.

This man sent for our bishop, and when he came he found a large tent with the heads of these one hundred twenty-eight families there, sitting in a circle, and "Yellow Face" was sitting right in front with one Indian woman. "Yellow Face" said to this bishop, "We want you to talk to us. We have been to your meetings. We have been to your parties. You have asked us to dine with you. Now we return the compliment. We want you to come and visit us." He was led to the center of the circle.

Bishop Parker did not know what to say. He had never been on a mission and wasn't prepared to preach the gospel, but he was struck with the sincerity he saw in the people's faces as they sat in the circle. They were pleased to see him, so he told them about the restoration of the gospel and about our work of colonizing in that country. They did not seem much interested in that.

After he got through, they said, "Is that all you know about your gospel?"

He thought and said, "Well, I believe I have told you all I know."

"Well," "Yellow Face" said, "don't you have any books that you talk about?"

"O yes," and Brother Parker then thought of the Book of Mormon.

"Well, tell us about that book." Brother Parker told all he could. It did not take very long and when he got through, the chief said, "That is all," and Brother Parker went home.

About a week later the chief sent for the bishop again. Brother Parker did not know this time what would be expected of him. But he went and found the same crowd there. This time "Yellow Face" said to Brother Parker, "When you were here before I sat there, and you stood here. This time I'll stand here and you sit there," and so he related the following story to Brother Parker:

"Two years ago the High Chief of our council had a vision," (mind you, this man never knew anything about our gospel, never knew there was such a thing as visions or heavenly manifestations). "Our High Chief, the great chief of the Kree Nation had a messenger come to him that he never knew, and he told this chief, you are going to die, but you won't die all over. When you die, I do not want you to be buried until you get cold all over. So the chief said, all right; and later he went with this messenger, so that they all thought he died. All the other chiefs thought he was dead, but he had told his nearest associates previously to watch his body when he went cold, from the extremities of his fingers to his bones, and to bury him if his body was cold all over; but if they found a warm spot over his heart not to bury him.

"So he was watched for five days and only above his heart was there a small warm place. On the end of the fifth day he came to, and he called all his council together and told them he had been into a country where he saw his forefathers, walked with them, talked with them; and they told him he would not yet die, for he would come back to earth and that he was to send all over the country until he found a people who had a book in which was recorded the history of the many people he had been with in the spirit world; and he said I will give unto you four signs by which you may know the people.

"First, they will not drive you out of their country.

"Second, you can turn your horses loose; they won't steal them.

"Third, they will go through your village, and they won't rob the virtue of your maiden women.

"Fourth, they will let you hunt and fish on their domain."

So he said to Brother Parker, "With my family for two years we have hunted for such a people. You invited us into your meetings. We sat at the table with you in your picnic parties. You have come through our village; you have not molested our women. We are fishing and hunting today on your Church land. So I tried you; I watched you; we have watched your old men, your young men; we have watched every action of all your people.

"When I heard you speak, it sounded like good music to me, and when you said that that was all you had to tell, I thought again, I am disappointed. So I asked you if you had a book. You told me you had and told me of your Book of Mormon. That is our book. That is our history, not yours; we want it."

So Brother Parker went and got the Book of Mormon and brought it back to the Indians. The Indians took it, gave it to the interpreter and had him sit down and read it by the hour, and when he got through, the Indian Chief kept the book—to take back to the High Chief who was waiting for them—he did not think he had to buy it. He had said, "It is our book, our history," and drew out a beautifully embroidered envelope of leather and wrapped it up and took it away.

They have visited us several times since, telling us other wonderful things. They are a very fine people, and only the Lord knows what this visit may portend. Not all that was related can be related here as it pertains to a sacred prophecy. It will come true in due time.

Relief Society Magazine, March 1917, 135–37. See also Conference Report, October 1915, 66–68.

"I DID NOT LOOK MUCH LIKE A PREACHER"

WILFORD WOODRUFF

On the 27th of March I arrived at Memphis, weary and hungry. I went to the best tavern in the place, kept by Mr. Josiah Jackson. I told him I was a stranger and had no money, and asked him if he would keep me over night. He inquired what my business was, and I told him I was a preacher of the gospel. He laughed and said that I did not look much like a preacher. I did not blame him, as most of the preachers he ever had been acquainted with rode on fine horses or in fine carriages, dressed in broadcloth, had large salaries, and would likely see this whole world sink to perdition before they would wade through one hundred and seventy miles of mud to save the people.

The landlord wanted a little fun, so said he would keep me if I would preach. He wanted to see if I could preach. I must confess that by this time I became a little mischievous, and pleaded with him not to set me preaching. The more I pleaded to be excused the more determined Mr. Jackson was that I should preach. He took my valise, and the landlady got me a good supper. I sat down in a large hall to eat. Before I got through, the room began to be filled by some of the rich and fashionable people of Memphis, dressed in their broadcloth and silk, while my appearance was such as you can imagine, after traveling through the mud as I had done. When I had finished eating, the table was carried out of the room over the heads of the people. I was placed in the corner of the room, with a stand having a Bible, hymn book, and candle on it, hemmed in by a dozen men, with the landlord in the center.

There were present some five hundred persons, who had come together, not to hear a gospel sermon, but to have some fun. I read a hymn, and asked them to sing. Not a soul would sing a word. I told them I had not the gift of singing; but with the help of the Lord, I would both pray and preach. I knelt down to pray, and the men around me dropped on their knees. I prayed to the Lord to give me His spirit and to show me the hearts of the people. I promised the Lord, in my prayer, that I would deliver to that congregation whatever He would give to me. I arose and spoke one hour and a half, and it was one of the best sermons of my life. The lives of the congregation were open to the vision of my mind, and I told them of their wicked deeds and the reward they would obtain. The men who surrounded me dropped their heads. Three minutes after I closed, I was the only person in the room.

Matthias F. Cowley, *Wilford Woodruff—His Life and Labors,* 55–56.

"THERE MIGHT BE SOMETHING TO IT"

S. DILWORTH YOUNG

Phinehas Young, Brigham's brother, was returning from a preaching tour when he stopped for lunch at the house of a family named Tomlinson. While he was sitting in the parlor, waiting, there walked into the room a tall, thin man who was dressed in the homespun of the day. He did not waste time on preliminaries (I tell it in the words of Phinehas):

"'There is a book, sir, I wish you to read.' The thing appeared so novel to me, [said Phinehas] that for a moment I hesitated, saying,—'Pray, sir, what book have you?' 'The Book of Mormon, or, as it is called by some, the Golden Bible.' 'Ah, sir, then it purports to be a revelation?' 'Yes,' said he, 'It is a revelation from God.' I took the book, and by his request looked at the testimony of the witnesses [which in that day, in the first editions, was in the back of the book]. Said he—'If you will read this book with a prayerful heart and ask God to give you a witness you will know of the truth of this work.' I told him I would do so, and then asked him his name. He said his name was Samuel H. Smith. 'Ah,' said I, 'you are one of the witnesses.' 'Yes,' said he, 'I know the book to be a revelation from God, translated by the gift and power of the Holy Ghost, and that my brother, Joseph Smith, Jun., is a Prophet, Seer and Revelator.'"

That book was read first, after Phinehas, by John Young, the father. In due course Brigham read it. There was talk about it. Brigham opined there might be something to it.

In the summer of 1831 there came into the community five young men from Columbia, Pennsylvania. At Victor, six miles away from Mendon, Phinehas invited them to stay with him, and there they preached about the restoration. All of the Youngs went over to Victor to hear them and, in addition, Heber C. Kimball and his wife, Vilate. What they said is not now known, but the results of their preaching were soon apparent. Brigham, Phinehas, and Heber C. Kimball decided to investigate the branch at Columbia, from whence these young men came, to learn more. It was now January 1832, so they hitched a team to a sleigh and bucked the winter drifts and forded the icy streams for the 125 miles it took to get to Columbia. They stayed a week with the members. . . .

Upon their return to Mendon, Brigham, now convinced that there was indeed "something to it," hitched his horse to a sleigh and with his brother-in-law for company drove to Kingston, Canada, and sought out Joseph, his brother. Joseph immediately left his preaching—for he was a Methodist preacher—and accompanied Brigham back to Mendon. They arrived in late February or early March. Then Joseph, Phinehas, and their father drove to Columbia where they were baptized, but Brigham waited at Mendon. His wife Miriam was very ill. One day, April 14, 1832, he told Eleazer Miller to baptize him. He was ready. And so on a cold, raw day with snow falling, they went to a stream half a mile away, and he was baptized. He was immediately confirmed and ordained an elder. He said, "I felt the sweet influence of the spirit testifying my sins were forgiven."

BYU Speeches, 17 March 1964, 3–4.

Obedience

"They Counselled Me Not to Go"

ANSON CALL

To some persons it may appear strange that the elders of the Church in their addresses to the Saints should so frequently dwell upon the necessity of constant obedience to counsel. But although this may seem strange, still the experience of both the elders and the Saints goes to prove that "to obey is better than sacrifice, and to hearken than the fat of rams."

The Bible, the Book of Mormon, and the book of Doctrine and Covenants contain many instances of the blessings that have attended obedience, and the serious consequences that have followed disobedience.

I will not, however, refer to any one of these divine books; but will give my readers an instance of the consequence of disobedience which occurred to me in my early experience in the Church, in the commencement of the year 1839.

At that time I was living with the Saints in Far West, though I owned property, which I had been driven from, at the Three Forks of Grand River, distant from Far West about thirty miles.

As I wished to learn whether I could dispose of this property or not, I asked Father Joseph Smith and President Brigham Young for counsel about visiting Grand River for this purpose. They counselled me not to go; but to stay at home.

I had been driven from my property by the mob that came against the Saints, and as the Saints were obliged to leave the state I desired to go with them to Illinois. But I did not want to be burdensome to others. If I could sell my property on Grand River I would not be, so I concluded that there could not be much harm in my going to Grand River, and I set out.

How I succeeded the following extract from my journal will show.

December 31, 1838, being anxious to obtain means to make a team, that I might be able to go with the Saints, I this morning mounted the only horse I had left, and started for the Three Forks of Grand River.

I arrived at my farm on New Year's Day, and learned that a man by the name of George Washington O'Niel had it in his possession.

I passed on two miles further to a family by the name of Day, who had come in from the Eastern States a few weeks before I was driven away. This family had taken no part with the mob. I found the lady at home, and received from her a history of my property. She informed me that O'Niel and Culp, Missouri mobbers, had said that if ever I came to the place they would kill me; and that one Henderson and others would help them.

When on my farm I had sold store goods to a number of the citizens, who were to pay me for them at Christmas. She said she had heard many of them say that if I came there, they would pay me just as "Mormons" should be paid.

Just at this time O'Niel and Culp came into the house. They demanded of me my reasons for being there. I told them that I was attending to my business. They said I had no business there, and if I got away from there I would be smart.

I replied that . . . it was time enough to be afraid when I saw danger, and that I should go when I pleased.

They told me that they would as soon kill me as a dog, and that there would be no more notice taken of my death than if a dog were killed. This I very well understood.

They then told me that they supposed I had come to get my property.

I informed them I had; to which they replied that there was no property for me.

After repeated threatenings I became convinced that it was in vain to think of obtaining anything, and started for my horse, which was hitched at the yard fence about five rods from the door.

They followed me. O'Niel picked up the end of a hoop pole which Mr. Day had left there, he having been hooping a barrel. With this pole he struck me a blow upon the head, which nearly brought me to the ground. I looked around for a club with which to defend myself, but there was none in sight. He continued striking me, and would doubtless have killed me, had it not been for a very thick woolen cap on my head.

Mrs. Day threw open the door and cried murder. I ran for the house to get something, if possible, to defend myself with; but before I reached the door, he struck me repeatedly, and gave me one blow over the eye, the scar of which I carry to this day.

As soon as I got into the house I clutched the fire shovel. At that moment Mrs. Day closed the door, so that I could not get out nor O'Niel in. He and Culp then passed the window, on which Mrs. Day supposed they had started for their guns, so I mounted my horse and rode for Far West as fast as I could.

My head and face soon commenced swelling. On my way home I washed myself, and resolved not to inform any one what had happened, as Father Smith and President Young had both told me not to go.

I reached home about eleven o'clock at night, and went to bed without making a light. In the morning I arose, and just as soon as I got out of bed, I fell upon the floor. My wife was alarmed and screamed. I told her what had happened; but told her to keep the matter from my family. Father Smith, however, soon heard of the occurrence, and came to see me. He hoped, he said, that the lesson would do me good, and that he was glad that I was not quite killed.

Had I obeyed the words "do not go, but stay at home," I should not have fallen into this trouble. May you who read this be wise, and in this particular, profit by my experience.

Fragments of Experience, 19–22.

"All This Is Mine"

SPENCER W. KIMBALL

One day, a friend took me to his ranch. He unlocked the door of a large new automobile, slid under the wheel, and said proudly, "How do you like my new car?" We rode in luxurious comfort into the rural areas to a beautiful new landscaped home, and he said with no little pride, "This is my home."

He drove to a grassy knoll. The sun was retiring behind the distant hills. He surveyed his vast domain. Pointing to the north, he asked, "Do you see that clump of trees yonder?" I could plainly discern them in the fading day.

He pointed to the east. "Do you see the lake shimmering in the sunset?" It too was visible.

"Now, the bluff that's on the south." We turned about to scan the distance. He identified barns, silos, the ranch house to the west. With a wide sweeping gesture, he boasted, "From the clump of trees, to the lake, to the bluff, and to the ranch buildings and all between—all this is mine. And the dark specks in the meadow—those cattle also are mine."

And then I asked from whom he obtained it. The chain of title of his abstract went back to land grants from governments. His attorney had assured him he had an unencumbered title.

"From whom did the government get it?" I asked. "What was paid for it?"

There came into my mind the bold statement of Paul: "For the earth is the Lord's, and the fulness thereof" (1 Corinthians 10:26).

And then the psalmist who declared: "The words of the Lord are pure words: as silver tried in a furnace of earth, purified seven times" (Psalms 12:6).

And then I asked, "Did the title come from God, Creator of the earth and the owner thereof? Did he get paid? Was it sold or leased or given to you? If gift, from whom? If sale, with what exchange or currency? If lease, do you make proper accounting?"

And then I asked, "What was the price? With what treasures did you buy this farm?"

"Money!"

"Where did you get the money?"

"My toil, my sweat, my labor, and my strength."

And then I asked, "Where did you get your strength to toil, your power to labor, your glands to sweat?"

He spoke of food.

"Where did the food originate?"

"From sun and atmosphere and soil and water."

"And who brought those elements here?"

I quoted the psalmist: "Thou, O God, didst send a plentiful rain, whereby thou didst confirm thine inheritance, when it was weary" (Psalms 68:9).

"If the land is not yours, then what accounting do you make to your landlord for his bounties? The scripture says: 'Render unto Caesar that which is Caesar's and to God that which is God's.' What percentage of your increase do you pay Caesar? And what percent to God?

"Do you believe the Bible? Do you accept the command of the Lord through the prophet Malachi? It reads:

"'Will a man rob God? Yet ye have robbed me. But ye say, Wherein have we robbed thee? In tithes and offerings. . . .

"'Bring ye all the tithes into the storehouse, . . . and prove me now herewith, saith the Lord of hosts, if I will not open you the windows of heaven, and pour you out a blessing, that there shall not be room enough to receive it' (Malachi 3:8, 10).

"And in the latter days, the Lord said again:

"'And if ye seek the riches which it is the will of the Father to give unto you, ye shall be the richest of all people, for ye shall have the riches of eternity; and it must needs be that the riches of the earth are mine to give' (D&C 38:39).

"And Moses confirmed to Pharaoh regarding the plagues: ' . . . that thou mayest know now that the earth is the Lord's'" (Exodus 9:29).

I said again: "I seem to find no place in holy writ where God has said, 'I give you title to this land unconditionally. It is yours to give, to have, to hold, to sell, despoil, exploit as you see fit.'

"I cannot find such scripture, but I do find this from Psalms: 'Those that wait upon the Lord, . . . shall inherit the earth' (Psalms 37:9).

"And I remember that our Creator covenanted in the council in heaven with us all: '[And] We will go down, for there is space there, and we will take of these materials, and ye will make an earth whereon these may dwell' (Abraham 3:24).

"It seems more of a lease on which a rental is exacted than of a fee simple title.

"Modern scripture says that if you live the commandments, 'the fulness of the earth is yours, the beasts of . . . field and the fowls of the air, . . .

"'Yea, all things which come of the earth, . . . are made for the benefit and the use of man' (D&C 59:16, 18).

"This promise does not seem to convey the earth but only the use and contents which are given to men on condition that they live all of the commandments of God."

But my friend continued to mumble, "Mine—mine," as if to convince himself against the surer knowledge that he was at best a recreant renter.

That was long years ago. I saw him lying in his death among luxurious furnishings in a palatial home. His had been a vast estate. And I folded his arms upon his breast, and drew down the little curtains over his eyes. I spoke at his funeral, and I followed the cortege from the good piece of earth he had claimed to his grave, a tiny, oblong area the length of a tall man, the width of a heavy one.

Yesterday I saw that same estate, yellow in grain, green in lucerne, white in cotton, seemingly unmindful of him who had claimed it. Oh, puny man, see the busy ant moving the sands of the sea.

Conference Report, April 1968, 73–74.

"WHAT DIFFERENCE WILL IT MAKE?"

MARION G. ROMNEY

Four Latter-day Saint boys set out from a Utah city on a cross-country trip. They had saved all their money during the last year of high school for this purpose, and now that graduation was over, they packed their suitcases into the trunk of their car and said good-byes to worrying parents and envious friends. It was a matter of considerable celebration when they crossed the Utah state line and entered into another state. . . .

One of the boys . . . proposed to his friends that they forget all about being Mormons for the duration of their adventure. Asked why by the other three puzzled boys, he said that they could now afford to "let their hair down" and sample some of the excitement enjoyed by other people, not of the Mormon church. "Anyway," he argued, "what difference will it make? Nobody out here in the world knows us or cares anything about our church connections."

The thrill of the new experience weighted their judgment, and the group made an agreement to give it a try. . . .

Nightfall on the first day of the journey found them at a famous tourist attraction spot, and they made arrangements for camping near the resort. After the evening meal they gathered at the large hotel for the night's entertainment. No sooner had they arrived when the ringleader of the boys suggested that they begin here and now sampling the things they had so long been denied by strict parents and teachers. The first thing that caught their eyes was a large neon sign at the far end of the lounge. It read, "Bar—beer, cocktails." Thinking it a moderate nod in the direction of "sinning just a little bit," they agreed to go into the bar and order a glass of beer for each one. There was a nervous air about them as they entered the gaudily lighted bar and surveyed the counters loaded with intriguing bottles of liquor. The boy who had been delegated to give the order lost his voice on the first try and had to swallow hard to get out an understandable, "Four glasses of beer, please."

What the beer lacked in palatability, the atmosphere and thrill more than made up. They grew bolder and began to talk of the next adventure they would undertake. The talk was growing racy when suddenly a well-dressed man entered the bar and walked straight toward their table. The look on the stranger's face and the determined pace at which he walked toward them left the boys completely unnerved.

When the man reached the table at which the boys were sitting, he extended his hand to one of them and said, "I beg your pardon, but aren't you George Redford's son from Utah?"

The boy was speechless and terrified. His fingers froze around the base of the glass of beer and he answered in a wavering voice. "Why, yes, sir, I am."

"I thought I recognized you when you came in the lobby of the hotel," the stranger continued. "I am Henry Paulsen, vice-president of the company your dad works for, and I met you and your mother last winter at a company dinner at the Hotel Utah. I have never forgotten how you explained your Mormon priesthood to one of the other executives of our company who asked you what it meant to be a Mormon boy. I must say I was a little surprised to see you head for the bar, but I suppose that with Mormons as well as non-Mormons, boys will be boys when they're off the roost."

These boys had heard a sermon they would never hear duplicated at the pulpit. They were sick, ashamed, and crestfallen. As they left their half-filled glasses and walked out through the hotel lobby, they had the feeling that everyone was looking at them. The cover of darkness was kind as they made their way to their camp. "You just can't win," said the boy who had proposed their dropping their true identity, trying to ease the tension.

"I'm not so sure," replied the boy to whom the stranger had spoken. "If we have any sense left, we can make this experience into the most winning lesson of our lives."

Conference Report, October 1974, 104–5.

"GIVE HEBER $10,000"

JOSEPH ANDERSON

There is another story I would like to tell you that President [Heber J.] Grant often told. Whenever the Church needed someone to collect funds for some important purpose, they called on Brother Grant. At the time, of course, he was an apostle. And he was a great financier and a wonderful man for contributing to funds and for collecting funds. On one occasion, it so happened that one of the banks in Salt Lake was in trouble, and it looked like it might fail. Some of the brethren were interested in the bank as directors, and if it had failed, it would have been quite an embarrassment to them. And the President of the Church called on Brother Grant to go out and collect funds that they might put into the bank to save it from disaster.

Now some people questioned the wisdom of that, but at any rate Brother Grant went forward on his mission. And one of the places he visited was Provo where he called on Jesse Knight and Reed Smoot. He asked Reed Smoot for $2,000, and he asked Jesse for $5,000. They were both men of means, Brother Knight particularly, as some of you well know.

Jesse wasn't altogether sold on the idea. He said, "No, I don't think that an apostle of the Lord ought to be going out gathering funds for that purpose. I don't think that that's a worthy cause to go out and make collections for."

And Brother Smoot said, "I'll give you $1,000, but I won't give you $2,000."

Brother Grant said, "Brother Smoot, you have offered $1,000. I'll not take it, but you go home tonight and get down on your knees and pray to the Lord and ask him to give you enlargement of the heart and give me $2,000."

Jesse said, "Brother Grant, why didn't you ask *me* to pray?"

"Oh," Brother Grant said, "why should I ask you to pray? You didn't offer me anything. No use of asking the Lord to give you enlargement of the heart."

Brother Knight had told him, "You can come here as often as you want, and there is a bed and breakfast for you at my home, but I'm not going to contribute to that." And he was a very generous contributor normally.

He said, "I'll tell you what I will do. I will go home tonight, and I will pray to the Lord about that. And if I get the inspiration to give you that $5,000, I'll do it."

"Well," Brother Grant said, "I might as well have the check in my pocket now. I am sure if you pray about it I'll get it."

And so, two or three days later there came through the mail two checks—one from Jesse M. Knight for $10,000, and one from Brother Smoot for $2,000.

When Brother Grant saw Jesse a few days later, he said, "What happened? I didn't ask you for $10,000. I only asked for $5,000."

Brother Knight said, "I'll tell you this, Brother Grant. When you come to me again with a mission from the President of the Church to raise funds, I'm going to pay without any question." He said, "You're much more liberal than the Lord is. I went home as I promised to do, and I told the Lord that Heber was asking me for this contribution, and I wanted to know how he felt about it. I got down on my knees, and it just kept going through my mind like a tune: 'Give Heber $10,000.' And I got into bed and that tune kept going through my mind: 'Give Heber $10,000. Give Heber $10,000.' I got down on my knees again and said, 'Lord, Heber didn't ask me for $10,000. He only asked for $5,000.' The tune kept going through my mind. 'Give Heber $10,000. Give Heber $10,000.' And so, in order to satisfy the situation and have peace of mind, I told the Lord, 'All right, I'll give him $10,000.'"

BYU Speeches, 29 July 1969, 6–7.

Pioneers

"The Recollection of It Unmans Me Even Now"

JOHN CHISLETT

We [the Willie Handcart Company] reached [Fort] Laramie about the 1st or 2nd of September, but the provisions, etc., which we expected, were not there for us. Captain Willie called a meeting to take into consideration our circumstances, conditions and prospects, and to see what could be done. It was ascertained that at our present rate of travel and consumption of flour the latter would be exhausted when we were about three hundred and fifty miles from our destination. It was resolved to reduce our allowance from one pound to three-quarters of a pound per day, and at the same time to make every effort in our power to travel faster. We continued at this rate of rations from Laramie to Independence Rock. About this time Captain Willie received a letter from Apostle Richards informing him that we might expect supplies to meet us from the Valley by the time we reached South Pass. An examination of our stock of flour showed that it would be gone before we reached that point. Our only alternative was to still further reduce our bill of fare. The issue of flour was then to average ten ounces per day. . . .

We had not travelled far up the Sweetwater before the nights, which had gradually been getting colder since we left Laramie, became severe. The mountains before us, as we approached nearer to them, revealed themselves to view mantled nearly to their base in snow, and tokens of a coming snow were discernable in the clouds which each day seemed to lower around us. . . .

Our seventeen pounds of clothing and bedding was now altogether insufficient for our comfort. Nearly all suffered more or less at night from cold. Instead of getting up in the morning strong, refreshed, vigorous, and prepared for the hardships of another day of toil, the poor Saints were to be seen crawling out from their tents haggard, benumbed, and showing an utter lack of that vitality so necessary to our success.

Cold weather, scarcity of food, lassitude and fatigue from overexertion soon produced their effects. Our old and infirm people began to droop, and they no sooner lost spirit and courage than death's stamp could be traced upon their features. Life went out as smoothly as a lamp ceases to burn when the oil is gone. At first the deaths occurred slowly and irregularly, but a few days at more frequent intervals, until we soon thought it unusual to leave a campground without burying one or more persons.

Death was not long confined in its ravages to the old and infirm, but the young and naturally strong were among its victims. . . . Many a father pulled his cart, with his little children on it, until the day preceding his death. I have seen some pull their carts in the morning, give out during the day, and die before the next morning. . . .

We travelled on in misery and sorrow day after day. Sometimes we made a pretty good distance, but at other times we were only able to make a few miles progress. Finally we were overtaken by a snowstorm which the shrill wind blew furiously about us. . . .

In the morning the snow was over a foot deep. Our cattle strayed wildly during the storm, and some of them died. But what was worse to us than all this was the fact that five persons of both sexes lay in the cold embrace of death.

The morning before the storm, or rather, the morning of the day on which it came, we issued the last ration of flour. On this fatal morning, therefore, we had none to issue. We had, however, a barrel or two of hard bread which Captain Willie had procured at Fort Laramie in view of our destitution. This was equally and fairly divided among all of the company. . . .

Being surrounded by snow a foot deep, out of provisions, many of our people sick, and our cattle dying, it was decided that we should remain in our present camp until the supply train reached us. . . . The scanty allowance of hard bread and poor beef, distributed as described, was mostly eaten the first day by the hungry, ravenous, famished souls.

We killed more cattle and issued the meat; but, eating it without bread did not satisfy hunger, and to those who were suffering from dysentery it did more harm than good. This terrible disease increased rapidly amongst us during these three days, and several died from exhaustion. . . . The recollection of it unmans me even now—those three days! During that time I visited the sick, the widows whose husbands died in serving them, and the aged who could not help themselves, to know for myself where to dispense the few articles that had been placed in my charge for distribution. Such craving hunger I never saw before, and may God in his mercy spare me the sight again.

LeRoy R. Hafen and Ann W. Hafen, *Handcarts to Zion,* 101–4.

"DELIVERANCE IS AT HAND"

ELIZABETH JACKSON KINGSFORD

We continued our toil day after day, pulling our handcarts with our provisions and rations, our little children, etc., through deep sand, rocky roads, or fording streams. It was a dreary journey. Many miles each day were traveled, ere with tired limbs we reached camp, ate and retired for the night to rest, to pursue our monotonous course the following day. After toilsome and fatiguing travel, we reached Laramie on the 8th of October. . . .

Shortly after leaving Ft. Laramie it became necessary to shorten our rations that they might hold out, and that the company be not reduced to starvation. The reduction was repeated several times. First, the pound of flour was reduced to three-fourths of a pound, then to half a pound, and afterwards to still less per day. However, we pushed ahead. The trip was full of adventures, hair breadth escapes, and exposure to attacks from Indians, wolves, and other wild beasts. When we reached the Black Hills, we had a rough experience. The roads were rocky, broken, and difficult to travel. Frequently carts were broken down and much delay caused by the needed repairs.

In crossing the Platte River some of the men carried a number of the women on their backs or in their arms across the stream. . . . We had scarcely crossed the river when we were visited with a tremendous storm of snow, hail, sand, and fierce winds. It was a terrible storm from which both the people and teams suffered. After crossing the river, my husband was unable to walk and consequently provision had to be made for him to ride in a wagon.

As soon as we reached camp, I prepared some refreshments and placed him to rest for the night. From this time my worst experience commenced. The company had now become greatly reduced in strength, the teams had become so weak that the luggage was reduced to ten pounds per head for adults and five pounds per head for children under eight years. And although the weather was severe, a great deal of bedding and clothing had to be destroyed—burned—as it could not be carried along. This occurrence very much increased the suffering of the company, men, women, and children alike.

On the 20th of October we traveled, or almost wallowed, for about ten miles through the snow. At night, weary and worn out, we camped near the Platte River, where we soon left it for the Sweetwater. We were visited with three days of more snow. The animals and emigrants were almost completely exhausted. We remained in camp several days to gain strength.

About the 25th of October, I think it was—I cannot remember the exact date—we reached camp about sundown. My husband had for several days previous been much worse. He was still sinking, and his condition became more serious. As soon as possible, after reaching camp, I prepared a little of such scant articles of food as we then had. He tried to eat, but failed. He had not the strength to swallow. I put him to bed as quickly as I could. He seemed to rest easy and fell asleep. About 9 o'clock, I retired. Bedding had become very scarce, so I did not disrobe.

I slept until, as it appeared to me, about midnight. It was extremely cold. The weather was bitter. I listened to hear if my husband breathed—he lay so still. I could not hear him. I became alarmed. I put my hand on his body when to my horror I discovered that my worst fears were confirmed. My husband was dead. He was cold and stiff—rigid in the arms of death. It was a bitter freezing night and the elements had sealed up his mortal frame.

I called for help to the other inmates of the tent. They could render me no aid; and there was no alternative but to remain alone by the side of the corpse till morning. The night was enveloped in almost Egyptian darkness. There was nothing with which to produce a light or kindle a fire. Of course I could not sleep. I could only watch, wait, and pray for the dawn. But oh, how those dreary hours drew their tedious length along.

When daylight came, some of the male part of the company prepared the body for burial. And oh, such burial and funeral service. They did not remove his clothing—he had but little. They wrapped him in a blanket and placed him in a pile with thirteen others who had died, and then covered him up in the snow. The ground was frozen so hard that they could not dig a grave. I will not attempt to describe my feeling at finding myself thus left a widow with three children, under such excruciating circumstances. I cannot do it. But I believe the Recording Angel has inscribed it in the archives above, and that my sufferings for the gospel's sake will be sanctified unto me for my good. . . .

A few days after the death of my husband, the male members of the company had become reduced in number by death; and those who remained were so weak and emaciated by sickness that on reaching the camping place at night, there were not sufficient men with strength enough to raise the poles and pitch the tents. The result was that we camped out with nothing but the vault of heaven for a roof and the stars for companions. The snow lay several inches deep upon the ground. The night was bitterly cold. I sat down on a rock with one child in my lap and one on each side of me. In that condition I remained until morning. . . .

It will be readily perceived that under such adverse circumstances I had become despondent. I was six or seven thousand miles from my native land, in a wild rocky mountain country, in a destitute condition, the ground covered with snow, the waters covered with ice, and I with three fatherless children with scarcely anything to protect them from the merciless storms.

When I retired to bed that night, being the 27th of October, I had a stunning revelation. In my dream, my husband stood by me, and said, "Cheer up, Elizabeth, deliverance is at hand." The dream was fulfilled, for the next day (October 28, 1856) Joseph A. Young, Daniel Jones, and Abel Garr galloped unexpectedly into camp, amid tears and cheers and smiles and laughter of the emigrants. These three men were the first of the most advanced relief company sent out from Salt Lake City to meet the belated emigrants.

Andrew Jenson, *LDS Biographical Encyclopedia,* 2: 528–31.

"WHO WOULD STAY IF CALLED UPON?"

DANIEL W. JONES

I attended the October conference of 1856. When conference was opened President Young arose and said: "There are a number of our people on the plains who have started to come with handcarts; they will need help and I want twenty teams to be ready by morning with two men to each team to go out and meet them." . . .

Brother Young called upon everyone present to lend a hand in fitting up these teams. As I was going out with the crowd, Brother Wells spoke to me, saying, "You are a good hand for the trip; get ready." . . .

I had a saddle horse. We were instructed to get everything we could ready and rendezvous between the Big and Little Mountains, a short day's drive out from Salt Lake. Next day teams and volunteer men were ready. A better outfit and one more adapted to the work before us I do not think could have possibly been selected if a week had been spent in fitting up. Besides the wagons and teams, several men went horseback. We had good teams and provisions in great abundance. But best of all, those going were alive to the work and were of the best material possible for the occasion. . . .

The weather soon became cold and stormy. We traveled hard, never taking time to stop for dinner. On getting into camp all were hungry and willing to help. No doubt many of the boys remember the hearty suppers eaten on this expedition. There was some expectation of meeting the first train, Brother Willie's, on or about Green River. We began to feel anxiety about the emigrants, as the weather was now cold and stormy, and we, strong men with good outfits, found the nights severe. What must be the condition of those we were to meet! Many old men and women, little children, mothers with nursing babes, crossing the plains pulling handcarts. Our hearts began to ache when we reached Green River and yet no word of them. Here an express was sent on ahead with a light wagon to meet and cheer the people up. Cyrus Wheelock and Stephen Taylor went with this express.

At the South Pass, we encountered a severe snowstorm. After crossing the divide we turned down into a sheltered place on the Sweetwater. While in camp and during the snowstorm two men were seen on horseback going west. They were hailed. On reaching us they proved to be Brothers Willie and J. B. Elder. They reported their company in a starving condition at their camp then east of Rocky Ridge and said our express had gone on to meet the other companies still in the rear.

We started immediately through the storm to reach Brother Willie's camp. On arriving we found them in a condition that would stir the feelings of the hardest heart. They were in a poor place, the storm having caught them where fuel was scarce. They were out of provisions and really freezing and starving to death. The morning after our arrival nine were buried in one grave. We did all we could to relieve them. The boys struck out on horseback and dragged up a lot of wood; provisions were distributed and all went to work to cheer the sufferers. . . .

The handcart company was moved over to a cove in the mountains for shelter and fuel, a distance of two miles from the fort. The wagons were banked near the fort. It became impossible to travel further without reconstruction or help. . . .

Each evening the elders would meet in council. I remember hearing Charles Decker remark that he had crossed the plains over fifty times (carrying the mail) and this was the darkest hour he had ever seen. Cattle and horses were dying every day. What to do was all that could be talked about. Five or six days had passed and nothing determined upon.

Steve Taylor, Al Huntington, and I were together when the question, "Why doesn't Captain Grant leave all the goods here with someone to watch them, and move on?" was asked. We agreed to make this proposal to him. It was near the time appointed for the meeting. As soon as we were together, Captain Grant asked if anyone had thought of a plan. We presented ours. Captain Grant replied, "I have thought of this, but there are no provisions to leave and it would be asking too much of anyone to stay here and starve for the sake of these goods; besides, where is there a man who would stay if called upon?" I answered, "Any of us would." . . .

There was a move made at once to adopt this suggestion. Accordingly, next morning storerooms in the fort were cleared and some two hundred wagons run in and unloaded. No one was allowed to keep out anything but a change of clothing, some bedding, and light cooking utensils. Hauling provisions was not a weighty question.

The unloading occupied three days. The handcart people were notified to abandon most of their carts. Teams were hitched up and the sick and feeble loaded in with such light weight as was allowed. All became common property.

When everything was ready Brother Burton said to me, "Now Brother Jones, we want you to pick two men from the Valley to stay with you. We have notified Captains Hunt and Horgett to detail seventeen men from their companies to stay with you. We will move on in the morning." . . .

There was not money enough on earth to have hired me to stay. I had left home for only a few days and was not prepared to remain so long away; but I remembered my assertion that any of us would stay if called upon. . . .

We were about out of anything fit to eat. . . .

Game soon became so scarce that we could kill nothing. We ate all the poor meat; one would get hungry eating it. Finally that was all gone; nothing now but hides were left. We made a trial of them. A lot was cooked and eaten without any seasoning, and it made the whole company sick. Many were so turned against the stuff that it made them sick to think of it. . . .

Things looked dark, for nothing remained but the poor rawhides taken from starved cattle. We asked the Lord to direct us what to do. The brethren did not murmur, but felt to trust in God. We had cooked the hide, after soaking and scraping the hair off until it was soft, and then ate it, glue and all. This made it rather inclined to stay with us longer than we desired.

Finally I was impressed how to fix the stuff and gave the

company advice, telling them how to cook it; for them to scorch and scrape the hair off; this had a tendency to kill and purify the bad taste that scalding gave it. After scraping, boil one hour in plenty of water, throwing the water away which had extracted all the glue, then wash and scrape the hide thoroughly, washing in cold water, then boil to a jelly and let it get cold, and then eat with a little sugar sprinkled on it. This was considerable trouble, but we had little else to do and it was better than starving.

We asked the Lord to bless our stomachs and adapt them to this food. We hadn't the faith to ask him to bless the rawhide, for it was "hard stock." On eating now, all seemed to relish the feast. We were three days without eating before this second attempt was made. We enjoyed this sumptuous fare for about six weeks.

Forty Years Among the Indians, 62–64, 69–72, 80–83.

PETTICOATS AND WAGON WHEELS

KENNETH AND
AUDREY ANN GODFREY

Though the days were often dull, there were other times when the excitement was almost more than these prairie women needed, as Rachel Lee found out near the end of her journey. As she walked beside her wagon, delighting in the wind that cooled her a little as she trudged along, an unexpected gust whipped her skirts into the wagon wheel. Historical writer Juanita

Brooks wrote that before Rachel knew it, her skirts were being "wrapped around and around the hub. She screamed for help as she tried to extricate them, but in an instant they were drawn so tight that she could only grasp two spokes in her hands, her feet between two others, and make a complete revolution with the wheel."

The wagon was finally stopped, and Rachel found herself almost right side up but still tightly bound to the wheel. Everyone gathered around, trying to decide how to get her loose. There was no question of cutting her clothing, as that would mean one less item for wear that she needed badly.

It was decided they would unhook her skirt and unbutton the petticoat, and by carefully slitting the placket, she could be pulled free. Her shoes were unlaced. Then, as one woman held a blanket to protect her from curious eyes, she was plucked from skirt, petticoats, and shoes "clean as though they were skinning the legs of a chicken." Later the clothing was easily removed from the wheel, and in the privacy of her wagon, Rachel shook them free of wrinkles and put them on again. As she took up her walk again, she kept a wary distance from the wheels.

Improvement Era, May 1969, 34.

"SHE MAY HAVE MY PLACE!"

LLEWELYN R. McKAY

After two years, the [William McKay] family moved to Iowa, and again settled down for another year's work saving money and preparing for the long trek across the plains to Utah. By the end of a year the family owned two two-year-old steers, two cows, one old ox, a wagon, and a scanty supply of provisions, and all were happy that the 1,000 mile journey could begin. They joined the company of Captain James Brown at Florence [Nebraska]. On the eve of departure, June 13, 1859, a council of instructions was held. Captain Brown reported that there was a widow with a small child in the camp who had no means of transportation and who was too ill to walk. "Is there anybody here who can make room for this widow and her child?" Every wagon was heavily loaded, and no answer came from the assembled men. William had always taken the best possible care of his wife, and he planned to have her ride in the wagon across the plains, intending to walk the whole distance himself.

He reported the incident to Ellen Oman [McKay], saying: "Mother, there is a widow who would like to cross the plains; she is helpless, unable to walk. Somebody will have to make room for her in the wagons. I said nothing tonight."

She answered immediately, "You go right back and tell her that she may have my place!" At her insistence, he did so, and Ellen walked with her husband the whole distance of 1,000 miles across the plains!

Llewelyn R. McKay, comp., *Home Memories of President David O. McKay,* 19–20.

"BE PATIENT AND FEAR NOT"

SUSA YOUNG GATES

[Lydia Knight's] little babe was a week old when a sudden severe rainstorm came up. It poured down into the cabin with much violence. Lydia told her daughter Sally to give her all the bedclothes they had, and these were put upon the bed and removed as they became soaked.

At last, finding the clothes were all wet completely through and that she was getting chilled sitting up in the wet, she said, "Sally, go to bed. It's no use doing any more unless some power beyond that which we possess is exercised; it is impossible for me to avoid catching cold. But we will trust in God; he has never failed to hear our prayers."

And so she drew her babe to her, and covered up as well as she could, and asked God to watch over them all through the night.

Her mind went back to the time when she had a noble companion, one who would never allow her to suffer any discomfort and who loved her as tenderly as man could woman. But now he was in the grave in a savage Indian country, and she was alone and in trouble.

As she thus mused, chilled with the cold rain and shivering, her agony at his loss became unbearable and she cried out, "Oh Newel, why could you not have stayed with and protected me through our journeyings?"

A voice plainly answered her from the darkness around her and said, "Lydia, be patient and fear not. I will still watch over you, and protect you in your present situation. You shall receive no harm. It was needful that I should go, and you will understand why in due time."

As the voice ceased, a pleasant warmth crept over her and seemed like the mild sunshine on a lovely spring afternoon.

Curling down in this comfortable atmosphere, she went immediately to sleep, and awoke in the morning all right, but wet to the skin.

Instead of receiving harm from this circumstance, she got up the next morning, although the child was but a week old, and went about her usual labors.

Susa Young Gates, *Lydia Knight's History,* 73.

"Will We Trust to Luck to Get the Tenth?"

SUSA YOUNG GATES

When first moving into their little home [in Utah], Lydia [Knight] had put all the cows but one upon the range. The following very remarkable instance is an example of what God will do for those who gladly keep his laws:

The one cow left at home stood out in the open air, staked a little way from the house. One morning in December Lydia awoke to find herself surrounded by a mountain of snow.

"Oh, the cow!" said Lydia, as she sprang from her bed. "Boys, something must be done."

Hurriedly dressing, she went to the door, and there stood the faithful beast, cold and shivering, and there was not a spear of feed to give her.

"Boys, take this blanket," said Lydia, taking a heavy, warm, homemade blanket from her bed, "and go down to Brother Drake, who lives in the Second Ward. I knew him in the Ponca camp, and something whispers to me that he will have some feed for the cow. Tell him I would like to get enough of some kind of feed to last until this storm is over, and we can turn the poor thing out. This blanket is a good, almost new one, and should be worth part of a load."

The boys hastened down to Brother Drake's, and in a little while Lydia was pleased and surprised to see them returning in a wagon, which was well loaded with feed.

You may be sure Lydia thanked and blessed her kind friend; the boys went to work and made a pen of poles that they had hauled for wood, and they soon had "Bossie" in a warm place.

In the course of a day or two, Lydia was able to churn, getting just about a pound of butter. When it was all worked over, she said to the children who had watched the operation with much interest, "Now, children, what shall we do? Here is just about a pound of butter; we may not be able to get the tenth from the cow, and shall we pay this, the first pound for tithing, or will we eat this and trust to luck to get the tenth?"

"Pay this for tithing," answered all the children with one breath. "We can do without, mother, till you churn again."

So the butter was taken to the tithing office. That cow was a "stripper" (had no calf for two years), and furthermore, the cow never got a spear of feed but what Brother Drake had brought, it having lasted until the grass grew in the spring.

As Lydia has since told me, she has made it a firm rule to pay the first instead of the tenth of everything for tithing, commencing always with New Year's Day. "And," added she in relating this circumstance, "I have never been without butter in the house from that day to this."

Susa Young Gates, *Lydia Knight's History,* 93–94.

HE SANG THE HYMN ALONE

OSCAR WINTERS

One night, as we were making camp, we noticed one of our brethren had not arrived, and a volunteer party was immediately organized to return and see if anything had happened to him. Just as we were about to start, we saw the missing brother coming in the distance. When he arrived, he said he had been quite sick; so some of us unyoked his oxen and attended to his part of the camp duties.

After supper, he sat down before the campfire on a large rock, and sang, in a very faint but plaintive and sweet voice, the hymn "Come, Come, Ye Saints."

It was a rule of the camp that whenever anybody started this hymn all in the camp should join, but for some reason this evening nobody joined him; he sang the hymn alone. When he had finished, I doubt if there was a single dry eye in the camp.

The next morning we noticed that he was not yoking up his

cattle. We went to his wagon and found that he had died during the night. We dug a shallow grave, and after we had covered his body with the earth we rolled the large stone to the head of the grave to mark it, the stone on which he had been sitting the night before when he sang:

"And should we die before our journey's through,
Happy day! all is well!"

Improvement Era, June 1914, 781–82.

Prayer

"It Was the Exact Amount Required"

AUTHOR UNKNOWN

When the Saints were preparing to leave Nauvoo, wagons for the journey were in great demand, and every person among them who had ever worked at wagon-making, and very many also who never had, set to work making them. Good timber was tolerably plentiful, but iron cost cash, and that was a scarce article. All sorts of nondescript vehicles were hastily improvised, many of them so rude in their construction as to put the veriest bungler of a wheelwright to the blush for their appearance. Yet under the blessing of God they did good service. Some of them, for the want of iron, were made almost entirely of wood. In some extreme cases they were even made without the usual iron tires, strips of rawhide being nailed on the felloes as a substitute. One, at least, of the wagons made in this fashion stood the trip across the plains, and was used for several years after its arrival in Salt Lake Valley.

Brother L—— had been fortunate enough to get the wood work of a wagon made, but how to procure the iron was a question which greatly perplexed him. However, he knew that he was engaged in the Lord's service, and he felt that he had a claim upon His mercy and blessings. Accordingly, he and his wife made their want a subject of earnest prayer, and then went on about their duties, trusting in the Lord to answer their petition.

Soon afterwards Brother L—— had occasion to go out on the prairie in search of his cow, which had strayed off, and during his absence encountered a drenching shower, so that when he returned home he found it necessary to change his clothing. He hung his wet clothes before a fire in the open fireplace to dry, and as he did so a bright gold sovereign, a ten and a five cent piece dropped to the floor, apparently from his pocket. He knew, however, that he had no money previously, and he could account for its presence there only by its having been sent by the Lord. It was the exact amount required to purchase the iron for his wagon, and it was soon obtained and the wagon finished.

Fragments of Experience, 85–87.

A New Pair of Shoes

AUTHOR UNKNOWN

A rather remarkable case of special providence occurred when Brother L——— was crossing the plains, coming to Salt Lake Valley. His shoes gave out, and his feet became very sore from having to walk so much while driving his ox-team, etc. Early one morning, when he, in company with another brother, were out hunting for their cattle, he exclaimed to his companion as he limped and hobbled over the rocky ground, "Oh! I do wish the Lord would send me a pair of shoes!"

He had not walked many rods after expressing this wish when he saw something lying a short distance ahead of him, and called the attention of his companion to it, who remarked that it must be the bell and strap lost off one of the oxen, but to the inexpressible joy of Brother L———, he found, on approaching the object, that it was a new pair of shoes, which had evidently never been worn, and which he found, on trying them on, to fit him as well as if they had been made for him. He thanked the Lord for them, for he felt that it was through His merciful providence that they had been left there, and went on his way rejoicing. The shoes did him good service.

Fragments of Experience, 84–87.

She Prayed All Night

HEBER J. GRANT

I met President George Q. Cannon, then our delegate to Congress, and he said: "Would you like to go to the Naval Academy, or to West Point?"

I told him I would.

He said: "Which one?"

I said, "The Naval Academy."

"All right, I will give you the appointment without competitive examination."

For the first time in my life I did not sleep well; I lay awake nearly all night long rejoicing that the ambition of my life was to be fulfilled. I fell asleep just a little before daylight; my mother had to awaken me.

I said: "Mother, what a marvelous thing it is that I am to have an education as fine as that of any young man in all Utah. I could hardly sleep; I was awake until almost daylight this morning."

I looked into her face; I saw that she had been weeping.

I have heard of people who, when drowning, had their entire life pass before them in a few seconds. I saw myself an admiral, in my mind's eye. I saw myself traveling all over the world in a ship, away from my widowed mother. I laughed and put my arms around her and kissed her and said, "Mother, I do not want a naval education. I am going to be a businessman and shall enter an office right away and take care of you and have you quit keeping boarders for a living."

She broke down and wept and said that she had not closed her eyes, but had prayed all night that I would give up my life's ambition so that she would not be left alone.

Heber J. Grant, as quoted in Bryant S. Hinckley, *Heber J. Grant,* 33–34.

"IN THE DEATH OF YOUR MAMMA THE WILL OF THE LORD WILL BE"

HEBER J. GRANT

My wife Lucy was very sick for nearly three years prior to her death. At one time I was in the hospital with her for six months. When she was dying, I called my children into the bedroom and told them their mamma was dying. My daughter Lutie said she did not want her mamma to die and insisted that I lay hands upon her and heal her, saying that she had often seen her mother, when sick in the hospital in San Francisco, suffering intensely, go to sleep immediately and have a peaceful night's rest when I had blessed her. I explained to my children that we all had to die sometime, and that I felt that their mamma's time had come. The children went out of the room, and I knelt down by the bed of my dying wife and told the Lord that I acknowledged his hand in life or in death, in joy or in sorrow, in prosperity or adversity; that I did not complain because my wife was dying, but that I lacked the strength to see my wife die and have her death affect the faith of my children in the ordinances of the gospel. I therefore pleaded with him to give to my daughter Lutie a testimony that it was his will that her mother should die. Within a few short hours, my wife breathed her last. Then I called the children into the bedroom and announced that their mamma was dead. My little boy Heber commenced weeping bitterly, and Lutie put her arms around him and kissed him, and told him not to cry, that the voice of the Lord had said to her, "In the death of your mamma the will of the Lord will be." Lutie knew nothing of my prayers, and this manifestation to her was a direct answer to my supplication to the Lord, and for it I have never ceased to be grateful.*

Improvement Era, June 1912, 726–27.

* To read this story from Lutie's point of view, see *Best-Loved Stories of the LDS People,* volume 1, page 267.

"I PRAYED FOR HER LIFE"

HEBER J. GRANT

When my wife died I took my oldest three daughters to Boston, New York, and other places in the hope that the sorrow caused by the death of their mother might be forgotten. When we reached Washington two of them were taken ill with diphtheria. They were as sick as any children I have ever seen. The younger of the two was so low that her pulse beat only twenty-eight times to the minute, and I felt sure she was going to die. I knelt down and prayed God to spare her life, inasmuch as I had brought my children east to relieve the terrible sorrow that had come to them, and prayed that I should not have the additional sorrow of taking one of my children home in a coffin. I prayed for her life, and shed bitter tears of humiliation.

While praying, the inspiration came to me that if I would administer to her, she would live. Some people say we cannot know for a certainty that we receive manifestations from the Lord.

Well, I know that I was shedding tears of sorrow, fear, and anguish while I was praying, and I know that immediately thereafter I received the witness of the Spirit that my little girl should live, and I shed tears of unbounding joy and gratitude and thanksgiving to God, thanking him for the inspiration that came to me to send for the elders that they might administer to my little girl.

Hiram B. Clawson and George Q. Cannon were in Washington at the time, and I sent for them. When George Q. Cannon laid his hands upon my daughter's head to seal the anointing wherewith she had been anointed, he made a statement that I have never heard before or since in all my life, in any prayer. He said, in substance: "The adversary, the destroyer, has decreed your death and made public announcement that you shall die; but by the authority of the priesthood of the Living God, we rebuke the decree of the adversary, and say that you shall live and not die; that you shall live to become a mother in the Church of Christ."

She did live to become a mother, and in the providences of the Lord her children are the great-grandchildren of the man who held the priesthood of God and gave her that blessing.

Conference Report, October 1941, 12–13.

"Come in and Get Your Shoes"

J. Golden Kimball

Father [Heber C. Kimball] had men working for him for a good many years, and he had one he called Colonel Smith. It was in the days of hardships and poverty, and men had great difficulty. They employed a great many people, the brethren did, that was a part of their religion. He employed the colonel, who had been a soldier in Great Britain, and on one occasion he went to father for a pair of shoes, and I guess father felt pretty cross, and answered him a little abruptly, perhaps. So the colonel went home feeling badly, and when he prayed that night, he made a complaint to God against father, saying that "thy servant Heber" was not treating him right.

When he came past that little place on Gordon Avenue, next morning, father came out and said, "Robert, what did you complain against me for? You come in and get your shoes, and don't do it again!" Now, how did he know that Colonel Robert Smith, who lived away down in the Nineteenth ward, had filed a complaint against him? Don't you think that we can get on friendly terms with God? Not on familiar terms, but friendly terms. I tell you, God will answer your prayers. If there was any one thing I knew better than another when I was traveling in the South, it was that God answers prayers, and softens the hearts of people towards you.

Conference Report, April 1913, 90.

"HOW ABOUT YOUR PRAYERS?"

ROBERT L. SIMPSON

It was thrilling to listen to a father relate this story about his three-year-old youngster recently, as they knelt by the crib in the usual manner for the little fellow to say his simple bedtime prayer. Eyes closed—heads bowed—seconds passed, and there were no words spoken by the child. Just about the time Dad was going to open his eyes to check the lengthy delay, little Tommy was on his feet and climbing into bed.

"How about your prayers?" asked Dad.

"I said my prayers," came the reply.

"But son, Daddy didn't hear you."

Then followed the child's classic statement: "But Daddy, I wasn't talking to you."

Conference Report, April 1970, 89.

"The Little Boy Is Nearly Frozen"

HEBER J. GRANT

Fifty-four years ago [1863], as a little child, I took a sleigh ride with President Brigham Young, that is, I ran out and took hold of the back of the sleigh, intending to ride a block and then drop off and walk home; but President Young was driving such a fine team, or at least his driver was, that I dared not let go, hence rode on till we reached the Cottonwood, and then when the sleigh slowed up, to pass through the stream, I jumped off, and the president saw me.

He said, "Stop, Brother Isaac, stop. The little boy is nearly frozen. Put him under the buffalo robe and get him warm." Isaac Wilson was his driver.

After I got warm he inquired my name, and told me about my father, and his love for him. He told me to tell my mother that he wanted her to send me up to his office in six months to have a visit with him; and in six months I went for the visit. From that time, fifty-four years ago, until the day of his death, I was intimately acquainted with President Young. . . .

I was almost as familiar in the homes of President Brigham Young as I was in the home of my own mother. . . . I have spent hours and hours, as a child, in the rooms of Eliza R. Snow, listening to her counsel and advice, and hearing her relate incidents in the life of Joseph Smith the Prophet, and bearing witness of the wonderful blessings of God to Brigham Young. As I say, I was familiar with the Prophet Brigham Young. I knelt down time and time again in his home in the Lion House at family prayers, as a child and as a young man; and I bear witness that as a little child, upon more than one occasion, because of the inspiration of the Lord to Brigham Young while he was supplicating God for guidance, I have lifted my head, turned and looked at the place where Brigham Young was praying, to see if the Lord was not there. It seemed to me that he talked to the Lord as one man would talk to another.

Heber J. Grant, *Gospel Standards,* 222–23.

A YOUNG MAN'S FAITH

OSCAR A. KIRKHAM

I shall not soon forget a young man at the hospital. He was entering the operating room. He was a very worthy man and very dear to me personally. As they were wheeling him to the operating room, the doctor noticed that the young man's eyes were closed. He said to the nurse, "Take his pulse quickly—he may be gone."

Just at that moment the young man opened his eyes and said, "No, I'm not gone, Doctor—I was just talking to the Lord. I told him to be sure and be with you when you perform this operation. You may go ahead now. I am ready."

Conference Report, April 1948, 94–95.

"I DON'T NEED TO BE AFRAID OF A PRAYING INDIAN"

AUTHOR UNKNOWN

The first sawmill in Escalante, Utah, was situated in North Creek Canyon, about fourteen miles from town. This mill was built and managed by Henry J. White.

One Sunday it became necessary for Mr. White to leave his young wife, Susannah, alone at the sawmill until the next day. He disliked doing this because Indians were camped close by, and one . . . was known to be the meanest Indian in the country.

About two hours after Mr. White left, this very Indian came to the mill. He rode up to the cabin and said, "Where is your Mormon?" Susannah pretended that she wasn't frightened, and told the Indian that Mr. White was in town. He said he wanted to hunt above the mill, so Susannah told him to go. He rode away, but reappeared in the late afternoon with two deer tied on his horse, and again asked, "Where is your Mormon?" She told him he was still in town. The Indian then asked to stay all night. She told him he could stay and for him to put his horse in the corral and feed it.

The deer were hung in a nearby tree and the horse cared for before the Indian came to the cabin. Susannah had supper ready when he came in, and after eating, they sat by the fire-place. He tried to tell her the town news and passed her a little . . . sack of pine nuts.

While sitting there the Indian asked, "You 'fraid?"

"No, I'm not afraid," replied Susannah. "I can shoot as good as any Indian."

The reply amused the Indian and laughingly he replied, "You no shoot Indian."

When the time came to retire, Susannah gave him some matches and said, "My Mormon always makes the fire in the morning." She then gave him a quilt and some rugs to make himself a bed by the fire.

Susannah, thinking she would have to remain awake all night and watch him, just slipped off her shoes and went to bed. When she looked around, she was amazed to see the Indian kneeling in prayer by the side of his bed.

Susannah had been terribly frightened all evening, but seeing the Indian now she said to herself, "I don't need to be afraid of a praying Indian." Soon after, she went to sleep and slept until next morning, when she was awakened by the Indian, who was building the fire. He insisted on helping milk the cows, but she explained that the cows would be afraid of him; but she told him he could cut her an armful of wood, which he gladly did. He cut a large pile instead of an armful.

After they had eaten breakfast, the Indian left. But before going, he cut two hind quarters off one of the deer and left them hanging in the tree for her.

Leon R. Hartshorn, *Remarkable Stories from the Lives of Latter-day Saint Women,* 1:243–44.

"We Will Fast for That Child"

MATTHEW COWLEY

I have got two friends down here from New Zealand—a couple. They had never had any children, and they finally thought they had adopted one, but one day along came the father and said he wanted his child. Maybe you saw it in the newspaper. It was in the headlines covering quite a period of time. He said, "I never put that child in that home to be adopted, just to be cared for." He had two other children. His wife was a drunkard, and she left him and left the children. "Now she is back with me. She has reformed. We want our children back." This couple had one of them. Well, they had had that child so long it was one of the family, and so they had a long drawn-out litigation.

I was there at conference a couple of months ago. This couple was here. They came up after one of the meetings on Sunday. I said, "How is the case coming out? What is happening?"

They said, "Well, the final hearing is on Tuesday."

I said, "All right. Tomorrow morning I have an engagement for breakfast. After that I will fast all day Monday until Tuesday evening. You join me. We will fast for that child, and then whatever happens is right." So they shed a few tears and we fasted, and I never heard any more about it until general conference. The lawyer was at conference.

I said, "How did the case come out?"

He said, "Well, it was the strangest thing. I called the witness to take the witness stand, and I said, 'You tell the judge now what you are doing for this child, what kind of home you have, what its prospects are for the future, the husband's ability to care for it, his job, the money he is making, and everything.' That's what I intended her to say. But I said, 'Tell the court what you are doing for this child.' Do you know what she said? She said, 'We are fasting and praying.' Do you know what the judge did? He had to declare a recess. He didn't say a word. He went back in his chambers and spent a few minutes, and he came out, and he awarded this child to these two, this couple. They have been married in the temple and had it sealed to them."

Address at San Fernando [California] Stake welfare meeting, 24 May 1952.

A Day in the Temple

MATTHEW COWLEY

I had a brother called in the first war. He was in Washington at school when he was called. My father had the idea that he should go to the temple and receive his blessings before he went overseas. Next door to us lived President Anthon H. Lund, counselor to the President of the Church. My father went over and talked to him and said, "I certainly would like to see my boy come home to receive the blessings of the temple before he goes overseas."

President Lund said, "Why not? You know how to do it."

My father knew what he meant, and he prayed, and President Lund helped him. In three or four days my father received a wire from my brother that said, "Our captain here has passed away. He is from San Diego. I have been appointed to escort the body to San Diego, and on my return I will pass through Salt Lake City, and I will be there for one day." That one day was spent in the temple.

Matthew Cowley, *Matthew Cowley Speaks,* 381–82.

Prophecy

"I Thought of the Old Prophet"

WILFORD WOODRUFF

When I was a boy, there was an old man who used to visit at my father's house. His name was Robert Mason, and I heard teachings from him from the time that I was eight years old and upwards, and they were teachings that I shall ever remember. And he taught my father's household many important truths concerning the church and kingdom of God, and told them many things in relation to the prophets and the things that were coming upon the earth. But his teachings were received by but few. They were unpopular with the Christian world, but nearly all who did receive his teachings have joined the Latter-day Saints.

Prophets were not popular in that day any more than now, and I have often thought of many things which the old man taught me in the days of my youth since I received the fulness of the gospel and became a member of the Church of Christ.

He said, "When you read the Bible, do you ever think that what you read there is going to be fulfilled? The teachers of the day," said he, "spiritualize the Bible, but when you read in the Bible about the dreams, visions, revelations and predictions of Ezekiel, Isaiah, Jeremiah, or any other of the prophets or apostles, relative to the gathering of Israel and the building up of Zion, . . . you may understand that it means just what it says, and that it will be fulfilled upon the earth in the last days. And when you read of men laying hands upon the sick and healing them, and casting out devils and working miracles in the name of Jesus Christ, it means what it says." And he further said, "The church of Christ and Kingdom of God is not upon the earth, but it has been taken from the children of men through unbelief and because they have taken away from the gospel some of its most sacred ordinances, and have instituted in their stead forms and ceremonies without the power of God, and have turned from the truth unto fables; but," said he, "it will soon be restored again unto the children of men upon the earth, with its ancient gifts and powers, for the scriptures cannot be fulfilled without it. I shall not live to see it, but," said he to me, "you will live to see that day, and you will become a conspicuous actor in that kingdom, and when you see that day, then that which the prophets have spoken will be fulfilled."

I did not join any church, believing that the church of Christ in its true organization did not exist upon the earth. But when the principles of the everlasting gospel were first proclaimed unto me, I believed it with all my heart, and was baptized the first sermon I heard, for the Spirit of God bore testimony to me in power that it was true.

And I believe that I should never have joined any church had I not heard the fulness of the gospel. I was greatly blessed in receiving it, and was filled with joy unspeakable, and I have never been sorry but I have rejoiced all the day long. . . . I thought of the teaching and words of the old prophet Mason, for he came the nearest to being a true prophet of God in his predictions and works of any man I ever saw, until I saw men administering in the Holy Priesthood.

. . . "But," said he, "I have no right to administer in the ordinances of the gospel, neither has any man unless he receives it by revelation from God out of heaven, as did the ancients. But if my family or friends are sick, I have the right to lay hands upon them, and pray for them in the name of Jesus Christ. And if we can get faith to be healed, it is our privilege." And I will here say that many were healed through his faith and prayers.

Journal of Discourses, 4:99–100.

"The Prophet Wept"

ERASTUS SNOW

I have just learned from the family of the late Andrew L. Lamoreaux that Joseph Smith, during his tour to Washington in 1839, stopped with them in Dayton, Ohio, and before leaving laid his hands on Elder Lamoreaux and blessed him, and prophesied upon his head, that he would go on a mission to France, learn another tongue, and do much good, but that he would not live to return to his family, as he would fall by the way as a martyr. The Prophet wept, as he blessed him and told him these things, adding that it was pressed upon him and he could not refrain from giving utterance to it. Elder Lamoreaux talked with his family about it when he left them in 1852, and endeavored to persuade them that this was not the time and mission upon which he should fall, but to believe that he would at this time be permitted to return again. When the "Luminary" brought the tidings of his death, they exclaimed, "Surely, Brother Joseph was a Prophet, for all his words have come to pass."

Andrew Jenson, *LDS Biographical Encyclopedia,* 3:667.

"THAT'S A BIG LIE"

ANNE KIRSTINE SMOOT

When Senator Reed Smoot was a small boy, Brigham Young came to Provo and, at a conference meeting, said that the day would come when the human voice would be heard from New York to San Francisco.

Reed's mother had taken him to this meeting, and on the way home he said (referring to what President Brigham Young had said), "Now that's a big lie. That's absolutely impossible. It couldn't be." His mother, who was a woman of very great faith, told her son, "Yes, you'll live to see the fulfillment of what the President has said today." But he did not believe it.

Time went by, and while he was in the United States Senate, a broadcasting system was built so one could speak from New York City to San Francisco. One of his colleagues in the Senate had charge of this enterprise, and when it was completed and they were to celebrate the event, he invited Senator Smoot to come to New York City and be the first man to speak over the completed network, which he did, and his voice was heard clearly and distinctly across the continent.

Thus he lived to literally fulfill the promise by President Brigham Young in Provo years before.

Bryant S. Hinckley, *The Faith of Our Pioneer Fathers,* 207.

"I TOLD HIM WE SHOULD SEE SOMETHING STRANGE"

WILFORD WOODRUFF

In the early days of the Church, it was a great treat to an elder in his travels through the country to find a "Mormon"; it was so with us. We were hardly in Arkansas when we heard of a family named Akeman. They were in Jackson County in the persecutions. Some of the sons had been tied up there and whipped on their bare backs with hickory switches by the mob. We heard of their living on Petit Jean River, in the Arkansas Territory, and we went a long way to visit them.

There had recently been heavy rains, and a creek that we had to cross was swollen to a rapid stream of eight rods in width. There was no person living nearer than two miles from the crossing, and no boat. The people living at the last house on the road, some three miles from the crossing, said we would have to tarry till the water fell before we could cross. We did not stop, feeling to trust in God.

Just as we arrived at the rolling flood a [man], on a powerful horse, entered the stream on the opposite side and rode through it. On our making our wants known to him, he took us, one at a time, behind him and carried us safely over, and we went on our way rejoicing.

We arrived that night within five miles of Mr. Akeman's and were kindly entertained by a stranger. During the night I had the following dream:

I thought an angel came to us, and told us we were commanded of the Lord to follow a certain straight path, which was pointed out to us, let it lead us wherever it might. After we had walked in it awhile we came to the door of a house, which was in the line of a high wall running north and south, so that we could not go around. I opened the door and saw the room was filled with large serpents, and I shuddered at the sight. My companion said he would not go into the room for fear of the serpents. I told him I should try to go through the room though they killed me, for the Lord had commanded it.

As I stepped into the room the serpents coiled themselves up, and raised their heads some two feet from the floor, to spring at me. There was one much larger than the rest in the center of the room, which raised its head nearly as high as mine and made a spring at me. At that instant I felt as though nothing but the power of God could save me, and I stood still. Just before the serpent reached me he dropped dead at my feet; all the rest dropped dead, swelled up, turned black, burst open, took fire and were consumed before my eyes, and we went through the room unharmed, and thanked God for our deliverance.

I awoke in the morning and pondered upon the dream. We took breakfast, and started on our journey on Sunday morning, to visit Mr. Akeman. I related to my companion my dream, and told him we should see something strange. We had great anticipations of meeting Mr. Akeman, supposing him to be a member of the Church. When we arrived at his house he received us very coldly, and we soon found that he had apostatized. He brought railing accusations against the Book of Mormon and the authorities of the Church.

Word was sent through all the settlements on the river for twenty miles that two "Mormon" preachers were in the place. A mob was soon raised, and warning sent to us to leave immediately or we would be tarred and feathered, ridden on a rail and hanged.

I soon saw where the serpents were. My companion wanted to leave; I told him no, I would stay and see my dream fulfilled.

There was an old gentleman and lady, named Hubbel, who had read the Book of Mormon and believed. Father Hubbel came to see us, and invited us to make our home with him while we stayed in the place. We did so, and labored for him some three weeks with our axes, clearing land, while we were waiting to see the salvation of God.

I was commanded of the Lord by the Holy Ghost to go and warn Mr. Akeman to repent of his wickedness, I did so, and each time he railed against me, and the last time he ordered me out of his house. When I went out he followed me, and was very angry. When he came up to me, about eight rods from the house, he fell dead at my feet, turned black and swelled up, as I saw the serpents do in my dream.

His family, as well as ourselves, felt it was the judgment of God upon him. I preached his funeral sermon. Many of the mob died suddenly. We stayed about two weeks after Akeman's death and preached, baptized Mr. Hubbel and his wife, and then continued on our journey.

Wilford Woodruff, *Leaves from My Journal,* 18–20.

"SHE SENT ME TO THE CITY TO FIND THESE MEN"

JOSE YAÑES

Shortly after the arrival of the first Mormon elders in Mexico, my mother had a dream, in which it was manifested to her that in the City of Mexico were some men publishing a pamphlet called "Voz del que Clama en el Desierto," and that this tract contained information highly important to her spiritual welfare.

The following day she sent me to the city to find these men and to bring her a copy of the paper.

I searched unsuccessfully for two days, then sat down in the Alameda somewhat discouraged, to decide what to do. A man came and sat down by me. In the conversation that followed between us, he said there were some men in Hotel San Carlos who were publishing a pamphlet by that name. This strengthened my faith, for I admit that I did not expect to find either men or paper.

I went to the hotel, and was received kindly by the elders, who informed me, unasked, that the literature I sought was at hand. To test their faith and knowledge, I denied being in search of any literature and told them that my mother had been dead many years.

The elders replied that it all had been made known to them; that my mother was living; that she was a descendant of Guatemozine, who succeeded Montezuma II as ruler of the Aztecs; and further, that she would be the first woman to embrace the gospel and be baptized in Mexico.

I then accepted the literature and returned home. When my mother saw me coming she ran to meet me, her face radiant with joy. She said, "You found the men; let me have the pamphlet."

Desiring to test her still further—for I was still skeptical—I said, "You were mistaken, mother: there are no such men and no such pamphlet in all Mexico."

Her countenance fell and she looked very much disappointed as she said, "You are trying to deceive me. In a dream I saw you talking to the men, and I saw you receive the literature!" Then I gave it to her.

After very carefully reading the papers brought her, she sent me to the city again this time to bring the elders. They returned with me and baptized her according to their vision.

Juvenile Instructor, 15 May 1906, 309–10.

PROTECTION

"I Defy Ten of Your Best Men"

JAMES S. BROWN

About the 5th of May, 1852, the whole people were called to assemble at the village of Tatake [in Tahiti] and prepare a feast, and at the same time to decide definitely what to do with [missionary James S. Brown] and his *pipis* (disciples). Everything was excitement. The young braves came armed with muskets, shouting and yelling, saying they were going to have a fat roast for tomorrow, while the old councillors, twenty-five or thirty in number, came with slow, quiet steps and grave countenances, and filed into the schoolhouse just at dark. Then the people gathered, loaded down with roast pig, and fruit, fish and poultry. They kindled fires and began shouting, singing, and dancing.

Soon the young braves were dancing around the house that they were in; for by this time every member of the Church had come to one place. The mob seemed to be fully enthused with the spirit of murder, as they shouted, "Tomorrow we will have a fat young missionary for a roast!" Just then they fired a salute, seemingly under the foundation or sill of the house—a frame building. Then they commenced to tear down the post and pole fence that enclosed the premises. This fence, together with other wood, was piled up in a heap, as people in timbered countries stack timber to burn it off their land. Then the natives covered the wood with coral rock, as if they were going to burn a lime kiln. They kept up a continual howl all the night long, firing their guns, singing their war songs, and burning their campfires.

While this was going on, we held prayer and testimony meeting, never sleeping a moment the whole night. Many times we could hear the crowd outside boasting what a fine, fat missionary roast they were going to have *enanahe* (tomorrow).

Daylight came, and the village was all alive with people, as in America on the Fourth of July, at a barbecue. Soon the feasting began. The council had been all night in deciding what they would do with the Mormons and their minister. The provisions at the feast were apportioned to each village according to its numbers, and subdivided among the families, so that a full allowance was made for the Mormon *pupu* (party). They sent to me the portion of ten men, saying: "Here, this is for you, *Iatobo* (James); eat it and get fat for the roast," laughing contemptuously as they did so. By this time the whole people were in high glee, eating, drinking, talking, laughing and jeering, as if all hands were bent on pleasure only. When the feasting was over, all became silent, and it seemed as though everybody had gone to sleep.

By one o'clock P.M. all were astir again. Two great ruffians came into my apartment, armed with long clubs. They said they had been sent to order me before the council, and if I refused to come they were to drag me there. . . . As quick as thought, the promises of President Brigham Young flashed through my mind; also the promise of Dr. Willard Richards, in which he told me, in the name of the Lord God of Israel, that though men should seek my life, yet I should return in safety to the bosom of the Saints, having done good and honor to myself and the Church and kingdom of God. He also gave me instructions what to do; this was when starting on my mission. The next thought that came to my mind was: Have I forfeited those promises? The answer that came quickly from the Spirit was no; and this drove away all fear. Not a doubt was left in my mind.

Without hesitation I arose and walked out to the beach, where the people had assembled, the Saints following me. We passed by the log heap to the assemblage, at the head of which stood twelve or fifteen stout, athletic, young braves, with hair cut close. They were stripped naked to their breechclouts, and were oiled. They stood with folded arms, and certainly seemed formidable, although they were without weapons, for they had a fierce and savage look about them that must be seen to be realized in its effect.

As we came near, the man Tabate stepped out from the crowd and said, "All the Britons stand to the right hand with the sheep, and all the Mormons stand to the left hand where the goats are." Everyone responded to the order except two men from the Mormon party, who drew off to themselves and were neutral. At that, one faithful Mormon man named Rivae, and his wife, with an eight months old babe in her arms, stepped forward, well knowing what the sentence was to be. This brave brother said, "If you burn this man," pointing to the writer, "you burn me first." His heroic wife stepped forward, holding her babe at arm's length, and shouted, "I am a Mormon, and this baby is a Mormon. . . . You will have to burn all of us, or Mormonism will grow again." . . .

Pointing to the left and rear of the prisoner, to the log heap, which was then at the zenith of its burning, with haughty demeanor and in an exulting voice, Tabate said, "Look there at that fire. It is made to consume the flesh off of your bones." In that moment the Spirit of the Lord rested mightily upon me, and I felt as though I could run through a troop and leap over a wall. "In the name of Israel's God," I said, "I defy ten of your best men, yea, the host of you, for I serve that God who delivered Daniel from the den of lions, and the three Hebrew children from the fiery furnace!"

. . . There was absolutely not one particle of fear or tremor in my whole being. But I did feel thankful for that great and marvelous deliverance, because in the very moment that I defied the host the spirit of division rested upon the judge who had passed the sentence, his counselors, and the executioners, insomuch that the counselors faced the executioners, and they grappled with each other in a sharp tussle. From that ensued a fight, until the whole people were mixed up in it. . . .

During all this time our enemies quarreled and fought with clubs and stones, pulled hair and screamed. They did not cease fighting till sundown. Then, with many sore heads, and more sore limbs, they dispersed, and I doubt very much if the majority of them knew what they had been fighting for. After they left, a feeling of quiet and safety pervaded the village, especially in and about our residence, such as we had not before known on the island, and for weeks everything was strangely peaceful. People who once seemed surly and defiant now had a tame and subdued expression in their countenances and appeared to prefer passing by unnoticed rather than otherwise.

Some two months later, I was traveling alone in the timber, and at a short turn in the road I chanced to meet one of the old councillors who decided that I should be burned. We were close together before we saw each other. At sight of me he turned and ran as hard as he could, and I, without any particular object in view, gave chase and ran him down. I seized him by the neck and asked why he ran from me and why he was afraid of me.

Said he: "Your God is a God of power, and I was afraid to meet his servant." I inquired how he knew that my God was a God of power, and why they had not burned me when they had decided to do so. He answered: "At the moment that you defied us there was a brilliant light, or pillar of fire, bore down close over your head. It was as bright as the sun. We remembered reading in the Bible about Elijah calling fire down from heaven so that it consumed the captains and their fifties, and we thought that you had prayed to your God of power, and that he had sent that fire to burn us and our people if we harmed you. The young men did not see the light. They were going to burn you, and we tried to stop them. So we got into a fight. Now we all know that you are a true servant of God."

James S. Brown, *Life of a Pioneer,* 245–51.

"PROVIDENCE HAD CAUSED HER DOOR TO BE HELD FAST"

KATE B. CARTER

One night [pioneer] Harriet Carter, who happened to be alone at the ranch except for her small children, was awakened by a terrible commotion out in the nearby corral. Cows were bellowing, calves bawling, and a most awful din broke the stillness of the night in the lonely ranch home. Accepting her responsibility as head of the house in the absence of any men folk, she struck a light, hastily dressed herself, and proceeded to investigate the cause of the trouble and disturbance.

As she hastily grabbed the heavy door, after warning the children to lie quiet until she returned, she found it held fast. Surprised but undismayed, she grabbed for the handle again, only to find that it would not budge an inch to her healthy grasp. Sensing that something was wrong, she quickly surveyed its surroundings to see if any heavy object could be holding it so tightly, but could find nothing whatever that should have prevented her from opening it as usual. A few more strenuous jerks, however, soon convinced her that she was locked tightly in the cabin, with no other openings large enough for her to get through. Stirred on by the uproar outside, she tried to peek through the tiny cracks, but only the blackness of the night met her anxious eye. After repeated attempts to open the fastened door, she finally gave up and went back to bed, after the bellowing and bawling had died down to an occasional snort of fear from one of the animals.

Awakening early, she at once dressed and upon going to the

door, found that it yielded readily to her touch and swung silently inward on its hinges. Looking quickly around, she proceeded to the corral. There, to her surprise and horror, she found the fresh remains of a newly slain calf, surrounded by numerous cougar tracks. So the lion had come to her own yard for the kill. Returning thoughtfully to the house, she carefully studied her door and wondered if a kind and merciful Providence had caused her door to be held fast.

Kate B. Carter, *Heart Throbs of the West,* 3:336.

"THERE FELL FROM HIS POCKET A LETTER"

BRYANT S. HINCKLEY

In the early days of the Southern States Mission, men of heroic mold were required to face persecutions and persist in their endeavors to reach the honest in heart. Many instances of heroism could be chronicled, but one of the most interesting was when a mother's letter played a very important part in saving a young elder from being cruelly whipped and possibly from being killed.

Elder Frank Croft was a missionary in the state of Alabama. Because he persisted in his legal rights guaranteed under the Constitution of the United States in preaching righteousness to the people, he was forcefully taken into a secluded spot of the backwoods for the purpose of receiving lashings across his bare back at the hands of armed and vicious men. Having arrived at the place where they had concluded to administer the torture, Elder Croft was commanded to remove his coat, shirt, and garments, and bare his body to his waist. Then he was stood against a nearby tree to which his arms and body were tied to prevent his moving while being lashed across the back until the blood would flow.

Having no alternative, he complied with the demands of the mob, but in so doing, there fell from his pocket a letter he had recently received from his mother who lived near Morgan, Utah. Elder Croft, a short time before, had written his parents and in this letter had seriously condemned mob violence, the Ku Klux Klan, and others for their cowardly treatment of the elders.

The letter that had fallen from his coat was an answer from his mother. In it she counseled, "My beloved son, you must remember the words of the Savior when He said, 'Blessed are they which are persecuted for righteousness' sake: for theirs is the kingdom of heaven'; also 'Blessed are ye, when men shall revile you and persecute you, and shall say all manner of evil against you falsely, for my name's sake. Rejoice, and be exceeding glad: for great is your reward in heaven: for so persecuted they the prophets which were before you.'

"Also remember the Savior upon the cross suffering for the sins of the world when he uttered these immortal words: 'Father, forgive them; for they know not what they do.' Surely, my boy, they who are mistreating you elders know not what they do, or they would not do it. Sometime, somewhere, they will understand and then they will regret their action and they will honor you for the glorious work you are doing. So be patient, my son; love those who mistreat you and say all manner of evil against you, and the Lord will bless you and magnify you in their eyes and your mission will be gloriously successful. Remember also, my son, that day and night, your mother is praying for you always."

Elder Croft, tied to the tree, was so situated that he could see that the leader of the mob had picked up the fallen letter and evidently had decided to read it before giving the word to his men to start the lashing. The elder observed the hardness of his features, the cruelty in his eyes. He then realized that no sympathy could be expected from him, for his every action was characteristic of cruelty and vindictiveness. He closed his eyes in resignation to his fate and, while awaiting the moment when the beating would begin, he thought of home and loved ones and particularly of his beloved mother. Then he silently uttered a prayer in her behalf.

Opening his eyes a moment or two later, and feeling that the leader had had time to finish reading the letter, he was amazed to see that the man had retired to a nearby tree stump and, having seated himself, was apparently reading the letter; but what was more amazing to the elder was the change in the man's countenance. Much of the hardness and cruelty in his face was gone; his eyes were slightly dimmed by moisture. His whole personality appeared to have changed. He would read a line or two or a paragraph and sit and ponder, and deep down in the elder's conscience was the hope—yes, the conviction—that the man's heart had been touched by the loveliness and beauty of his mother's letter.

To Elder Croft, it seemed that an interminable time had elapsed before the mob leader arose and, approaching the helpless elder, said: "Feller, you must have a wonderful mother. You see, I once had one, too." Then, addressing the other members of the mob, he said, "Men, after reading this Mormon's mother's letter, I just can't go ahead with the job. Maybe we had better let him go." Elder Croft was released and went his way, and the loving influence of his mother seemed very near.

Bryant S. Hinckley, *The Faith of Our Pioneer Fathers,* 257–59.

"I TALKED TO THEM IN THEIR OWN LANGUAGE"

JANE GROVER

One morning [on the pioneer trail near Council Bluffs, Iowa, in 1846], we thought we would go and gather gooseberries. Father Tanner, as we familiarly called the good, patriarchal Elder Nathan Tanner, harnessed a span of horses to a light wagon and, with two sisters by the name of Lyman, his little granddaughter, and me, started out. When we reached the woods we told the old gentleman to go to a house in sight and rest himself while we picked the berries.

It was not long before the little girl and I strayed some distance from the rest, when suddenly we heard shouts. The little girl thought it was her grandfather and was about to answer, but I restrained her, thinking it might be Indians. We walked forward until within sight of Father Tanner, when we saw he was running his team around. We thought nothing strange at first, but as we approached we saw Indians gathering around the wagon, whooping and yelling as others came and joined them. We got into the wagon to start when four of the Indians took hold of the wagon wheels to stop the wagon, and two others held the horses by the bits, and another came to take me out of the wagon.

I then began to be afraid as well as vexed, and asked Father Tanner to let me get out of the wagon and run for assistance. He said, "No poor child; it is too late!" I told him they should not take me alive. His face was as white as a sheet. The Indians had commenced to strip him—had taken his watch and handkerchief—

and while stripping him, were trying to pull me out of the wagon. I began silently to appeal to my Heavenly Father.

While I was praying and struggling, the Spirit of the Almighty fell upon me and I arose with great power; and no tongue can tell my feelings. I was happy as I could be. A few moments before I saw worse than death staring me in the face, and now my hand was raised by the power of God, and I talked to those Indians in their own language. They let go the horses and wagon, and all stood in front of me while I talked to them by the power of God. They bowed their heads and answered "Yes," in a way that made me know what they meant.

The little girl and Father Tanner looked on in speechless amazement. I realized our situation; their calculation was to kill Father Tanner, burn the wagon, and take us women prisoners. This was plainly shown me. When I stopped talking they shook hands with all three of us and returned all they had taken from Father Tanner, who gave them back the handkerchief, and I gave them berries and crackers. By this time the other two women came up, and we hastened home.

The Lord gave me a portion of the interpretation of what I had said, which was as follows:

"I suppose you Indian warriors think you are going to kill us? Don't you know the Great Spirit is watching you and knows everything in your heart? We have come out here to gather some of our father's fruit. We have not come to injure you; and if you harm us, or injure one hair of our heads, the Great Spirit shall smite you to the earth, and you shall not have power to breathe another breath. We have been driven from our homes, and so have you; we have come out here to do you good, and not to injure you. We are the Lord's people and so are you; but you must cease your murders and wickedness; the Lord is displeased with it and will not prosper you if you continue in it. You think you own all this land, this timber, this water, all the horses.

Why, you do not own one thing on earth, not even the air you breathe—it all belongs to the Great Spirit."

Edward Tullidge, *The Women of Mormondom,* 475–77.

WARNINGS OF THE SPIRIT

H. G. B.

There are no people on the earth, that we are acquainted with, that exercise so much faith in God our Heavenly Father as do the Latter-day Saints. No other people seek for His protecting care as they do. Nor are there any people to whom His protection is oftener extended or made manifest more visibly than unto this people.

Especially has this been the case with hundreds of our elders, when traveling and preaching the gospel. A few of these instances of divine protection in my own experience I wish to relate.

While on my way to Nauvoo, Illinois, in the month of June 1845, going down the Ohio River, the steamer I was aboard of ran aground on the "Flint Island Bar," just above Evansville, Indiana.

I remained on the boat for thirty-six hours; when, the water in the river being very low, and getting lower every day, and, seeing no prospect of our getting past this bar, I concluded to go ashore and work a few days, as I understood laborers were in demand in Evansville. The captain of the steamer aground, accordingly, refunded me a just proportion of the passage money I had paid him.

I procured work for one week, at the end of which time the river began to rise. Being very anxious to pursue my journey, I went aboard the first boat that landed at Evansville, which I learned was going as far up the Mississippi River as Galena. I made arrangements with the clerk for passage to Nauvoo, but did not pay him at the time, as he said the boat would not leave for two hours.

I was never more desirous of pursuing my journey than I was on this occasion, yet soon after going aboard a feeling of aversion to going on that steamer took possession of me. Instead of a sensation of joy, an undefinable dread, or foreboding of coming evil was exercising an influence over me, that increased in its power every moment, until I could resist no longer, and, snatching up my trunk, I fled with it to shore, just as the deck hands stopped to haul in the gangway, and the boat moved off.

I put my trunk down on the bank of the river, and sat down on it, too weak to stand on my feet longer.

This was a new experience to me, then. What did it mean? One thing was certain, I felt as if I had just escaped from some great calamity to a place of safety.

Two days after this I took passage on another steamer for St. Louis, where in due time I arrived in safety. As I walked ashore I met a newsboy crying his morning paper, and among the items of news it contained the most prominent was an account of the ill-fated steamer that I had made my escape from at Evansville, on the Ohio River. I purchased the paper, and found the boat had been snagged in the Mississippi River, below St. Louis, in the night, and sank, with a loss of nearly all that were onboard.

The mysterious feeling that impelled me to leave that boat was cleared up to my satisfaction. There remained not the shadow of a doubt that Providence had interposed between me and the great danger.

The thanks, gratitude, and joy that filled my whole being on this occasion, I will not try to describe.

Gems for the Young Folks, 22–24.

AN ACCIDENT IN THE CANYON

MARRINER W. MERRILL

During the winter of 1855 and '56 I worked in North Mill Creek Canyon as I had done the previous winter. And in this connection I will here relate a circumstance that occurred with me that winter while working in the canyon. During the month of January 1856, the weather was very cold, the temperature ranging 20 to 30 degrees below zero at times.

On one occasion I found myself in the canyon alone, as it was so cold no one else cared to risk going out in the canyon that day. I was at that time hauling house logs, usually five to a load. After getting my logs cut and dragged down to the loading place I commenced loading them on my bob sled, one end on the sled and the small end to drag on the snow. I had the five logs lying side by side. The loading place being very slippery, I was as I thought very careful. But after getting the first one loaded on the sled I turned around to load another one. The one I had on the sled slipped off like it was shot out of a gun and struck me in the hollow of the legs and threw me forward on my face across the four logs lying on the ground, or ice.

In falling, my hand spike, which I had used in loading the first log, slipped out of my hand and out of my reach. And thus I found myself with my body lying face downwards across the four logs and the fifth log lying across my legs, and I was pinned to the ground with a heavy red pine log 10 inches through at the large end and 22 feet long lying across my legs. And there I was with no visible means to extricate myself and there was no aid at hand, as no one but myself was in the canyon that day. I made up my mind that I must freeze and die all alone in the mountains of Utah.

Many serious thoughts passed through my mind, as you may imagine. In falling on the logs my breast and stomach were hurt and it was difficult for me to breathe. I did not conceive what to do under the trying ordeal, but concluded to ask the Lord to help me, which I did in earnest prayer. After calling upon the Lord for some time I began to make an effort to extricate myself but all in vain, as I could not move the log that was lying on me. I, however, continued my efforts until I was exhausted and lost all recollection of my situation.

And the first I remembered afterward I was one mile down the canyon sitting on my load of logs and the oxen going gently along. My overcoat by the side of me, and feeling very cold, I spoke to my oxen and stopped them and looked around in wonder and astonishment. Then I remembered being under the log at the loading place some time previous. But how long I was there I could not determine, but supposed about two hours, as I was two hours later getting home than usual.

I looked at the load and found I had the five logs on the sled, three on the bottom and two on the top, nicely bound, my ax sticking in the top log, my whip lying on the load by my side, my sheepskin (with the wool on, which I used to sit on) also on the load and I sitting on it. I made an effort to get off the load and put on my overcoat but found I could not do it, as I was so sore in my legs and breast that it was with great difficulty that I could move at all.

I put my overcoat on in a sitting position as I was and wrapped it around my legs the best I could and started on down the canyon. My oxen being gentle and tractable and the road smooth and all down hill, I arrived home without difficulty. On arriving there I found my wife was anxiously waiting for me and quite uneasy about me, as I was so much later than usual. She . . . helped me into the house, placed me by the fireside and made me as comfortable as possible and took care of my team. I was confined to the house for some days before I could get around again.

Who it was that extricated me from under the log, loaded my sled, hitched my oxen to it, and placed me on it, I cannot say, as I do not now, or even then at the time, remember seeing any one, and I know for a surety no one was in the canyon that day but myself. Hence I give the Lord . . . credit for saving my life in extricating me from so perilous a situation.

Utah Pioneer and Apostle Marriner Wood Merrill and His Family, 44–46.

"I FELT IMPRESSED TO STOP"

GEORGE ALBERT SMITH

Late one evening [during my mission] in a pitch-dark night, Elder Stout and I were traveling along a high precipice. Our little walk was narrow; on one side was the wall of the mountain, on the other side, the deep, deep river. We had no light and there were no stars and no moon to guide us. We had been traveling all day and we knew that we would have hospitality extended to us if we could reach the McKelvin home, which was on the other side of a high valley. We had to cross this mountain in order to reach the home of Mr. McKelvin.

Our mode of travel of necessity was very halting. We walked almost with a shuffle, feeling each foot of ground as we advanced, with one hand extended toward the wall of the mountain. Elder Stout was ahead of me and as I walked along I felt the hard surface of the trail under my feet. In doing so I left the wall of the mountain which had acted as a guide and a steadying force. After I had taken a few steps away I felt impressed to stop immediately, that something was wrong.

I called to Elder Stout and he answered me. The direction from which his voice came indicated I was on the wrong trail, so I backed up until I reached the wall of the mountain and again proceeded forward. He was just a few steps in front of me, and as I reached him we came to a fence piling. In the dark we carefully explored it with our hands and feet to see whether it would be safe for us to climb over. We decided that it would be secure and made the effort.

While I was on the top of this big pile of logs, my little suitcase popped open and the contents were scattered around. In the dark I felt around for them and was quite convinced I had recovered practically everything. We arrived safely at our destination about eleven o'clock at night. I soon discovered I had lost my comb and brush, and the next morning we returned to the scene of my accident. I recovered my property and while there my curiosity was stimulated and aroused to see what had happened the night before when I had lost my way in the dark.

As missionaries, we wore hob-nails in the bottom of our shoes to make them last longer, so that I could easily follow our tracks in the soft dirt. I retraced my steps to the point where my tracks left and wandered to the edge of a deep precipice. Just one more step and I would have fallen over into the river and had been drowned.

I felt very ill when I realized how close I had come to death. I was also very grateful to my Heavenly Father for protecting me. I have always felt that if we are doing the Lord's work and ask him for his help and protection, he will guide and take care of us.

A Story to Tell, 156–58.

THEY BROUGHT THE TAR AND FEATHERS

DANIEL TYLER

The gift of prophecy was poured out upon me. I also received the gift and interpretation of tongues. But what then, and ever since, has seemed to me the greatest gift I received was to speak easily and fluently in my own language. This was the first gift I received. It came upon me in great power.

A few months after my baptism, several leading elders from Kirtland, Ohio, were about to be dragged from our schoolhouse by a mob who had assembled to tar and feather them. When the elders and others failed to stop them from disturbing the meeting, I stepped upon a form or bench and began to talk to the people. Five minutes had not elapsed when, aside from my voice, a pin dropping upon the floor might have been easily heard. After I had spoken about ten or fifteen minutes the mob left the house, and, after consulting outside a few moments, retired, and we had a good meeting.

This circumstance had gone out of my mind until about 1849, while stopping overnight at the house of a brother named Brim. Alfred O. Brim, who was one of the mob, called my attention to it, and asked me if I knew that they had a keg of tar and a feather bed in the carriage in which they came to the meeting.

I replied that I did not think I ever heard of it. He said they brought the tar and the feathers with the full intent to use them on the elders, but they were so surprised at the power with which I spoke that they knew I was helped by some invisible spirit. They had known me since I was seven years old, and were satisfied that I had not made up the speech, and that I was not capable of doing so. They decided that it must be of the Lord or of the devil. Of this they could not be the judges, not, as they said, having the discerning of spirits. Hence one of them suggested that lest they be found fighting against God, they had better retire. All agreed to it and they left.

Classic Experiences, 28–29.

"A BRIGHT LIGHT SUDDENLY SHONE AROUND US"

WILFORD WOODRUFF

On the sixteenth of November, I preached at Brother Camp's, and baptized three. On the day following, it being Sunday, I preached again at Brother Clapp's, and baptized five. At the close of the meeting I mounted my horse to ride to Clark's River, in company with Seth Utley, four other brethren, and two sisters. The distance was twenty miles.

We came to a stream which was so swollen by rains that we could not cross without swimming our horses. To swim would not be safe for the females, so we went up the stream to find a ford. In the attempt we were overtaken by a severe storm of wind and rain, and lost our way in the darkness and wandered through creeks and mud. But the Lord does not forsake his Saints in any of their troubles. While we were in the woods suffering under the blast of the storm, groping like the blind for the wall, a bright light suddenly shone around us, and revealed to us our dangerous situation on the edge of a gulf. The light continued with us until we found the road. We then went on our way rejoicing, though the darkness returned and the rain continued.

Tullidge's Quarterly Magazine, October 1883, 9.

A Voice of Warning

HAROLD B. LEE

I have a believing heart that started with a simple testimony that came when I was a child—I think maybe I was around ten or eleven years of age. I was with my father out on a farm away from our home, trying to spend the day busying myself until my father was ready to go home. Over the fence from our place were some tumbledown sheds that would attract a curious boy, and I was adventurous. I started to climb through the fence, and I heard a voice as clearly as you are hearing mine, calling me by name and saying, "Don't go over there!" I turned to look at my father to see if he were talking to me, but he was way up at the other end of the field. There was no person in sight. I realized then, as a child, that there were persons beyond my sight, for I had definitely heard a voice. Since then, when I hear or read stories of the Prophet Joseph Smith, I too have known what it means to hear a voice, because I've had the experience.

Harold B. Lee, *Stand Ye in Holy Places,* 139.

"There Is Something Seriously Wrong"

GEORGE ALBERT SMITH

I am standing on what to me is sacred ground. My grandparents and my parents and many other relatives lived here in Provo, and some still live here. My father, as a young man, came near losing his life in the Provo River, not far from where we are now. His father, who was in Salt Lake City, felt impressed to go into a room that had been set apart for prayer. He . . . said: "Heavenly Father, I feel that there is something seriously wrong with my family in Provo. Thou knowest that I cannot be with them there and be here. Heavenly Father, wilt thou preserve and safeguard them, and I will be grateful to thee and honor thee."

At the time when he was praying, just as near as it was possible to indicate by checking the time, my father had fallen into the river. It was at flood time. Logs and rocks were pouring down from the canyon, and he was helpless. Those who were near saw his predicament, but they could not reach him. The turbulence of the water was such that nobody could live in it. They just stood there in horror. Father was doing everything he could to keep his head above water, but he was being thrown up and down and being dashed against the rocks and logs. All at once a wave lifted him bodily from the water and threw him upon the shore. It was a direct answer of the prayer of a servant of the Lord.

George Albert Smith, *Sharing the Gospel with Others,* 83–84.

"HE MADE WAR UPON ME"

WILFORD WOODRUFF

The prospect in London at that time was the darkest it had ever been in since entering the vineyard; but the Lord was with us, and we were not discouraged. On Sunday we met with the Saints three times at Brother Corner's, read the Book of Mormon, gave instruction, and broke bread unto them. We had a good time, although there were only about half a dozen present. I felt the Spirit bear testimony that there would be a work done in London.

Having retired to rest in good season, I fell asleep and slept until midnight, when I awoke and meditated upon the things of God until three o'clock in the morning. And, while forming a determination to warn the people in London, and by the assistance and inspiration of God to overcome the power of darkness, a person appeared to me whom I consider as the prince of darkness. He made war upon me and attempted to take my life. As he was about to overcome me I prayed to the Father, in the name of Jesus Christ, for help. I then had power over him and he left me, though I was much wounded. Afterwards three men dressed in white came to me and prayed with me, and I was healed immediately of all my wounds, and delivered of my troubles.

Matthias F. Cowley, *Wilford Woodruff,* 130.

Revelation

"The Spirit of God Rested Upon Me"

HARRISON BURGESS

The Lord blessed His people abundantly in [the Kirtland] Temple with the Spirit of prophecy, the ministering of angels, visions, etc. I will here relate a vision which was shown to me. It was near the close of the endowments. I was in a meeting for instruction in the upper part of the temple, with about a hundred of the High Priests, Seventies and Elders. The Saints felt to shout "Hosannah!" and the Spirit of God rested upon me in mighty power and I beheld the room lighted up with a peculiar light such as I had never seen before. It was soft and clear and the room looked to me as though it had neither roof nor floor to the building, and I beheld the Prophet Joseph and Hyrum Smith and Roger Orton enveloped in the light: Joseph exclaimed aloud, "I behold the Savior, the Son of God." Hyrum said, "I behold the angels of heaven." Brother Orton exclaimed, "I behold the chariots of Israel." All who were in the room felt the power of God to that degree that many prophesied, and the power of God was made manifest, the remembrance of which will remain with me while I live upon the earth.

Labors in the Vineyard, 67.

A RADIANT LIGHT

SUSA YOUNG GATES

The early days of April in the year 1893 were heavy with storm and gloom. A leaden sky stretched over the earth; every day the rain beat down upon it, and the storm-winds swept over it with terrific force. Yet the brightness and the glory of those days far outshone the gloom. It was during those tempestuous days of early April that the Salt Lake Temple was dedicated.

During the dedicatory services, it was my privilege to transcribe the official notes of the various meetings. At the first service, which was known as the "official dedication," I was sitting on the lower side of the east pulpits, at the recorder's table. Brother John Nicholson, who had been busy at the outer gate, came in and sat down beside me. Just as President Joseph F. Smith began to address the Saints, there shone through his countenance a radiant light that gave me a peculiar feeling. I thought that the clouds must have lifted, and that a stream of sunlight had lighted on the President's head.

I turned to Brother Nicholson and whispered: "What a singular effect of sunlight on the face of President Smith! Do look at it."

He whispered back: "There is no sunlight outdoors—nothing but dark clouds and gloom."

I looked out of the window, and somewhat to my surprise, I saw that Brother Nicholson had spoken the truth. There was not the slightest rift in the heavy, black clouds above the city; there was not a gleam of sunshine anywhere.

Whence, then, came the light that shone from the face of

President Smith? I was sure that I had seen the actual presence of the Holy Spirit, focused upon the features of the beloved leader and prophet, Joseph F. Smith. It was but an added testimony to me that he was the "Chosen of the Lord." I cherish the occurrence as one of the most sacred experiences of my life.

Susa Young Gates, as quoted in Preston Nibley, *Faith-Promoting Stories,* 47–48.

"I RAN OUT OF IDEAS"

HEBER J. GRANT

Do we not often take the credit when we excel instead of giving it to God? We are not yet humble enough, and therefore, when we offer a fine prayer or speech, or whatever it may be, we allow Satan to flatter us, and say, "How beautiful." To the Lord alone is due the praise.

I shall make a confession. When I was made the president of the Tooele Stake of Zion and made my maiden speech I ran out of ideas in seven and one-half minutes by the watch. That night I heard in a very contemptuous voice in the dark, "Well, it is a pity if the General Authorities of the Church had to import a boy from the city to come out here to preside over us they could not have found one with sense enough to talk ten minutes." So you see, he held his stop watch on me; he knew I did not take ten minutes. I knew I did not, because I timed myself—seven and one-half minutes was the limit. The next speech, and the next, and the next were the same. One of them was only five minutes. The next speech was at a little town called Vernon, sometimes called Stringtown, as it spread over twelve miles as I remember it.

As we were going to the meeting I was with the bishop, Brother John C. Sharp, and I did not see anybody going to meeting. The Bishop said, "Oh, there will be somebody there." We were going up a little hill, and when we got to the top of the hill we found a number of wagons and white tops at the meetinghouse—it was a log meetinghouse—but did not see anybody going in.

I said: "There doesn't seem to be anybody going to meeting."

He said, "Oh, I think you'll find somebody there."

When we got inside, the meetinghouse was crowded. We went in at two minutes to two and nobody else came in afterwards. I congratulated the bishop after the meeting on having educated his people to be so prompt.

He said: "Most of them have to hitch up a team to come here, and I have told them they could just as well hitch it up a few minutes earlier and be here at two minutes to two o'clock, so there will be no disturbance."

I had taken a couple of brethren with me that day to do the preaching. I got up expecting to take five or six minutes and talked forty-five minutes with as much ease, if not more, than I have ever enjoyed since. I shed tears of gratitude that night to the Lord for the inspiration of his Spirit.

The next Sunday I went to Grantsville, the largest town in Tooele County, and got up with all the assurance in the world and told the Lord I would like to talk forty-five minutes, and ran out of ideas in five. I not only ran out of ideas in five minutes, but I was perspiring, and [I] walked fully two and one-half, if not three, miles, after that meeting, to the farthest haystack in Grantsville, and kneeled behind that haystack and asked the Lord to forgive me for my egotism in that meeting. And [I] made a pledge to the

Lord that never again in my life would I stand before an audience without asking for his Spirit to help me, nor would I take personally the credit for anything I said; and I have kept this pledge.

BYU Quarterly, November 1934, 24–26.

"He Presented the Name of Melvin J. Ballard"

FRANCIS M. GIBBONS

Heber J. Grant was ordained and set apart as the seventh President of the Church on November 23, 1918. As he and his counselors, Anthon H. Lund and Charles W. Penrose, considered filling the vacancy in the Twelve caused by President Grant's ordination, they focused on Richard W. Young, grandson of Brigham Young and Heber's lifelong friend. A retired general of the army, a lawyer, and a former stake president, he had every qualification to serve in the Twelve. Deciding he was the man, President Grant wrote Richard W. Young's name on a slip of paper before going to the temple meeting where filling the vacancy was to be discussed. In the temple, he removed the paper with the name written on it, fully intending to present Richard W. Young to the council for approval. But for a reason he could never fully explain, he was unable to do so; instead, he presented the name of Melvin J. Ballard, president of the Northwestern States

Mission, a man with whom he had had very little personal contact. This experience had a profound influence on President Grant. It taught him to heed the sudden flashes of insight that came to him in making decisions affecting the Church.

Francis M. Gibbons, *Dynamic Disciples, Prophets of God,* 169–70.

LISTENING TO THE RIGHT SOURCES OF POWER

HAROLD B. LEE

A very grievous case came before a high council and stake presidency that resulted in the excommunication of a man.

The very next morning I was visited in my office by the brother of this man. He said, "I want to tell you that my brother wasn't guilty of what he was charged with."

"How do you know he wasn't guilty?" I asked.

"Because I prayed, and the Lord told me he was innocent," the man answered.

I asked him to come into the office. As we sat down, I asked, "Would you mind if I ask you a few personal questions?"

He said, "Certainly not."

"How old are you?"

"Forty-seven."

"What priesthood do you hold?"

He said he thought he was a teacher.

"Do you keep the Word of Wisdom?"

"Well, no." He used tobacco, which was obvious.

"Do you pay your tithing?"

He said, "No"—and he didn't intend to as long as that blankety-blank-blank man was the bishop of the ward.

I said, "Do you attend your priesthood meetings?"

He replied, "No, sir!" and he didn't intend to as long as that man was bishop.

"You don't attend your sacrament meetings either?"

"No, sir."

"Do you have your family prayers?" and he said no.

"Do you study the scriptures?" He said well, his eyes were bad, and he couldn't read very much.

I then said to him: "In my home I have a beautiful instrument called a radio. When everything is in good working order we can dial it to a certain station and pick up the voice of a speaker or a singer all the way across the continent or sometimes on the other side of the world, bringing them into the front room as though they were almost right there. But after we have used it for a long time, the little delicate instruments or electrical devices on the inside called radio tubes begin to wear out. When one of them wears out, we may get some static—it isn't so clear. Another wears out, and if we don't give it attention, the sound may fade in and out. And if another one wears out—well, the radio may sit there looking quite like it did before, but because of what has happened on the inside, we can hear nothing.

"Now," I said, "you and I have within our souls something like what might be said to be a counterpart of those radio tubes. We might have what we call a 'go-to-sacrament-meeting' tube, a 'keep-the-Word-of-Wisdom' tube, a 'pay-your-tithing' tube, a 'have-your-family-prayers' tube, a 'read-the-scriptures' tube, and, as one of the most important—one that might be said to be the master tube of our whole soul—we have what we might call the 'keep-yourselves-morally-clean' tube. If one of these becomes worn out by disuse or inactivity—if we fail to keep the commandments of God—it has the same effect upon our spiritual selves that a worn-out tube has in a radio.

"Now, then," I said, "fifteen of the best-living men in that stake prayed last night. They heard the evidence and every man was united in saying that your brother was guilty. Now you, who do none of these things, you say you prayed and got an opposite answer. How would you explain that?"

Then this man gave an answer that I think was a classic. He said, "Well, President Lee, I think I must have gotten my answer from the wrong source." And, you know, that's just as great a truth as we can have. We get our answers from the source of the power that we wish to obey. If we're following the ways of Satan, we'll get answers from Satan. If we're keeping the commandments of God, we'll get our answers from God.

Harold B. Lee, *Stand Ye in Holy Places,* 135–38.

"MY MOTHER WAS UNYIELDING"

JOHN A. WIDTSOE

Two months before we were to sail from Oslo, I was sent to my father's oldest sister, who with her husband lived in the country some twenty-five miles north of Oslo. There I spent happy weeks among the fields and forests on the two large estates that my uncle was managing.

My aunt was scandalized that any member of the family had become besmirched with Mormonism. She was determined to prevent the oldest son of her beloved brother from going to Utah. . . . Therefore, she arranged that a few days before my mother's expected arrival, I was to be sent into the mountain districts, so far away that I could not be brought back in time for the sailing of the boat. And should the stubborn mother miss the boat to recover her son, no one would know where her son was. It was a perfect plan, which, of course, was unknown to me. I understood only that I was going into the mountains for an outing.

The day for my departure came. My belongings were all packed. The horses were at the door. We were at breakfast. Suddenly there was the sound of the daily mail cart, which also carried passengers. It stopped in front of the house. Out stepped my mother with my brother Osborne, just one week earlier than the set date! My aunt's consternation was inexpressible. Even now I must smile at the episode. Yet, even then, my aunt wanted to take me into the mountains, "for a change." She also was of the stern kind. But my mother was unyielding.

"We leave for Oslo this afternoon." Thus, I was not kidnapped, and another "best-laid" plan was foiled. Why my mother left her home a week early she could not explain. "I just had to leave then." So the Lord guides his faithful children.

John A. Widtsoe, *In a Sunlit Land,* 7–8.

"Take Your Team and Go to the Farm"

WILFORD WOODRUFF

After attending a large annual conference in Salt Lake City, and, having a good deal of business to attend to, I was somewhat weary. And at the close of the conference I thought I would repair to my home and have a rest.

As I went into the yard the Spirit said to me, "Take your team and go to the farm," which is some three miles south of the Tabernacle.

As I was hitching the horse to the wagon, Mrs. Woodruff asked where I was going.

I said, "To the farm."

"What for?" she asked.

"I do not know," I replied; but when I arrived there I found out.

The creek had overflowed, broken through my ditch, surrounded my home, and filled my barnyard and pig pen. . . .

Through my own exertions I soon turned it and prevented

much damage that might have occurred had I not obeyed the voice of the Spirit.

This same Spirit of revelation has been manifested to many of my brethren in their labors in the kingdom of God.

Wilford Woodruff, *Leaves from My Journal*, 103.

"Joseph Smith Visited Me after His Death"

WILFORD WOODRUFF

One morning, while we were at Winter Quarters, Brother Brigham Young said to me and the brethren that he had had a visitation the night previous from Joseph Smith. I asked him what he said to him. He replied that Joseph had told him to tell the people to labor to obtain the Spirit of God; that they needed that to sustain them and to give them power to go through their work on the earth.

Now I will give you a little of my experience in this line. Joseph Smith visited me a great deal after his death, and taught me many important principles. The last time he visited me was while I was in a storm at sea. I was going on my last mission to preside in England. My companions were Brother Leonard W. Hardy, Brother Milton Holmes, Brother Dan Jones, and another brother, and my wife and two other women. We had been traveling three days and nights in a heavy gale, and were being driven backwards. Finally I asked my companions to come into the cabin with me, and I told them to pray that the Lord would change the wind. I had no fears of being lost; but I did not like the idea of being driven back to New York, as I wanted to go on my journey. We all offered the same prayer, both men and women; and when we got through we stepped on to the deck and in less than a minute it was as though a man had taken a sword and cut that gale through, and you might have thrown a muslin handkerchief out and it would not have moved it. The night following this Joseph and Hyrum visited me, and the Prophet laid before me a great many things. Among other things, he told me to get the Spirit of God; that all of us needed it. He also told me what the Twelve Apostles would be called to go through on the earth before the coming of the Son of Man, and what the reward of their labors would be; but all that was taken from me, for some reason. Nevertheless I know it was most glorious, although much would be required at our hands.

Joseph Smith continued visiting myself and others up to a certain time, and then it stopped. The last time I saw him was in heaven. In the night vision I saw him at the door of the temple in heaven. He came and spoke to me. He said he could not stop to talk with me because he was in a hurry. The next man I met was Father Smith; he could not talk with me because he was in a hurry. I met half a dozen brethren who had held high positions on earth, and none of them could stop to talk with me because they were in a hurry. I was much astonished. By and by I saw the Prophet again, and I got the privilege to ask him a question. "Now," said I, "I want to know why you are in a hurry. I have been in a hurry all through my life; but I expected my hurry would be over when I got into the kingdom of heaven, if I ever did." Joseph said: "I will tell you, Brother Woodruff. Every dispensation that has had the Priesthood on the earth and has gone into the celestial kingdom, has had a certain amount of work to do to prepare to go to the earth with the Savior when He goes to reign on the earth. Each dispensation has had ample time to do this work. We have not. We are the last dispensation, and so much work has to be done, and we need to be in a hurry in order to accomplish it." Of course, that was satisfactory to me, but it was new doctrine to me.

Deseret Weekly, 7 November 1896, 642–43.

"I SLEPT NO MORE THAT NIGHT"

LORENZO DOW YOUNG

In the autumn of 1816, when about nine years old, I had a peculiar dream. I thought I stood in an open, clear space of ground, and saw a plain, fine road, leading, at an angle of 45 degrees, into the air, as far as I could see. I heard a noise like a carriage in rapid motion, at what seemed the upper end of the road. In a moment it came in sight. It was drawn by a pair of beautiful, white horses. The carriage and harness appeared brilliant with gold. The horses traveled with the speed of the wind. It was made manifest to me that the Savior was in the carriage, and that it was driven by His servant. The carriage stopped near me, and the Savior inquired where my brother Brigham was. After informing Him, He further inquired about my other brothers, and our father. After I had answered His inquiries, He stated that He wanted us all, but He especially wanted my brother Brigham. The team then turned right about, and returned on the road it had come.

I awoke at once, and slept no more that night. I felt frightened, and supposed we were all going to die. I saw no other solution to the dream. It was a shadowing of our future which I was then in no condition to discern.

In the morning I told my father the dream, and my fears that we were going to die. He comforted me with the assurance that he did not think my interpretation was correct.

Fragments of Experience, 23–24.

"The Lord Doeth All Things Well"

BRYANT S. HINCKLEY

Elder [Marriner W.] Merrill [of the Quorum of the Twelve] was a man of many interests. His business of farming, merchandising, milling, stock-raising, dairying, etc., called for careful supervision and wise management. These latter tasks were largely entrusted to his older sons. His oldest son, and namesake, was the one upon whom he leaned most heavily. In the prime of his life this oldest son died. This loss Elder Merrill endured with great difficulty and much sorrow. In truth, it seemed that his son's departure caused him to mourn unduly.

Apostle Merrill presided over the Logan Temple. He frequently traveled by horse and carriage from Logan to Richmond where his families were located.

On one occasion soon after the death of his son, as he was returning to his home, he sat in his carriage so deeply lost in thought about his son that he was quite oblivious to things about him. He suddenly came into a state of awareness when his horse stopped in the road. As he looked up, his son stood in the road beside him. His son spoke to him and said, "Father, you are mourning my departure unduly! You are over concerned about my family (his son left a large family of small children) and their welfare. I have much work to do and your grieving gives me much concern. I am in a position to render effective service to my family. You should take comfort, for you know there is much work to be done here and it was necessary for me to be called. You know that the Lord doeth all things well." So saying the son departed.

After this experience Elder Merrill was comforted, for he realized that the death of his son was in keeping with God's will.

Bryant S. Hinckley, *The Faith of Our Pioneer Fathers,* 182–83.

TWO BRIGHT SOVEREIGNS

ANNIE EMMA DEXTER NOBLE

It was my practice before my husband joined the Church to pay my tithing on my monthly allowance that he gave me to keep up the house, but since he did not yet believe in the law of tithing, I did not tell him about this.

One month I ran short and had to ask for some extra money. He looked surprised and rebuked me, saying, "You must learn to cut your coat according to your cloth."

This hurt me terribly and I decided that I would never again ask him for extra money. I worked hard to make ends meet so that I would have enough to pay my tithing. But try as I would, I found it very difficult, and once again several months later I faced the same problem. I did not have enough money to finish out the month.

When I was trying to decide what to do, I suddenly found myself complaining that the Lord expected too much of us when he asked for a tenth. This questioning of his demands only lasted a moment or two and then a feeling of deep remorse came over me for having had such a thought. Immediately I knelt down before the chair that stood by the cupboard and asked the Lord to forgive me for my ingratitude, for I truly felt that I had received from his hands a "pearl of great price," and for me to begrudge a paltry tenth to him was indeed inexcusable. I begged him to forgive me, and with tears streaming down my face I promised him that I would never again question the law of tithing.

After I had asked the Lord's forgiveness I began to wonder what I should do. I was very sad that day, for I still felt that I could not ask my husband for more money. It was Tuesday, and on that evening, we always had a cottage meeting at the home of Brother and Sister Harrison. I was especially happy to go there that night, for their home had always been to me like a haven in a storm at sea. There I was safe from the frowns and disapprovals of all my friends and relatives. As I went upstairs to dress for the meeting, I still felt very sad and troubled. I knelt down and prayed that the Lord would take from me this troubled feeling so that I could enjoy the cottage meeting. Just as I finished my prayer, I heard these words: "Go and look in the little jewel box in the back of your drawer."

I quickly obeyed and hastily took out the jewel box and opened it. There lay side by side two bright sovereigns. Needless to say, I was amazed and so filled with joy that I recall that I had the sensation of walking on air as I went to the meeting. The sovereign at that time was equal to a five-dollar gold piece in American money.

Annie Emma Dexter Noble, as quoted in *Supplement to the Seagull, Home Builder Lesson Book,* 1951, 50–51.

"PUT THE PRIESTHOOD OF GOD TO WORK"

HAROLD B. LEE

I had a lesson years ago as to the greatness of priesthood. A call came for me from the First Presidency, asking me to come to their office on a day that I shall never forget—April 20, 1935.

I was a city commissioner at the time, as well as a stake president. In our stake there were 4,800 of our 7,300 people who were wholly or partially dependent. There were few government work programs; the finances of the Church were low; and we had been told that not much could be done so far as outside help was concerned. We had only one place to go, and that was to apply the Lord's program as set forth in the revelations.

It was from our humble efforts in helping our people that the First Presidency, knowing of our experience, called me asking if I would come to their office. It was Saturday morning and they had no other appointments on their calendar, so for hours they talked with me. They told me they wanted me to resign from the city commission and they would release me from being stake president; they wished me now to head up the welfare movement to turn the tide from government relief and help put the Church in a position where it could take care of its own needy.

After that morning I drove my car up to the head of City Creek Canyon into what was then called Rotary Park, and there, all by myself, I offered one of the most humble prayers of my life.

There I was, just a young man in my thirties. My experience had been limited. I was born in a little country town in Idaho and had hardly been outside the boundaries of the states of Utah and Idaho. And now, to put me in a position where I was to reach out to the entire membership of the Church worldwide, was one of the most staggering contemplations I could imagine. How could I do it with my limited understanding?

As I knelt down, my petition was, "What kind of an organization should be set up in order to accomplish what the Presidency has assigned?" And there came to me on that glorious morning one of the most heavenly realizations of the power of the priesthood of God. It was as though something were saying to me, "There is no new organization necessary to take care of the needs of this people. All that is necessary is to put the priesthood of God to work. There is nothing else that you need as a substitute."

Conference Report, October 1972, 123–24.

SEIZED WITH A PECULIAR FEELING

RULON S. WELLS

I was measuring lumber as it came from the mill and was being stacked nearby, when I was seized with a peculiar feeling over which I had no control, and which impelled me to descend from the pile of lumber and go to the office, a little board shanty which served the purpose of office, store and bedroom combined. It was situated about 300 or 400 feet from where I was working.

After entering the door and locking it, I knelt down and prayed to the Lord "to send me where He wanted me to go." This was the whole burden of my prayer, which lasted only about one minute. The whole proceeding was to me a very strange one, for I did not understand the meaning of it, and it was so unusual and out of the ordinary.

On this very day, and probably at the same moment, my name was being called in the Tabernacle at Salt Lake City, where the conference was then being held, for a mission. The first intimation I had of this call was when my mother, then fifty-one years old, rode on horseback, in company with Archibald Livingstone, who was superintendent of the mills, on the following day to mill F and apprised me of this fact.

Andrew Jenson, *LDS Biographical Encyclopedia,* 1:212.

"They Died in Just That Order"

JOSEPH ANDERSON

On one occasion when Orson Pratt visited the Tooele Stake, at which time President [Heber J.] Grant was the president of the stake and Brother Rowberry was the patriarch, Patriarch Rowberry, in meeting him at the train to take him down to Tooele, said to him, "Brother Pratt, I have had a rather remarkable dream. I can't understand it. I wish you would tell me the interpretation of it."

Brother Pratt said, "Tell me the dream and I will pray about it, and if I can get the interpretation before I go back to Salt Lake I'll tell you what it is."

Brother Rowberry said, "I dreamed that I was on a big ship on the ocean, and as we traveled along the way, people began to fall off that ship one after another. And finally I fell off and fell into the water and made my way to the shore. And lo and behold, when I got there I met a man." (He didn't tell him his name because the man happened to be Orson Pratt himself.) He said, "I met a man, and he showed me around the place where we were, whatever it was, the spirit world, I suppose. And, oh, it was such a beautiful place. Brother Pratt," he said, "this man said to me, this guide, 'Is there any place you would like to see especially?'

"I said, 'Yes, I have always had a great love for the Prophet Joseph, and I would appreciate it if I might see his home.'"

And so he showed him the Prophet's home and other places.

Brother Pratt said, "I'll pray to the Lord about it, and if I get the interpretation I'll tell you."

As Brother Rowberry was taking him to the train after his visit in the stake and visiting the wards, Brother Pratt said to him, "By the way, Brother Rowberry, I have the interpretation of that dream for you." He said, "The ship that you saw was the world, and the people who fell off were people dying, and," he said, "if you'll make a record of those who fell off the ship, in the order that you saw them fall off, as nearly as you can, they will pass away in that particular order." And he said, "When your time comes and you meet the man whom you saw in your dream, he will tell you that the dream was of the Lord and so also was the interpretation."

Some time later while President Grant was president of the stake, Brother Rowberry came to him and said, "Brother Grant, you remember my dream. Well, I wrote down the names of those people in the order in which they fell off that ship and," he said, "they've done it. They have died just in that order."

Some time later a request came from the headquarters of the Church for the people in the stake to pray for Brother Pratt. He was very sick. They had a prayer circle room in the building where they met, and on the way up to the prayer circle room on Sunday morning Brother Rowberry said to Brother Grant, "Now, Brother Grant, you remember my dream?"

Brother Grant said, "Yes, I remember your dream."

He said, "It's all right to pray for Brother Pratt, but," he said, "it's his turn next."

Brother Pratt died on time; he didn't get well. Later, after Brother Grant became an apostle and was visiting out in Tooele, he met Brother Rowberry. Brother Rowberry reminded him of that dream and he said those people had passed away in just the order that they had been listed. And he said, "Brother Grant, it's my turn next. I just can't wait to get over on the other side to meet Brother Pratt and to meet the Prophet Joseph and your father." He said, "I'll tell them what a wonderful work you are doing as an apostle of the Lord."

The next time Brother Grant visited Grantsville, he visited Brother Rowberry's grave.

BYU Speeches, 29 July 1969, 4–6.

"I Am Her Child"

Melvin S. Tagg

Mrs. Newlun from Portland, a convert to the Church, was in a sealing room [of the Alberta Temple] to be sealed to her dead husband and to have their dead children sealed to them. Friends were to act as proxy for the husband and children.

As President Wood was ready to seal the children to the parents, he said he felt impressed to ask if the information on the sealing sheet was complete. After being assured that the record was right, he again began the ceremony. He said he again felt impressed to ask if she had other children whose names should be on the sheet. She said she had other living adult children who were not members of the Church and hence their names should not be included. The third time the President started the ceremony, whereupon he stopped and said, "I heard a voice quite distinctly saying 'I am her child.'" He again asked the mother if she had another child that was not on the sheet. She answered, with tears running down her face, "Yes, I had another daughter who died when twelve days old and she was overlooked in preparing the information." When the group learned how the President knew of the other child, "all in the room shed tears of joy to know of the apparent nearness of our kindred dead."

A very similar incident to the above was also related by Edward J. Wood. He told of a widow who came to have two living children sealed to her and her dead husband. The two children, ages nine and twelve, were standing just inside the sealing room door to witness the sealing of the parents, when a peculiar light appeared over the two children and President Wood said, "I saw another child standing with the two." He asked the mother about a third child and found there had been such, but by neglect, the information was not recorded. "As I told her how I knew," said President Wood, "the child disappeared from the other two."

Melvin S. Tagg, "The Life of Edward James Wood, Church Patriot," 118–19.

Temple Work

"Today You Will Find Records"

ARCHIBALD F. BENNETT

I remember one day in the temple at Manti, a brother from Mount Pleasant rode down to the temple to take part in the work, and as he passed the cemetery in Ephraim, he looked ahead (it was early in the morning), and there was a large multitude all dressed in white, and he wondered how that could be. Why should there be so many up here? It was too early for a funeral, he thought; but he drove up and several of them stepped out in front of him and they talked to him.

They said, "Are you going to the temple?"

"Yes."

"Well, these that you see here are your relatives and they want you to do work for them."

"Yes," he said, "but I am going down today to finish my work. I have no more names, and I do not know the names of those whom you say are related to me."

"But when you go down to the temple today you will find there are records that give our names."

He was surprised. He looked until they all disappeared, and drove on. As he came into the temple, Recorder Farnsworth came up to him and said, "I have just received records from England and they all belong to you."

And there were hundreds of names that had just arrived, and what was told him by these persons that he saw was fulfilled. You can imagine what joy came to his heart, and what a testimony it was to him that the Lord wants this work done.

Archibald F. Bennett, *Saviors on Mount Zion,* 156.

"The Lord Bless You for Your Faith!"

Thomas Briggs

The temple in St. George had been completed . . . , and Thomas [Briggs] was strongly reminded of his father's dying injunction to "never forget the dead." He was so strongly impressed with the fact that it was his duty to go to St. George and have the work done for all of his ancestors whose names he had, that he talked the matter over with his neighbor, Newton Tuttle, who became so enthusiastic on the subject that he proffered to go to St. George with him, and to furnish the team to convey them on the trip.

Some time after that he asked Bishop Call some questions concerning the dead, which the Bishop did not venture to answer, but suggested that he go and talk with President Brigham Young, and offered to go with him.

They accordingly visited President Young, who answered the questions that Thomas wanted to be enlightened upon in a way that was satisfying and very comforting to him, and explained temple work to him in a way that he had never fully understood before.

After conversing about an hour, he said: "Brother Briggs, how many of the names of your dead kindred have you?" On learning that he had only seven names, he asked:

"And have you faith to travel to St. George, over three hundred miles distant, to do the work for seven dead persons?"

Thomas told him he had, and seemed surprised at his asking,

for it had not occurred to him that it required a great amount of faith to do so.

"Well, the Lord bless you for your faith!" said President Young. "Go to St. George, and have the work done for those whose names you have. Travel comfortably and independently, making your own camp and sleeping in or under your wagon. Put the people along the way and in St. George to as little trouble as possible. If you require hay, bread or other supplies, pay for them. Then all the honor will be yours. You shall be blessed on the trip, and you shall never want for names of the dead to work for as long as you live."

He and Brother Tuttle secured their recommends to admit them to the temple and commenced preparations for the journey.

Brother Tuttle and his daughter Emily, and Thomas and his daughter Emma, [along with] Thomas's prospective wife, soon set out for St. George, where they arrived on the 24th of May, 1877.

When his daughter Emma was baptized for his grandmother he received a powerful testimony that his ancestor had accepted of the work done in her behalf.

After finishing the work for all the dead whose names and genealogies they had, they drove out on their return journey a few miles and camped. That night, soon after Thomas had retired to rest in his bed under the wagon, his mother appeared to him.

"You have made a mistake in giving in my genealogy," she said. "You have given the date upon which I was married instead of the date of my birth; but you need not go back now, as some of the family will soon come here, and then you can have the error corrected." She disappeared when Thomas was about to embrace her. This visit, and the purpose of it, were testimonies to Thomas that the dead have a knowledge of the work being done in their behalf. It was also an answer to the prayer offered by Thomas when he sought for information upon that point. It was an evidence too, that the dead have some foreknowledge of things that are going to transpire; for, although Thomas was not aware that any of his family would visit the St. George Temple soon, he was informed by his son, David, almost as soon as he reached home, that he had decided to marry, and he accepted the father's advice to go to St. George and be married in the temple.

George C. Lambert, comp., *Precious Memories,* 37–41.

"This Is the Man You Want to See"

B. F. CUMMINGS

When I was twenty years of age I went on a mission to New England, and was laboring there when the St. George Temple was dedicated. The completion and dedication of this sacred structure greatly stimulated among the Latter-day Saints in the stakes of Zion a desire to procure records necessary for temple work, and a number of brethren and sisters, who had migrated from New England to Utah, wrote to me and asked me to procure genealogical data for them.

I was kept too busy at missionary work to do very much record searching, but I complied with such requests in a number of instances, and soon came to feel an intense interest in genealogical work, a sentiment that influenced my course of life for many years, and still remains with me.

I returned from this mission in September 1877, and soon

after reaching my home, which was in Salt Lake City, I had a conversation with Elder Wilford Woodruff, who was then one of the Twelve Apostles, in which I told him that I felt that it was my duty to return to New England for the purpose of procuring genealogies for such of the Saints as might desire to employ me in that work. He approved my sentiments, and introduced me to President John Taylor, who likewise approved them. At the April conference, 1878, I was set apart by Elder Orson Pratt to go on a mission to New England and the eastern states to preach the gospel to the living, but more especially to procure the records of the dead kindred of Latter-day Saints. I was profoundly impressed by the blessing Elder Pratt gave me.

Immediately after conference I started on this mission and was soon engrossed with my labors in the interest of the dead, labors that consumed much of my time for many years. Although I was but a youth of limited education and at the outset of my genealogical work was almost totally ignorant of those branches of knowledge that are commonly considered absolutely essential to success in such work, such as local history, local laws and usages, systems of records in towns, cities and states, etc., I often met with a degree of success which surprised me.

Many a time I was made to believe that I was receiving assistance from the other side of the veil, and my faith to this effect has always been unshaken; and it is my present purpose to relate a few incidents that tended to create this faith within me.

One of the first genealogies I undertook to trace on this mission was that of a Williams family. An aged widow named Sister F——— employed me to trace it, and the data she gave me to start from pointed to Newark, N. J., as the place in and near which her Williams kindred had lived, and thither I went. At this time I was an utter novice at such work, with not a soul to teach me the first lesson in it. I made my way to the surrogate's office and told the clerk in charge that I desired to trace the genealogy of the

Williams family of Newark and vicinity. He replied to the effect that I had a big job on my hands, and advised me to call on Judge Jesse Williams of Orange, a town a few miles from Newark, who, he said, could probably give me some information. Accordingly I took a car to Orange and soon found myself near the center of that town. The clerk had given me directions for finding Judge Williams' residence, and I started to go to it. I soon came to a marble yard which had a sign extending over the sidewalk. The sign gave the name of the proprietor. It was Williams. Something seemed to say to me: "This man belongs to the family you are tracing, and you had better speak with him."

A lady customer was selecting a gravestone, and the proprietor of the marble yard was walking about with her, directing her attention first to one monument and then to another, apparently in an effort to suit both her taste and her purse. As it would have been impolite to interrupt them, I waited. The lady could not decide. It was getting late in the afternoon and I was uneasy at losing time. Mr. Williams had not noticed me, and I decided to go on to Judge Williams' residence. But something seemed to say to me:

"This is the man you want to see."

"But," I argued with myself, "the clerk in the surrogate's office advised me to see Judge Williams, and the clerk is likely to know whom I had better see." For about an hour this debate continued in my mind. The lady was about that long in choosing the stone and I chafed at the loss of time. Again and again I started to leave the marble yard, but each time came the same prompting: "This is the man for you to see; do not leave until you have talked with him."

Yielding to my unseen adviser, I waited. When the lady had selected a stone, Mr. Williams approached me and asked what he could do for me. I told him I desired to trace the genealogy of the Williams family of that vicinity, and seeing that his name was Williams I had thought he might give me some information.

"I am the man for you to see," he said promptly. I was struck with his words. Except that they were in the first person, they were the same that my invisible monitor had many times repeated to me during the preceding hour, an hour of impatient chafing on my part. As he spoke he turned on his heel and without another word walked to a desk some distance away, opened and took from it two sheets of foolscap paper. With these sheets of paper in his hands he walked back to where I stood and proceeded to tell me that he had been desiring to know more about his ancestors, that he had traced his father's line back to the first settler of the name in New Jersey, that he had arranged the pedigree in the form of a "broadside" (which was the old-fashioned form for such a record), that he had made two copies of this "broadside," which he held in his hands as he spoke, and that I was welcome to one of them. So saying he handed me one of the sheets, to my great surprise and delight.

We conversed a few moments during which I thanked him heartily, and then I returned to Newark. When I came to examine carefully the record he had given me, I found it to be of great value to me, or rather to Sister F———. It embraced her trunk line of ancestry as well as his own. In fact, they were near cousins. I spent two or three weeks in the surrogate's office making abstracts of wills left on record by members of this Williams family, which was very numerous, and collecting other data; and the pedigree given me by the marble cutter, which contained some 200 names and six or seven generations, was of great aid to me in establishing proper connections. I was successful in obtaining and connecting many hundreds of names of this family, although I was slow and awkward at the work.

How came the marble cutter to make a duplicate of his record? The only answer that I can give is this: So that a copy might be in readiness to give to me for use in the house of the Lord.

George C. Lambert, comp., *Gems of Reminiscence,* 77–81.

Opposition to Temple Work

N. B. Lundwall

One occasion I heard the late Apostle Marriner W. Merrill, president of the Logan Temple, relate this extraordinary incident:

He was sitting in his office one morning, he said, when he noticed from the window a company of people coming up the hill to the temple. As they entered the temple grounds they presented rather a strange appearance. . . .

A little later a person unknown to Brother Merrill entered the room. Brother Merrill said to him: "Who are you and who are these people who have come up and taken possession of the temple grounds unannounced?"

He answered and said: "I am Satan and these are my people."

Brother Merrill then said: "What do you want? Why have you come here?"

Satan replied: "I don't like the work that is going on in this temple and feel that it should be discontinued. Will you stop it?"

Brother Merrill answered and said emphatically, "No, we will not stop it. The work must go on."

"Since you refuse to stop it, I will tell you what I propose to do," the adversary said. "I will take these people, my followers, and distribute them throughout this temple district, and will instruct them to whisper in the ears of people, persuading them not to go to the temple, and thus bring about a cessation of your temple work." Satan then withdrew.

The spirit of indifference to temple work took possession of the people and very few came to the house of the Lord for a period after this incident. It is not to be wondered at that Satan, who is the enemy of all righteousness, is displeased with temple work.

N. B. Lundwall, *Temples of the Most High,* 99.

Testimony

"We Were in the Presence of an Angel"

Oliver Cowdery

The Lord, who is rich in mercy, and ever willing to answer the consistent prayer of the humble, after we had called Him in a fervent manner, aside from the abodes of men, condescended to manifest to us His will. On a sudden, as from the midst of eternity, the voice of the Redeemer spake peace to us. While the veil was parted and the angel of God came down clothed with glory, and delivered the anxiously looked for message, and the keys of the gospel of repentance. What joy! What wonder! What amazement! While the world was racked and distracted—while millions were groping as the blind for the wall, and while all men were resting upon uncertainty, as a general mass, our eyes beheld, our ears heard, as in the "blaze of day"; yes, more—above the glitter of the May sunbeam, which then shed its brilliancy over the face of nature! Then His voice, though mild, pierced to the center, and his words, "I am thy fellow-servant," dispelled every fear. We listened, we gazed, we admired! 'Twas the voice of an angel, from glory, 'twas a message from the Most High! And as we heard we rejoiced, while His love enkindled upon our souls, and we were wrapped in the vision of the Almighty! Where was room for doubt? Nowhere; uncertainty had fled, doubt had sunk no more to rise, while fiction and deception had fled forever!

But, dear brother, think, further think for a moment, what joy filled our hearts, and with what surprise we must have bowed, (for who would not have bowed the knee for such a blessing?) when we received under his hand the Holy Priesthood as he said, "Upon you my fellow-servants, in the name of Messiah, I confer this Priesthood and this authority, which shall remain upon earth, that the Sons of Levi may yet offer an offering unto the Lord in righteousness!"

I shall not attempt to paint to you the feelings of this heart, nor the majestic beauty and glory which surrounded us on this occasion; but you will believe me when I say, that earth, nor men, with the eloquence of time, cannot begin to clothe language in as interesting and sublime a manner as this holy personage. No; nor has this earth power to give the joy, to bestow the peace, or comprehend the wisdom which was contained in each sentence as they were delivered by the power of the Holy Spirit! Man may deceive his fellow-men, deception may follow deception, and the children of the wicked one may have power to seduce the foolish and untaught, till naught but fiction feeds the many, and the fruit of falsehood carries in its current the giddy to the grave; but one touch with the finger of his love, yes, one ray of glory from the upper world, or one word from the mouth of the Savior, from the bosom of eternity, strikes it all into insignificance, and blots it forever from the mind. The assurance that we were in the presence of an angel, the certainty that we heard the voice of Jesus, and the truth unsullied as it flowed from the pure personage, dictated by the will of God, is to me part description, and I shall ever look upon this expression of the Savior's goodness with wonder and thanksgiving while I am permitted to tarry; and in those mansions where perfection dwells and sin never comes, I hope to adore in that day which shall never cease.

Times and Seasons, 1 November 1840, 201.

TESTIMONY

"This Is the Way, Walk Ye in It"

ANNIE EMMA DEXTER NOBLE

I was born on the 15th of February in the little English village of Friezland, near the city of Nottingham, in the year 1861.

My parents had thirteen children, six girls and seven boys. I was the tenth child.

Abraham and I were married and we had five lovely daughters. In the year 1906 my husband became very ill. The doctor ordered a rest from his work, so we went to Gainsborough to visit some friends. One afternoon while we were there, two gentlemen called and, to my great surprise, I learned that they were "Mormons." Almost as soon as I knew who they were, I felt a great desire to hear something of their beliefs. Question after question I put to them, and they answered each one to my entire satisfaction. The scriptures were opened to me in a manner I had never known before. My husband, not feeling well, took no part in the conversation, and neither did the other members of the household, but they listened attentively.

After two weeks of complete rest, my husband felt very much improved, and he went back to work. It was not long, however, before he had a relapse. Again the doctor prescribed a rest, and a sea voyage was decided upon. We decided to visit some friends in Brooklyn, New York. It was a very sad time for us all. We left our dear children in the care of my husband's two maiden sisters and sailed from Liverpool on January 22, 1907.

When we left England we thought three months change would fully restore my husband's health, but seven months passed and we realized that he was not yet well enough to hold his position. One morning I was alone in my bedroom. I was unusually troubled and I knelt down and poured out my feelings to my Father in heaven. I asked him to make known to me whether or not my husband would recover, and promised him that if he would spare his life, we would devote our lives to his service.

I had no sooner uttered the prayer than a voice spoke these words: "Your husband shall be made completely well and he shall preach the gospel." I stood up, amazed, but full of joy. I knew without a doubt that my husband would be made well and strong again. But the second promise puzzled me greatly. I finally came to the conclusion that he was to enter college and prepare for the Baptist ministry. Such an idea as Mormonism had never seriously entered my mind.

From that time my husband began to get better. A month later we were homeward bound. My heart was full of hope and joy at the prospect of seeing our beloved children, and the precious assurance that God would fulfill his promise made us equal to the many trials that came our way for long months after.

Eighteen months passed, and still there was no sign that the second promise would be fulfilled. One day, as I was preparing dinner, a knock came to our door. I answered it. A young man asked me if I would accept a gospel tract. I quickly turned it over and saw the words Church of Jesus Christ of Latter-day Saints. I told him that I had met some of his people two years before and that I had hoped ever since to hear more of their teachings. Every week after that the elders visited our home, explaining the principles of the gospel. Two years passed away and no elder had mentioned the subject of baptism.

One day the thought came to me that I could not expect to go on forever taking up the valuable time of these young men, and if

I believed the truths that they were teaching, I should be baptized. This was a most disturbing thought to me. I was afraid to discuss my feelings with my husband, for he was not particularly interested in the gospel. I became unhappy and ill at ease. I felt more and more that I could not go on with Mormonism; that meant that I must give it up—and oh, how dreadful it would be to give it up! Soon after, when Elder Brown came, he saw at once that something was wrong. He asked me if I were unhappy and I answered feverishly, "Yes, I am wretched. I feel I cannot go on any longer with Mormonism. I must give it up or accept it."

He stood up before me and in a most decided manner told me that the time had come for me to be baptized. I answered bitterly, "But I have already been baptized."

He said, "Have you been baptized by one having authority?" I hung my head and could not answer. Then without another word he put out his hand and said, "Good afternoon, Mrs. Noble," and was quickly gone.

How dreadful I felt and how alone. I went immediately to my room and dropped to my knees and cried out, "Father, I am ignorant and cannot see the way; tell me whether this is the true church or not."

Instantly I heard these words, "This is the way, walk ye in it." That was all, but it was enough. No words of mine can express the convincing power that came into my whole being, and with it came peace. I stood up and said, "Now I know beyond a doubt."

It took me three weeks to get enough courage to ask my husband to allow me to be baptized. One night after my husband had put out the light and we were in bed, I told myself that I could not wait any longer, so I tried to make my voice natural and softly asked, "Abe, would you mind very much if I were baptized into the Mormon Church?"

I felt him start, and then came his answer, "No, I don't think I would. I have seen this coming and I know what kind of woman you are. You have not come to this decision in a hurry and if I could keep you from it, I would not dare. I dare not come between you and God."

Never have I forgotten the deep love that I felt for him at that moment, and I felt sure that God would show to him also that Mormonism was true.

I was baptized by Elder Brown on Saturday, November 5, 1910. My daughter Julia was baptized the Sunday following.

Fifteen months after I joined the Church, my husband and my daughter Dora were baptized. A few days following his baptism, my husband was deeply impressed to go to Utah, although just before his baptism he had expressed his unwillingness to leave his own country. Three months later we were on our way. We immigrated to Utah and settled in Ogden. There the last member of our family of five was baptized. We were happy in our new home and made many friends, and each of us tried to do what was asked of us in the Church.

We had lived in Ogden eight years when my husband and I were called on a mission to England. When the call came my mind went back to that day so long ago when a voice spoke to me and said, "Your husband shall be made well and shall preach the gospel." For more than twenty-five years I had waited for the fulfillment of the second promise, and at last it was fulfilled; my husband was called to preach the gospel. I felt like singing all day long, for truly the Lord had manifest his power unto us. We fulfilled a mission in England among our friends and relatives and we rejoice that we had the opportunity to help in the work of the Lord. Our only desire is to do his gracious will and be faithful to the end.

Annie Emma Dexter Noble, as quoted in Mary Pratt Parrish, *Supplement to the Seagull, Home Builder Lesson Book,* 1951, 47–52.

PRAYER ANSWERED IN GOD'S OWN DUE TIME

DAVID O. McKAY

One day in my youth I was hunting cattle. While climbing a steep hill, I stopped to let my horse rest, and there, once again, an intense desire came over me to receive a manifestation of the truth of the restored gospel. I dismounted, threw my reins over my horse's head, and there under a serviceberry bush I prayed that God would declare to me the truth of his revelation to Joseph Smith. I am sure that I prayed fervently and sincerely and with as much faith as a young boy could muster.

At the conclusion of the prayer, I arose from my knees, threw the reins over my faithful pony's head, and got into the saddle. As I started along the trail again, I remember saying to myself: "No spiritual manifestation has come to me. If I am true to myself, I must say I am just the same 'old boy' that I was before I prayed."

The Lord did not see fit to give me an answer on that occasion, but in 1899, after I had been appointed president of the Scottish conference, the spiritual manifestation for which I had prayed as a boy in my teens came as a natural sequence to the performance of duty.

David O. McKay, *Cherished Experiences,* 16.

Acquiring That Special Witness

HAROLD B. LEE

I shall never forget my feelings of loneliness the Saturday night after I was told by the President of the Church that I was to be sustained the next day as a member of the Quorum of the Twelve Apostles. That was a sleepless night. There ran through my mind all the petty things of my life, the nonsense, the foolishness of youth. I could have told you about those against whom I had any grievances and who had any grievance against me. And before I was to be accepted the next day, I knew that I must stand before the Lord and witness before him that I would love and forgive every soul that walked the earth and in return I would ask Him to forgive me that I might be worthy of that position.

I said, as I suppose all of us would say as we are called to such a position, or any position, "President Grant, do you feel that I am worthy of this call?" And just as quick as a flash, he said, "My boy, if I didn't think so, you would never be called to this position."

The Lord knew my heart and He knew that I was not perfect and that all of us have weaknesses to overcome. He takes us with imperfections and expects us to begin where we are and make our lives conform fully with the principles and doctrines of Jesus Christ.

The following day I went to the temple where I was ushered into the room where the Council of the Twelve meet with the First Presidency each week in an upper room. I thought of all the great men who have occupied those chairs and now here I was, just a young man, twenty years younger than the next youngest of the

Twelve, being asked to sit in one of those chairs. It was frightening and startling.

And then one of the brethren, who arranged for Sunday evening radio programs, said, "Now you know that after having been ordained, you are a special witness to the mission of the Lord Jesus Christ. We want you to give the Easter talk next Sunday night." The assignment was to bear testimony of the mission of the Lord concerning His resurrection, His life, and His ministry, so I went to a room in the Church Office Building where I could be alone, and I read the Gospels, particularly those that had to do with the closing days and weeks and months of the life of Jesus. And as I read, I realized that I was having a new experience.

It wasn't any longer just a story; it seemed as though I was actually seeing the events about which I was reading, and when I gave my talk and closed with my testimony, I said, "I am now the least of all my brethren and want to witness to you that I know, as I have never known before this call came, that Jesus is the Savior of this world. He lives and He died for us." Why did I know? Because there had come a witness, that special kind of a witness, that may have been the more sure word of prophecy that one must have if he is to be a special witness.

Address given at Joint Nottingham and Leicester conference, Nottingham England Stake, 2 September 1973. See *Ensign,* February 1974, 18.

"Today I Found a Prophet"

Arch Madsen

I remember being in New York when President [David O.] McKay returned from Europe. Arrangements had been made for pictures to be taken, but the regular photographer was unable to go, so in desperation the United Press picked their crime photographer—a man accustomed to the toughest type of work in New York. He went to the airport, stayed there two hours, and returned later from the darkroom with a tremendous sheaf of pictures. He was supposed to take only two. His boss immediately chided him. "What in the world are you wasting time and all those photographic supplies for?"

The photographer replied very curtly, saying he would gladly pay for the extra materials, and they could even dock him for the extra time he took. It was obvious that he was very touchy about it. Several hours later the vice-president called him to his office, wanting to learn what happened. The crime photographer said, "When I was a little boy, my mother used to read to me out of the Old Testament, and all my life I have wondered what a prophet of God must really look like. Well, today I found one."

Improvement Era, February 1970, 72.

"I FELT SUCH A DESIRE TO READ THE BOOK"

MARY LIGHTNER

Quite a number of the residents of Kirtland accepted baptism. Mother and myself also, in the month of October, 1830. A branch of the Church was organized, and Father Morley was ordained an elder to preside over it. He owned a large farm, about a mile from Kirtland, and some three or four families went there to live, and meetings were held there. A good spirit and one of union prevailed among the brethren for some time.

After Oliver Cowdery and his brethren left there for Missouri on their mission to the Lamanites, a wrong spirit crept into our midst, and a few were led away by it. About this time, John Whitmer came and brought a Book of Mormon. There was a meeting that evening, and we learned that Brother Morley had the book in his possession—the only one in that part of the country.

I went to his house just before the meeting was to commence, and asked to see the book; Brother Morley put it in my hand; as I looked at it, I felt such a desire to read it, that I could not refrain from asking him to let me take it home and read it, while he attended meeting. He said it would be too late for me to take it back after meeting, and another thing, he had hardly had time to read a chapter in it himself, and but few of the brethren had even seen it, but I pled so earnestly for it, he finally said, "Child, if you will bring this book home before breakfast tomorrow morning, you may take it." He admonished me to be very careful, and see that no harm came to it.

If any person in this world was ever perfectly happy in the possession of any coveted treasure, I was when I had permission to read that wonderful book. Uncle and Aunt were Methodists, so when I got into the house, I exclaimed, "Oh, Uncle, I have got the 'Golden Bible.'" Well, there was consternation in the house for a few moments, and I was severely reprimanded for being so presumptuous as to ask such a favor, when Brother Morley had not read it himself. However, we all took turns reading it until very late in the night. As soon as it was light enough to see, I was up and learned the first verse in the book.

When I reached Brother Morley's they had been up for only a little while. When I handed him the book, he remarked, "I guess you did not read much in it." I showed him how far we had read. He was surprised and said, "I don't believe you can tell me one word of it." I then repeated the first verse, also the outlines of the history of Nephi. He gazed at me in surprise, and said, "Child, take this book home and finish it, I can wait."

Before or about the time I finished the last chapter, the Prophet Joseph Smith arrived in Kirtland, and moved into a part of Newel K. Whitney's house (Uncle Algernon's partner in the Mercantile Business), while waiting for his goods to be put in order. Brother Whitney brought the Prophet Joseph to our house and introduced him to the older ones of the family (I was not in at the time). In looking around he saw the Book of Mormon on the shelf, and asked how that book came to be there. He said, "I sent that book to Brother Morley."

Uncle told him how his niece had obtained it. He asked, "Where is your niece?" I was sent for; when he saw me he looked at me so earnestly, I felt almost afraid. After a moment or two he came and put his hands on my head and gave me a great blessing, the first I ever received, and made me a present of the book, and said he would give Brother Morley another. He came in time to rebuke the evil spirits, and set the Church in order. We all felt that he was a man of God, for he spoke with power, and as one having authority in very deed.

In the fall of 1831, in company with Bishop Partridge, Father Morley, W. W. Phelps, Cyrus Daniels and their families, mother and myself, my brother Henry and sister Caroline, under the guardianship of Algernon S. Gilbert, left Kirtland for Independence, Jackson County, Missouri. Soon, quite a number of the Saints settled in Independence. Uncle Gilbert opened a store of dry goods, and groceries; while his partner, Newel K. Whitney, kept one in Kirtland, where they had one for several years before the gospel came to them.

Mary Elizabeth Rollins Lightner, "The Life and Testimony of Mary Lightner."

The Restoration

"I Can Swear before High Heaven"

B. H. Roberts

In a manuscript history of his father's life, filed in the Historian's Office, Salt Lake City, John W. Rigdon, near the close of that history, makes final reference to the coming of Cowdery, Pratt, et al. to his father's home in Mentor with the Book of Mormon. He relates how he himself visited the then territory of Utah in 1863, where he spent the winter among the "Mormon" people. He was not favorably impressed with their religious life, and came to the conclusion that the Book of Mormon itself was a fraud. He determined in his own heart that if ever he returned home and found his father, Sidney Rigdon, alive, he would try and find out what he knew of the origin of the Book of Mormon. "Although," he adds, "he had never told but one story about it, and that was that Parley P. Pratt and Oliver Cowdery presented him with a bound volume of that book in the year 1830, while he (Sidney Rigdon) was preaching Campbellism at Mentor, Ohio."

What John W. Rigdon claims to have seen in Utah, however, together with the fact that Sidney Rigdon had been charged with writing the Book of Mormon, made him suspicious; "and," he remarks, "I concluded I would make an investigation for my own satisfaction and find out, if I could, if he had all these years been deceiving his family and the world, by telling that which was not true, and I was in earnest about it. If Sidney Rigdon, my father, had thrown his life away by telling a falsehood and bringing sorrow and disgrace upon his family, I wanted to know it and was determined to find out the facts, no matter what the consequences might be.

"I reached home in the fall of 1865, found my father in good health and [he] was very much pleased to see me. . . . Shortly after I had arrived home, I went to my father's room; he was there and alone, and now was the time for me to commence my inquiries in regard to the origin of the Book of Mormon, and as to the truth of the Mormon religion.

"I told him what I had seen at Salt Lake City, and I said to him that what I had seen at Salt Lake had not impressed me very favorably toward the Mormon church, and as to the origin of the Book of Mormon I had some doubts. 'You have been charged with writing that book and giving it to Joseph Smith to introduce to the world. You have always told me one story; that you never saw the book until it was presented to you by Parley P. Pratt and Oliver Cowdery; and all you ever knew of the origin of that book was what they told you and what Joseph Smith and the witnesses who claimed to have seen the plates had told you. Is this true? If so, all right; if it is not, you owe it to me and to your family to tell it. You are an old man and you will soon pass away, and I wish to know if Joseph Smith, in your intimacy with him for fourteen years, has not said something to you that led you to believe he obtained that book in some other way than what he had told you. Give me all you know about it, that I may know the truth.'

"My father, after I had finished saying what I have repeated above, looked at me a moment, raised his hand above his head and slowly said, with tears glistening in his eyes: 'My son, I can swear before high heaven that what I have told you about the origin of that book is true. Your mother and sister . . . were present when that book was handed to me in Mentor, Ohio, and all I ever knew about the origin of that book was what Parley P. Pratt, Oliver Cowdery, Joseph Smith and the witnesses who claimed they saw the plates have told me, and in all of my intimacy with Joseph

Smith he never told me but one story, and that was that he found it engraved upon gold plates in a hill near Palmyra, New York, and that an angel had appeared to him and directed him where to find it; and I have never, to you or to any one else, told but the one story, and that I now repeat to you.' I believed him, and now believe he told me the truth. He also said to me after that that Mormonism was true; that Joseph Smith was a Prophet, and this world would find it out some day.

"After my father's death, my mother, who survived him several years, was in the enjoyment of good health up to the time of her last sickness, she being eighty-six years old. A short time before her death I had a conversation with her about the origin of the Book of Mormon and wanted to know what she remembered about its being presented to my father. She said to me in that conversation that what my father had told me about the book being presented to him was true, for she was present at the time and knew that was the first time he ever saw it, and that the stories told about my father writing the Book of Mormon were not true. This she said to me in her old age and when the shadows of the grave were gathering around her; and I believed her."

B. H. Roberts, *Comprehensive History of the Church,* 1:233–35.

THE HEAVENS WERE OPENED

JOSEPH SMITH

About three o'clock, P.M., I dismissed the school, and the Presidency retired to the attic story of the printing office, where we attended the ordinance of washing our bodies in pure water. We also perfumed our bodies and our heads in the name of the Lord.

At early candlelight I met with the Presidency at the west school room, in the temple, to attend to the ordinance of anointing our heads with holy oil; also the Councils of Kirtland and Zion met in the two adjoining rooms, and waited in prayer while we attended to the ordinance. I took the oil in my left hand, Father Smith being seated before me, and the remainder of the Presidency encircled him round about. We then stretched our right hands towards heaven, and blessed the oil, and consecrated it in the name of Jesus Christ.

We then laid our hands upon our aged Father Smith, and invoked the blessings of heaven. I then anointed his head with the consecrated oil, and sealed many blessings upon him. The Presidency then in turn laid their hands upon his head, beginning at the oldest, until they had all laid their hands upon him, and pronounced such blessings upon his head, as the Lord put into their hearts, all blessing him to be our Patriarch, to anoint our heads, and attend to all duties that pertain to that office. The Presidency then took the seat in their turn, according to their age, beginning at the oldest, and received their anointing and blessing under the hands of Father Smith. And in my turn, my father anointed my head, and sealed upon me the blessings of Moses, to lead Israel in the latter days, even as Moses led him in days of old; also the blessings of Abraham, Isaac and Jacob. All of the Presidency laid their hands upon me, and pronounced upon my head many prophecies and blessings, many of which I shall not notice at this time. But as Paul said, so say I, let us come to visions and revelations.

The heavens were opened upon us, and I beheld the celestial kingdom of God, and the glory thereof, whether in the body or out I cannot tell. I saw the transcendent beauty of the gate through which the heirs of that kingdom will enter, which was like unto circling flames of fire; also the blazing throne of God, whereon was seated the Father and the Son. I saw the beautiful streets of that kingdom, which had the appearance of being paved with gold. I saw Fathers Adam and Abraham, and my father and mother, my brother, Alvin, that has long since slept, and marvelled as that he had obtained an inheritance in that kingdom, seeing that he had departed this life before the Lord had set His hand to gather Israel the second time, and had not been baptized for the remission of sins.

Thus came the voice of the Lord unto me, saying—

All who have died without a knowledge of this gospel, who would have received it if they had been permitted to tarry, shall be heirs of the celestial kingdom of God; also all that shall die henceforth without a knowledge of it, who would have received it with all their hearts, shall be heirs of that kingdom, for I, the Lord, will judge all men according to their works, according to the desire of their hearts.

And I also beheld that all children who die before they arrive at the years of accountability, are saved in the celestial kingdom of heaven. I saw the Twelve Apostles of the Lamb, who are now upon the earth, who hold the keys of this last ministry, in foreign lands, standing together in a circle, much fatigued, with their clothes tattered and feet swollen, with their eyes cast downward, and Jesus standing in their midst, and they did not behold Him. The Savior looked upon them and wept.

I also beheld Elder M'Lellin in the south, standing upon a hill, surrounded by a vast multitude, preaching to them, and a lame man standing before him supported by his crutches; he threw them down at his word and leaped as a hart, by the mighty power of God. Also, I saw Elder Brigham Young standing in a strange land, in the far south and west, in a desert place, upon a rock in the midst of about a dozen men of color, who appeared hostile. He was preaching to them in their own tongue, and the angel of God standing above his head, with a drawn sword in his hand, protecting him, but he did not see it. And I finally saw the Twelve in the celestial kingdom of God. I also beheld the redemption of Zion, and many things which the tongue of man cannot describe in full.

Many of my brethren who received the ordinance with me saw glorious visions also. Angels ministered unto them as well as to myself, and the power of the Highest rested upon us, the house was filled with the glory of God, and we shouted Hosanna to God and the Lamb. My scribe also received his anointing with us, and saw, in a vision, the armies of heaven protecting the Saints in their return to Zion, and many things which I saw.

The Bishop of Kirtland with his counselors, and the Bishop of Zion with his counselors, were present with us, and received their anointings under the hands of Father Smith, and this was confirmed by the Presidency, and the glories of heaven were unfolded to them also.

We then invited the High Councilors of Kirtland and Zion into our room, and President Hyrum Smith anointed the head of the President of the Councilors in Kirtland, and President David Whitmer the head of the President of the Councilors of Zion. The President of each quorum then anointed the heads of his colleagues, each in his turn, beginning at the oldest.

The visions of heaven were opened to them also. Some of them saw the face of the Savior, and others were ministered unto by holy angels, and the spirit of prophecy and revelation was poured out in mighty power; and loud hosannas, and glory to God in the highest, saluted the heavens, for we all communed with the heavenly host. And I saw in my vision all of the Presidency in the celestial kingdom of God, and many others that were present. Our meeting was opened by singing, and prayer was offered up by the head of each quorum; and closed by singing, and invoking the benediction of heaven, with uplifted hands. Retired between one and two o'clock in the morning.

Joseph Smith, *History of the Church,* 2:379–82.

THE SAVIOR APPEARS

MARY LIGHTNER

Well, my young brethren, I can say I never was more surprised in my life than to be called upon to speak to you young men who are called upon to go into the mission field to preach the gospel to the nations of the earth. It is true I have been in the Church from its beginning. Just six months after it was organized I joined it. I have been acquainted with all of those who were first members of this church, with all of those who saw the plates and handled them. I am well acquainted with every one of them, and I have known them from the time that they came to Ohio until their death, and I am the only living witness who was at the first meeting that the Prophet held in Kirtland [1831].

The Smith family were driven from New York, and a small church had been organized. Oliver Cowdery, Peter Whitmer, and Ziba Peterson were members. Well, I being anxious, though young, to learn about the plates from those who knew all about it, my mother and I went up to the Smith family, from the old gentleman and his wife to all the sons and daughters.

As we stood there talking to them, Joseph and Martin Harris came in. Joseph looked around very solemnly. It was the first time some of them had ever seen him. Said he, "There are enough here to hold a little meeting."

They got a board and put it across two chairs to make seats. Martin Harris sat on a little box at Joseph's feet. They sang and prayed. Joseph got up and began to speak to us. As he began to speak very solemnly and very earnestly, all at once his countenance changed and he stood mute. Those who looked at him that day said there was a searchlight within him, over every part of his body. I never saw anything like it on the earth. I could not take my eyes off him. He got so white that anyone who saw him would have thought he was transparent. I remember I thought I could almost see the cheek bones through the flesh.

I have been through many changes since, but that is photographed on my brain. I shall remember it and see it in my mind's eye as long as I remain upon the earth. He stood some moments. He looked over the congregation as if to pierce every heart, and said, "Do you know who has been in your midst?" One of the Smiths said an angel of the Lord. Martin Harris said, "It was our Lord and Savior, Jesus Christ." Joseph put his hand down on Martin and said, "God revealed that to you."

[Joseph continued:] "Brothers and Sisters, the Spirit of God has been here. The Savior has been in your midst this night, and I want you to remember it. There is a veil over your eyes; you could not endure to look upon Him. You must be fed with milk, not with strong meat. I want you to remember this as if it were the last thing that escapes my lips. He has given all of you to me and has sealed you up to everlasting life that where He is, there you may be also. And if you are tempted of Satan, say, 'get behind me, Satan.'"

These words are figured upon my brain and I never took my eyes off his countenance. Then he knelt down and prayed. I have never heard anything like it before or since. I felt that he was talking to the Lord and that power rested down upon the congregation. Every soul felt it. The spirit rested upon us in every fiber of our bodies, and we received a sermon from the lips of the representative of God.

Much has come to and gone from me through the power and vicissitudes of this church. I have been in almost every mob. I have been driven about and told I would be shot and had a gun pointed at me, but I stayed with the Church until it was driven from Nauvoo.

The words of the Prophet that had been revealed to him have always been with me from the beginning to the end of the gospel. Every principle that has been given in the Church by the Prophet is true. I know whereon I stand, I know what I believe, I know what I know, and I know what I testify to you is the living truth. As I expect to meet it at the bar of the eternal Jehovah it is true. And when you stand before His bar, you will know.

Mary Elizabeth Rollins Lightner, "The Life and Testimony of Mary Lightner," 55–57.

"DO YOU WANT TO FIGHT, SIR?"

LUCY MACK SMITH

Despite opposition,] the work of printing [the Book of Mormon] still continued with little or no interruption, until one Sunday afternoon, when Hyrum became very uneasy as to the security of the work left at the printing office, and requested Oliver to accompany him thither, to see if all was right. Oliver hesitated for a moment, as to the propriety of going on Sunday, but finally consented, and they set off together.

On arriving at the printing establishment, they found it occupied by an individual by the name of Cole, an ex-justice of the peace, who was busily employed in printing a newspaper. Hyrum was much surprised at finding him there, and remarked, "How is it, Mr. Cole, that you are so hard at work on Sunday?"

Mr. Cole replied that he could not have the press, in the day time during the week, and was obliged to do his printing at night and on Sundays.

Upon reading the prospectus of his paper, they found that he had agreed with his subscribers to publish one form of "Joe Smith's Gold Bible" each week, and thereby furnish them with the principal portion of the book in such a way that they would not be obliged to pay the Smiths for it. His paper was entitled, *Dogberry Paper on Winter Hill.* In this, he had thrown together a parcel of the most vulgar, disgusting prose, and the meanest, and most low-lived doggerel, in juxtaposition with a portion of the Book of Mormon, which he had pilfered. At this perversion of common sense and moral feeling, Hyrum was shocked, as well as indignant at the dishonest course which Mr. Cole had taken, in order to possess himself of the work.

"Mr. Cole," said he, "what right have you to print the Book of Mormon in this manner? Do you not know that we have secured the copyright?"

"It is none of your business," answered Cole, "I have hired the press, and will print what I please, so help yourself."

"Mr. Cole," rejoined Hyrum, "that manuscript is sacred, and I forbid your printing any more of it."

"Smith," exclaimed Cole, in a tone of anger, "I don't care a d——n for you: that d————d gold bible is going into my paper, in spite of all you can do."

Hyrum endeavored to dissuade him from his purpose, but finding him inexorable, left him to issue his paper, as he had hitherto done; for when they found him at work, he had already issued six or eight numbers, and had managed to keep them out of our sight.

On returning from the office, they asked my husband what course was best for them to pursue, relative to Mr. Cole. He told them that he considered it a matter with which Joseph ought to be made acquainted. Accordingly, he set out himself for Pennsylvania, and returned with Joseph the ensuing Sunday. The weather was so extremely cold, that they came near perishing before they arrived at home; nevertheless, as soon as Joseph made himself partially comfortable, he went to the printing office, where he found Cole employed, as on the Sunday previous. "How do you do, Mr. Cole?" said Joseph. "You seem hard at work."

"How do you do, Mr. Smith," answered Cole, dryly.

Joseph examined his *Dogberry Paper,* and then said firmly, "Mr. Cole, that book [the Book of Mormon], and the right of publishing it, belongs to me, and I forbid you meddling with it any further."

At this Mr. Cole threw off his coat, rolled up his sleeves, and came towards Joseph, smacking his fists together with vengeance, and roaring out, "Do you want to fight, sir? Do you want to fight? I will publish just what I please. Now, if you want to fight just come on."

Joseph could not help smiling at his grotesque appearance, for his behavior was too ridiculous to excite indignation. "Now, Mr. Cole," said he, "you had better keep your coat on—it is cold, and I am not going to fight you, nevertheless, I assure you, sir, that you have got to stop printing my book, for I know my rights, and shall maintain them."

"Sir," bawled out the wrathy gentleman, "if you think you are the best man, just pull off your coat and try it."

"Mr. Cole," said Joseph, in a low, significant tone, "there is law, and you will find that out, if you do not understand it, but I shall not fight you, sir."

At this, the ex-justice began to cool off a little, and finally concluded to submit to an arbitration, which decided that he should stop his proceedings forthwith, so that he made us no further trouble.

Lucy Mack Smith, *History of Joseph Smith by His Mother,* 164–66.

"YOU DO NOT KNOW HOW HAPPY I AM"

LUCY MACK SMITH

After attending to the usual services, namely, reading, singing, and praying, Joseph arose from his knees, and approaching Martin Harris with a solemnity that thrills through my veins to this day, when it occurs to my recollection, said, "Martin Harris, you have got to humble yourself before God this day, that you may obtain a forgiveness of your sins. If you do, it is the will of God that you should look upon the plates, in company with Oliver Cowdery and David Whitmer."

In a few minutes after this, Joseph, Martin, Oliver and David repaired to a grove, a short distance from the house, where they commenced calling upon the Lord, and continued in earnest supplication, until he permitted an angel to come down from his presence and declare to them, that all which Joseph had testified of concerning the plates was true.

When they returned to the house it was between three and four o'clock P.M. Mrs. Whitmer, Mr. Smith and myself were sitting in a bedroom at the time. On coming in, Joseph threw himself down beside me and exclaimed, "Father, Mother, you do not know how happy I am: the Lord has now caused the plates to be shown to three more besides myself. They have seen an angel, who has testified to them, and they will have to bear witness to the truth of what I have said, for now they know for themselves, that I do not go about to deceive the people, and I feel as if I was relieved of a burden which was almost too heavy for me to bear, and it rejoices my soul, that I am not any longer to be entirely alone in the world."

Upon this, Martin Harris came in: he seemed almost overcome with joy, and testified boldly to what he had both seen and heard. And so did David and Oliver, adding that no tongue could express the joy of their hearts and the greatness of the things which they had both seen and heard.

Lucy Mack Smith, *History of Joseph Smith by His Mother,* 151–53.

A PATHWAY THROUGH THE ARMY

LUCY MACK SMITH

A messenger came and told us that if we ever [wanted to see] our sons alive, we must go immediately to them, for they were in a wagon that would start in a few minutes for Independence, and in all probability they would never return alive. Receiving this intimation, Lucy [Lucy Mack Smith's daughter] and myself set out directly for the place. On coming within about a hundred yards of the wagon, we were compelled to stop, for we could press no further through the crowd. I therefore appealed to those around me, exclaiming, "I am the mother of the Prophet—is there not a gentleman here, who will assist me to that wagon, that I may take a last look at my children, and speak to them once more before I die?"

Upon this, one individual volunteered to make a pathway through the army, and we passed on, threatened with death at every step, till at length we arrived at the wagon. The man who led us through the crowd spoke to Hyrum, who was sitting in front, and, telling him that his mother had come to see him, requested that he should reach his hand to me. He did so, but I was not allowed to see him; the cover was of strong cloth, and nailed down so close that he could barely get his hand through. We had merely shaken hands with him, when we were ordered away by the mob, who forbade any conversation between us, and, threatening to shoot us, they ordered the teamster to drive over us.

Our friend then conducted us to the back part of the wagon, where Joseph sat, and said, "Mr. Smith, your mother and sister are here, and wish to shake hands with you." Joseph crowded his hand through between the cover and wagon, and we caught hold of it; but he spoke not to either of us, until I said, "Joseph, do speak to your poor mother once more—I cannot bear to go till I hear your voice."

"God bless you, Mother!" he sobbed out. Then a cry was raised, and the wagon dashed off, tearing him from us just as Lucy was pressing his hand to her lips, to bestow upon it a sister's last kiss—for he was then sentenced to be shot.

Lucy Mack Smith, *History of Joseph Smith by His Mother*, 290–91.

"I Do Not Feel Like Singing"

B. H. ROBERTS

The Prophet Joseph, his brother Hyrum, John Taylor, and Willard Richards were imprisoned in the Carthage Jail. Elder Taylor, to cheer the Prophet, sang the following sacred song, which had recently been introduced into Nauvoo.

Once when my scanty meal was spread
He entered—not a word he spake!
Just perishing for want of bread;
I gave him all; he blessed it, brake.

In prison I saw him next,—condemned
To meet a traitor's doom at morn;
The tide of lying tongues I stemmed,
And honored him 'mid shame and scorn.

My friendship's utmost zeal to try,
He asked if I for him would die;
The flesh was weak, my blood ran chill,
But the free spirit cried, "I will."

Then in a moment to my view,
The stranger started from disguise;
The tokens in his hands I knew;
The Savior stood before mine eyes.
He spake, and my poor name he named—
"Of me thou hast not been ashamed;
These deeds shall thy memorial be;
Fear not, thou didst them unto me."

The afternoon was sultry and hot. The four brethren sat listlessly about the room with their coats off, and the windows of the prison were open to receive such air as might be stirring. Late in the afternoon Mr. Stigall, the jailor, came in and suggested that they would be safer in the cells. Joseph told him that they would go in after supper.

Hyrum Smith asked Elder Taylor to sing again "A Poor Wayfaring Man of Grief."

Elder Taylor: "Brother Hyrum, I do not feel like singing."

Hyrum: "Oh, never mind; commence singing and you will get the spirit of it."

Soon after finishing the song the second time, as he was sitting at one of the front windows, Elder Taylor saw a number of men, with painted faces, rushing round the corner of the jail towards the stairs. They were halted at the entrance but a moment. "The guards were hustled away from the door, good naturedly resisting until they were carefully disarmed."

The brethren must have seen this mob simultaneously, for they all leaped to the door to secure it, as the lock and latch were of little use. The mob reaching the landing in front of the door fired a shot into the lock. Hyrum and Doctor Richards sprang back, when instantly another ball crashed through the panel of the door and struck Hyrum in the face; at the same instant a ball, evidently from the window facing the public square where the main body of the Carthage Greys were stationed, entered his back, and he fell, calmly exlaiming: "I am a dead man!"

With an expression of deep sympathy in his face, Joseph bent over the prostrate body of the murdered man and exclaimed: "Oh, my poor, dear brother Hyrum!"

While Joseph was firing the pistol, Elder Taylor stood close behind him.

Elder Taylor beat down the muzzles of those murderous guns.

"That's right, Brother Taylor, parry them off as well as you can," said the Prophet, as he stood behind him.

Meantime the crowd on the landing grew more dense and were forced to the door by the pressure of those below crowding their way upstairs. The guns of the assailants were pushed further and further into the room—the firing was more rapid and accompanied yells and horrid oaths. Certain that they would be overpowered in a moment, Elder Taylor sprang for the open window directly in front of the prison door, and also exposed to the fire of the Carthage Greys from the public square. As he was in the act of leaping from the window, a ball fired from the doorway struck him about midway of his left thigh. He fell helplessly forward towards the open window, and would have dropped on the outside of the jail, but that another ball from the outside, striking the watch in his vest pocket, threw him back into the room.

As Elder Taylor was thrown back from the window Joseph Smith attempted to leap out, but in doing so was instantly shot and fell to the ground with the martyr-cry upon his lips: "O Lord, my God!"

B. H. Roberts, *Comprehensive History of the Church,* 2:283–86.

Word of Wisdom

"I Will Smoke with You"

N. ELDON TANNER

I was driving along and had two young men with me in my car, and a young man thumbed a ride with us. I asked the boys who were with me if we should take him with us, and they said yes. I picked him up, and after we had driven along a little way he said, "Do you mind if I smoke in your car?"

I said, "No, not at all if you can give me any good reason why you should smoke." And I said, "I will go farther than that." (I was stake president at this time.) "If you can give me a good reason why you should smoke, I will smoke with you."

Well, these two young men looked at me and wondered. We drove on for some distance, about twenty minutes, I think, and I turned around and said, "Aren't you going to smoke?"

And he said, "No."

I said, "Why not?"

And he said, "I can't think of a good reason why I should."

Conference Report, April 1965, 93.

"Why I Keep the Word of Wisdom"

SOLOMON F. KIMBALL

Arizona's rainy season generally occurs during the summer months, and after the water has subsided, the farmers in that section of the country usually spend a few days repairing dams that have been damaged by the floods. One hot summer day I was hauling rocks for the Mesa dam, on the Salt River. The wind was blowing quite hard at the time. The rushing of the waters over the dam, mingling its voice with the moaning and sighing of the wind, almost makes one believe that he hears beautiful music, or human beings crying, singing or talking.

I had just driven my team into the river with a load of rocks and unloaded them, and was in the act of taking a chew of tobacco, when, to my great surprise, I heard a voice saying, "Don't chew any more tobacco." I looked around to see if I could see anyone close by, and then drove away for another load. While doing so I felt like a big simpleton, for allowing myself to believe such apparent nonsense as hearing a voice repeat those words, since there was no one within a hundred yards of me. I gathered up another load, and drove back to the same place, and threw it onto the brush, on the dam. I had come to the conclusion that the Arizona wind and water had perpetrated a huge joke on me. My tobacco was a great comfort to me, and I felt that I did not wish to be deceived by the elements of that hot and sultry country. I then looked all around again, to make sure that no one was near, and just as I was biting off a chew, I heard the same voice, only in a little louder tone, saying, "Never take another chew of tobacco as long as you live."

I hardly knew what to think, but said to myself, it is not the wind and water this time, but really and truly a human voice. In years gone by I was not a man to believe in such things, and had been severe in my criticism of others in relation to such matters; but now I had something to think about sure enough. I continued my work until noon, at the same time discussing this subject in my mind.

I said nothing to the boys about it during the dinner hour, although they could see that I was considerably agitated over something. I knew that by telling them about it, it would make me the laughing stock of the whole crowd. In the afternoon it was hard for me to keep from taking a chew, and there was quite a strong influence working with me by this time. It was bringing all kinds of arguments to bear upon this subject, and trying to convince me that it was my imagination pure and simple, and that the wind and water combined, had a good deal to do with it.

There were other things that made it hard for me to overcome this habit. I had an appetite for liquor, but had not touched it for about two years, and was determined never to taste it again, as long as I lived. Under these circumstances I felt that it would be more than I could bear, to put my old friend tobacco behind me. I understood what a curse the liquor habit is, and felt that if I could overcome it, I would be doing very well. I believed that by using tobacco it would help me to overcome the greater evil.

When I had driven my team into the river with my last load, that afternoon, I had convinced myself that I had heard no voice at all, and had also made up my mind to take a chew of tobacco, if it were the last act of my life. The gnawing, craving and hankering after it was almost driving me crazy. I then took it out of my pocket for the third time, and just as I was going to take a chew I heard the same voice again, plainly and distinctly, saying, "Solomon, never touch tobacco again as long as you live."

I made up my mind to do as I was told, let the consequences be what they may. I said nothing about it to anyone, except my wife, who was a good Latter-day Saint. From that time on, the craving for tobacco gradually left me, but the appetite for liquor began to get in its deadly work, just at a time when I needed help and encouragement the most. It seemed to me like the powers of darkness had begun to gather around me, thicker than ever. For two years I had made the effort of my life to overcome my weaknesses, and live the life of a Latter-day Saint, but it seemed like fate was against me.

I commenced to fast and pray and humble myself mightily before the Lord, crying unto him day and night, to deliver me from this cursed viper. I had to use all the energy and will power that I could possibly muster in order to resist this terrible disease that was getting the upper hand of me. There was no Keeley cure in those days, and we were left to ourselves, unless we could get help from above. I would dream of drinking it nights, and thirst for it in the daytime. One evening, after fasting for twenty-four hours, and spending a goodly portion of that time in praying to the Lord for help, his Spirit whispered these words to me, "If you will observe the Word of Wisdom, the liquor habit will leave you."

This to me was like a clap of thunder out of a clear sky. I had been drinking a good deal of strong tea and coffee up to this time, and it seemed so strange to me afterwards, that I should overlook so important a revelation as was the Word of Wisdom upon this subject. If I had obeyed its teachings when I left Pinal and joined the Mesa ward, two years before, what a blessing it would have been to me in many respects!

I obeyed the instructions received, and from that day until the present time, I have never drunk a cup of intoxicants of any description, neither have I used tea, coffee, or tobacco. In less than two months after this, I could master all these habits pretty well, and in less than a year, I had no desire for them whatever.

Improvement Era, August 1906, 768–70.

He Had Quit Several Times

Eldred G. Smith

Humility is one of the qualities that helps build faith. Would a missionary be successful if he were not humble? He has to be teachable, with a receptive mind, before he can teach others. And to be teachable, he must be humble. And we should all be missionaries.

All the requirements of living the gospel become easier through humility.

A young man told me his experience in becoming a member of the Church, which is typical of many in their activities of investigating the Church. He said the missionaries came to the lesson on the Word of Wisdom. He and his wife were both users of tobacco. After the meeting was over and the missionaries had left, they talked it over with each other and decided among themselves, "Well, if that is what the Lord wants and if this is the Lord's Church, we will try it." He said that he was not particularly concerned about himself, he thought he could do it easily. He was worried about his wife; she had never tried to quit before. On the other hand, he had quit several times. After proving to himself that he could quit, of course, he went back to the use of cigarettes again. But he said in this case it was just the reverse.

His wife quit without any apparent difficulty, but he had tremendous difficulty. He became nervous and irritable. He could not rest. He was cranky among his fellow workers. He could not sleep at night. But inasmuch as his wife had quit, he was not going to be outdone by her. So, one night, he became so restless, so disturbed that he could not sleep, and his wife suggested to him that he pray about it. He thought that was a good joke. He ridiculed the idea of prayer; he said, "This is something I have to do. Nobody can help me with this. I can do this." But as the night passed and he had done everything he could to stimulate sleep and rest without any success, finally in despair, he humbled himself enough to kneel at the side of the bed and pray vocally.

According to his own testimony, he said that he got up from his prayer, got into bed, went to sleep, and has never been tempted by cigarettes since. He has absolutely lost his taste for tobacco. He said, "The Word of Wisdom was not a health program for me. It was a lesson of humility." He said, "I had to learn humility." That is what it meant to him. As it is with many of the requirements of the Church, we have to demonstrate humble obedience.

Conference Report, April 1955, 42.

The Seven Goblets Were Still Full

Spencer W. Kimball

May I tell you another goal that I set when I was still a youngster.

I had heard all of my life about the Word of Wisdom and the blessings that could come into my life through living it. I had seen people chewing tobacco, and it was repulsive to me. I had seen men waste much time in "rolling their own" cigarettes. They would buy a sack of "Bull Durham" tobacco or some other brand, then some papers, and then they would stop numerous times in a day to fill the paper with tobacco, roll it, bend over the little end of it, and then smoke it. It seemed foolish to me and seemed such a waste of time and energy. Later when the practice became more sophisticated, they bought their cigarettes readymade. I remember how repulsive it was to me when women began to smoke.

I remember as a boy going to the Fourth of July celebration on the streets of my little town and seeing some of the men as they took part in the horse racing as participator or as gambler, betting on the horses, and I noted that many of them had cigarettes in their lips and bottles in their pockets and some were ugly drunk with their bleary eyes and coarse talk and cursing.

It took a little time to match the ponies and arrange the races, and almost invariably during this time there would be someone call out, "Fight!" "Fight!" and all the men and boys would gravitate to the fight area, which was attended with blows and blood and curses and hatreds.

Again I was nauseated to think that men would so disgrace themselves, and again I made up my mind that while I would drink the pink lemonade on the Fourth of July and watch the horses run, I never would drink liquor or swear or curse as did many of these fellows of this little town.

And I remember that without being pressured by anyone, I made up my mind while still a little boy that I would never break the Word of Wisdom. I knew that when the Lord said it, it was pleasing unto him for men to abstain from all these destructive elements, and the thing I wanted to do was to please my Heavenly Father. And so I made up my mind firmly and solidly that I would never touch those harmful things. Having made up my mind fully and unequivocably, I found it not too difficult to keep the promise to myself and to my Heavenly Father.

I remember once in later years, when I was district governor of the Rotary Clubs of Arizona, that I went to Nice, France, to the international convention. As a part of that celebration there was a sumptuous banquet for the district governors, and the large building was set for an elegant meal. When we came to our places, I noted that at every place there were seven goblets, along with numerous items of silverware and dishes; and everything was about the best that Europe could furnish.

As the meal got underway, an army of waiters came to wait on us, seven waiters at each place, and they poured wine and liquor. Seven glass goblets were filled at every plate. The drinks were colorful. I was a long way from home; I knew many of the district governors; they knew me. But they probably did not know my religion nor of my stand on the Word of Wisdom. At any rate, the evil one seemed to whisper to me, "This is your chance. You are thousands of miles from home. There is no one here to watch you. No one will ever know if you drink the contents of those goblets. This is your chance!"

Then a sweeter spirit seemed to whisper, "You have a covenant with yourself; you promised yourself you would never do it. With your Heavenly Father you made a covenant, and you have gone these years without breaking it, and you would be stupid to break it now." Suffice it to say that when I got up from the table an hour later, the seven goblets were still full of colorful material that had been poured into them but never touched.

Ensign, May 1974, 88–89.

WINE WAS PLACED AT EACH PLATE

DAVID O. McKAY

When I visited the beautiful Island of Tahiti in 1921 I learned of an incident associated with Brother Vaio (a member of the Church), who was then captain of one of the government schooners.

The newly appointed governor of the island was to make a tour of inspection of a government-owned vessel. Captain Vaio and his associates decorated their ship, placed fruits and delicacies on the table, and made ready for a suitable and appropriate reception to his excellency. A glass of wine was placed at each plate with which at the proper time all would respond to the toast and drink to the health of the governor. There was one exception however—at Captain Vaio's plate there was placed a glass of lemonade. One of his associates protested saying that he would offend the governor if he drank only lemonade at the toast, but notwithstanding these protestations Brother Vaio insisted that he would drink only lemonade when the toast was proposed.

It was Captain Vaio's responsibility and honor to make the welcome speech. This he did, and at the conclusion he explained in substance:

"Your Excellency, before proposing the toast I wish to explain why I am drinking lemonade instead of the customary wine. I am a member of The Church of Jesus Christ of Latter-day Saints. Every Sunday morning I teach a class of young people. It is one of our tenets not to drink wine or strong drink, tea, nor coffee, nor use tobacco. I cannot consistently tell them not to use intoxicating liquor and then indulge myself; therefore, you will understand why on this occasion I am drinking lemonade. And now I propose a toast to the health and happiness of his Excellency, governor of Tahiti."

There was a tense silence among the ship's crew as the governor arose to make his response. He was a true gentleman and appreciated the loyalty and manhood of the man who had given the welcoming speech. In substance the governor said:

"Captain Vaio, I thank you and your associates for this hearty welcome, and I am glad to learn that you maintain the ideals of your Church in regard to temperance. I wish we had more men with such sterling character to take charge of the government's ships."

As we sailed that evening toward Rarotonga, I wondered in admiration how many of the members of the Church were as loyal to the ideals and teachings of the gospel as was Captain Vaio; and the words of the Savior came to my mind as they come again as I dictate these lines. "Not every one that saith unto me Lord, Lord, shall enter into the kingdom of heaven; but he that doeth the will of my father which is in heaven" (Matthew 7:21).

I have learned that Captain Vaio has gone to his eternal reward. Perhaps he knows how many times I have told this story to Sunday School children, not a few of whom let us hope have been encouraged along the pathway of duty, because of his courage and loyalty to what he knew was right.

David O. McKay, *Cherished Experiences,* 199–200.

"What Kind of a Heart Did I Have?"

Heber J. Grant

I leave my testimony with you that I believe as firmly as I believe anything in this world that I would not be standing here today talking to you if I had not obeyed the Word of Wisdom. When my appendix was removed it had broken, and blood poisoning, so they said, . . . had set in. There were nine doctors present and eight said I had to die. The chief surgeon in the Catholic hospital turned to President Joseph F. Smith, and said: "Mr. Smith, you need not think of such a possibility or probability as that this man shall live. Why, if he should live it would be a miracle, and this is not the day of miracles." That was the message delivered to me by Joseph F. Smith himself during his last sickness, and he said: "Our doctor friend who said it would be a miracle has passed away. I never saw you looking healthier in my life than you do today, Heber."

I said to the nurse who told me regarding these nine doctors that I did not want to meet any of them, except the one who said and believed that I would pull through. She said: "He is the house doctor; I will call him in."

I asked him why he disagreed with the others, and he smiled, . . . and he said: "Mister Grant, I just took a chance, sir. I have felt the pulse . . . of thousands of patients, being a house doctor, in many many hospitals, but I never felt a pulse just like yours. . . . Why, do you know, . . . in all of the tests that I made during an hour and three quarters that you were under the knife your heart never missed one single, solitary beat, and I made up my mind that that heart would pull you through."

What kind of a heart did I have? I had a heart that had pure blood in it, that was not contaminated by tea, coffee or liquor. That is why the poison in my system was overcome. The doctor who operated upon me had made an agreement with me that he was to tell me if I had to die—and he did—so that I could write a couple of letters. But I did not write them because in the kind providences of the Lord it had been revealed in a manifestation that I did not have to die. Men say we cannot receive communications from the other world, but my wife whose body lies in the grave visited my wife who is alive and told her that my mission was not yet ended; and I had received before that a blessing by the gift of tongues from that identical wife whose body was in the grave. And what was in that blessing? That I should live to lift up my voice in many lands and in many climes proclaiming the restoration to the earth of the Gospel of the Lord Jesus Christ.

I had not lifted up my voice in many lands and many climes at the time I was in the hospital, but subsequently I have lifted up my voice in England, Ireland, Scotland, Wales, Germany, France, Belgium, Holland, Switzerland, Italy, Norway, Sweden, Denmark,

Canada and Mexico; from Portland, Maine, to Portland, Oregon; from the Canadian border down to Florida; in the Hawaiian Islands and in far-off Japan, proclaiming the restoration to the earth of the Gospel of the Lord Jesus Christ, the plan of life and salvation: bearing my witness that I know that God lives, that Jesus is the Christ, the Redeemer of mankind, the Savior of the world, and that Joseph Smith was a prophet of the true and living God.

Conference Report, April 1933, 10–11.

"We'll See What You Americans Are Drinking"

JOHN R. TALMAGE

In 1891 James E. Talmage traveled to England for scientific meetings and genealogical research. In Liverpool he had the following experience with a customs inspector.]

The customs inspector was a most sarcastic man, and perhaps he was in a bad humor for personal reasons. Whatever the cause, his actions were maddeningly slow and often deliberately offensive. Dr. Talmage, his baggage waiting in the "T" section, had a disagreeably long wait but bore it with fortitude, having carefully filled out the customs declaration form.

When at last the inspector reached the waiting professor, the official snatched the declaration held out to him, glanced rapidly over it, and said accusingly:

"But you have declared nothing dutiable."

"I believe I have nothing dutiable to declare," the traveler replied calmly.

"Come, come, my man, *everyone* has something to declare!" the inspector said with a show of indignation, as though he had received a personal affront. "Personal effects, jewelry, liquor, tobacco . . . they're all dutiable."

Professor Talmage, his patience worn thin, kept his outward composure and replied in a level voice: "I don't carry expensive jewelry and it so happens that I don't smoke and I don't drink liquor. I believe my declaration has been accurately filled out and that I have nothing at all to declare."

The customs inspector snorted disdainfully and proceeded to give the professor's luggage a most thorough examination. He would show this ignorant American, and all the other waiting boat passengers, that *every traveller* has *something* dutiable to declare.

Now Dr. Talmage had come prepared to be something more than a mere spectator at the forthcoming meeting of the Royal Microscopical Society. In case he, as a new member and coming from a far country, should be called on for a contribution to the proceedings, he had written a short paper on the Great Salt Lake and the surrounding desert. For illustration, he had brought a sample of the lake water containing the tiny *artemis fertilis,* or brine shrimp, the only animal form able to live in the lake water, and three horned lizards, commonly called "horned toads," as illustrative of animal life on the desert shore. Though a non-smoker and non-drinker as he had informed the customs inspector, Professor Talmage was acquainted with men who indulged in both practices, and had secured a cigar box and a flat pint whiskey bottle as convenient carriers for his exotic fauna. The customs inspector had barely started his thorough search of the professor's baggage when he encountered the cigar box.

"Ha!" he cried triumphantly, holding the box aloft for all to see. "I thought you said you were carrying no tobacco."

"No, no tobacco," Dr. Talmage replied quietly, and offered no further comment.

"We'll see what you Americans are smoking these days in place of tobacco," the inspector said with a wink to the crowd which had gathered around. He opened the box.

Most Westerners have sometime seen a "horned toad," a perfectly harmless but poisonous-looking little creature, whose appearance is bound to be alarming to anyone seeing it for the first time. One of the lizards promptly jumped from the box in which it had been so long confined onto the inspector's hand.

The official, in near-panic, leaped backward and tripped over a piece of baggage. Professor Talmage retrieved the lizard and returned it to the box while the embarrassed customs official arose red-faced, fuming with anger, and gingerly rubbing assorted sore spots on his anatomy. Most of the spectators, thoroughly annoyed with the inspector's petty officiousness, were openly laughing, adding to the official's mounting rage.

He said no more but grimly set about a further search of Professor Talmage's luggage, determined to find some dutiable object—and *then* this upstart American would taste the full severity of British law. Articles of clothing were recklessly flung about, but Dr. Talmage kept his studied composure. He perceived a vague possibility which was becoming less vague by the moment. Hopefully he awaited the almost inevitable next act in the little farce.

He did not have long to wait. The inspector encountered, carefully wrapped in layers of clothing for protection against breakage—although in the outraged official's eyes it seemed obviously for purposes of concealment—a pint bottle of the size and shape traditionally used to contain whiskey. Holding it to the light he could see it was filled with liquid. The colored glass of the bottle prevented any exact determination of the nature of the liquid. But the inspector was certain he had what he wanted.

"I thought you said you had no liquor," he said fiercely, holding the bottle up for dramatic effect.

"No liquor," Dr. Talmage said laconically. The vague possibility had now become a virtual certainty, but he took no action to interfere.

"We'll *see* what you Americans are drinking instead of whiskey," the inspector said scornfully, and he uncapped the bottle and put it to his lips.

Everyone who has ever bathed in the Great Salt Lake has at some time accidentally taken a mouthful of water, and knows the unpleasantness of swallowing even the tiniest amount of the supersaturated brine. The shock of quaffing deeply, even greedily, of the lake water in the belief that it is a choice liquor may well be imagined. The customs inspector gasped, choked, coughed, and spat as he flopped about the customs shed in agony, undoubtedly thinking that he was literally strangling and that the end might come any moment.

Dr. Talmage had alertly taken the bottle from the inspector's hand lest it be broken and its scientifically precious contents lost. He then sat quietly by as the stricken inspector went through his agonized contortions, saying nothing except to assure awed fellow passengers that the bottle contained no poison, but merely the over-salty water from the far-off Great Salt Lake.

The inspector's next act was awaited with hushed interest, as the anticipated explosion of personal temper and official ire might well be of historic proportions. But the customs official was through. He made one last attempt to assert his authority, but it failed miserably. When he tried to glare angrily, his watering eyes only rolled weakly in their sockets and closed right in pain. When he tried to roar authoritatively he could only manage a hoarse croak.

In desperation, the inspector grabbed a piece of chalk and marked each piece of the professor's baggage to show that it had passed inspection. Pausing for a brief moment, he then suddenly turned and moved rapidly about the shed, marking *all* items of uninspected luggage. After that, he dashed out of the door and disappeared from the view of the ship's passengers, possibly in search of a bottle whose contents could be trusted to match their container.

In later years, Dr. Talmage would say, mock-seriously, that he had no idea how many professional smugglers he may have provided with a free pass through British customs on this occasion.

John R. Talmage, *The Talmage Story,* 93–96.

"THE COFFEE IS HOT AND I AM COLD"

EZRA TAFT BENSON

Many years ago, a member of our district council in the mission in Washington was traveling by plane. He had been in Canada, and on the flight back the plane developed trouble and had to land on an auxiliary landing field in Pennsylvania. It was a cold night, and the passengers were told that the plane would probably be on the ground for an hour. They got out and stretched and wandered around a little, and then they noticed over in the brush a light. They walked over toward this light and found a CCC camp, and as they opened the door they got an aroma of hot food. So they got courage and walked in, and they were invited to join the CCC boys at dinner.

Now, the member of our district council found himself seated between two CCC boys, and when they brought around the hot coffee our friend, who didn't use it ordinarily, thought, "The coffee is hot and I am cold and there isn't anything else readily available to drink." So he took some and engaged in conversation with the two boys beside him.

One of them said, "Where do you come from?" He said, "I come from Washington, but originally I came from Utah."

"You don't happen to be a Mormon, do you?"

"Yes," he replied, "I am a Mormon."

The boy said, "You are not a very good one, are you?"

Well, he was a pretty good one, and it was an awful shock to him to hear this comment. He said, "What do you know about the Mormons?"

The boy said, "Well, a couple of years ago I was in St. George, Utah, and I attended Mormon services. I know you Mormons have in your church what you call the Word of Wisdom, and that good Mormons live it."

Can you imagine how the district councilor felt? It wasn't the cup of coffee—that is not going to destroy anyone—but it was the fact that he hadn't maintained that which he believed in. He hadn't kept the standards.

It never pays to let down your standards in this church. You will be thought more of if you live the gospel, if you will be what you profess to be. You will be happier, you will have a better feeling inside, you will do more good in the world, and you will be more effective missionaries. So live church and missionary standards wherever you go.

Ezra Taft Benson, *God, Family, Country,* 62–63.

"HER MIND WAS MADE UP"

JOHN A. WIDTSOE

My mother, Anna Widtsoe] had not been taught the Word of Wisdom, except as it had been mentioned casually in her Gospel conversations. Now, she began to understand its real meaning and purpose and the necessity of obeying it, as it was the desire of the Father that his children should heed it. Like nearly all of her country people she had drunk coffee from her childhood, and was an occasional user of tea. Alcoholic beverages she did not use. She set about to give up the use of tea and coffee, but found it difficult. When she sewed every night far beyond midnight, the cup of coffee seemed to freshen her, she thought. After a two months' struggle she came home one day, having given serious consideration to the Word of Wisdom problem. Her mind was made up. She stood in the middle of the room and said aloud, "Never again. Get behind me, Satan!" and walked briskly to her cupboard, took out the packages of coffee and tea and threw them on the fire. From that day she never used tea or coffee.

John A. Widtsoe, *In the Gospel Net,* 73.

HE BECAME A HERO

N. ELDON TANNER

When I was president of the Edmonton (Alberta, Canada) Branch we had a young man there who was the only member of the Church on his high school basketball team. That young man and I were pretty close friends, though he was only a sixteen-year-old boy. He said to me, "You know, I don't know how I am going to hold up."

I said, "Listen, you have something that these boys don't have. They don't know anything about our Word of Wisdom. They don't know several things that we have in the Church. They don't know that they are spirit children of God. If I were you, I would just tell these boys something about the Word of Wisdom, and how these things may destroy your body, and how detrimental they are to you, and how they will impede your playing, and so on."

You know, he set out to do that, and he became more or less a hero with those boys. Before that year was over, there wasn't a single boy on the team who was using tobacco.

Conference Report, October 1968, 103.

"ARE YOU GOING TO BE MASTER?"

SUSA YOUNG GATES

As a young man my father [Brigham Young] chewed tobacco. In after years he told the story of that conquered appetite. "I carried a half plug of tobacco in my pocket for a long time," he said. "When the gnawing for it seemed unbearable I would take it out, look at it, and say 'Are you, or is Brigham going to be master?' Then it went back untouched into my pocket."

Susa Young Gates and Leah D. Widtsoe, *Life Story of Brigham Young,* 333.

Sources

A Story to Tell. Salt Lake City: The Church of Jesus Christ of Latter-day Saints, 1945.

Bennett, Archibald F. *Saviors on Mount Zion.* Salt Lake City: The Church of Jesus Christ of Latter-day Saints, 1950.

Benson, Ezra Taft. *God, Family, Country: Our Three Great Loyalties.* Salt Lake City: Deseret Book Co., 1974.

Brown, James S. *Life of a Pioneer.* Salt Lake City: George Q. Cannon and Sons Co., 1900.

Burton, Alma P. *Karl G. Maeser, Mormon Educator.* Salt Lake City: Deseret Book Co., 1953.

Cannon, George Q. *Gospel Truth: Discourses and Writings of President George Q. Cannon.* Edited by Jerreld L. Newquist. Salt Lake City: Deseret Book Co., 1987.

———. *A String of Pearls.* Second Book of the Faith Promoting Series. Salt Lake City: Juvenile Instructor Office, 1882.

Cannon, George Q. [George C. Lambert, pseud.], comp. *Gems of Reminiscence.* Seventeenth Book of the Faith Promoting Series. Salt Lake City: George C. Lambert, 1915.

———. *Precious Memories.* Sixteenth Book of the Faith Promoting Series. Salt Lake City: George C. Lambert, 1914.

———. *Treasures in Heaven.* Fifteenth Book of the Faith Promoting Series. Salt Lake City: George C. Lambert, 1914.

Carter, Kate B. *Heart Throbs of the West.* 3 vols. Salt Lake City: Daughters of Utah Pioneers, 1939–1951.

Classic Experiences and Adventures. Salt Lake City: Bookcraft, 1969.

Conference Reports. Salt Lake City: The Church of Jesus Christ of Latter-days Saints, 1899–1998.

Cowley, Matthew. *Matthew Cowley Speaks.* Salt Lake City: Deseret Book Co., 1954.

Cowley, Matthias F. *Wilford Woodruff: His Life and Labors.* Salt Lake City: Bookcraft, 1964.

Crocheron, Augusta Joyce, comp. *Representative Women of Deseret.* Salt Lake City: J. C. Graham and Co., 1884.

Davis, Troy, Richard Nelson, and David Salmons. *Our Miraculous Heritage.* Orem, Utah: Cedar Fort, 1991.

Dew, Sheri L. *Ezra Taft Benson: A Biography.* Salt Lake City: Deseret Book Co., 1987.

Early Scenes in Church History. Eighth Book of the Faith Promoting Series. Salt Lake City: Juvenile Instructor Office, 1882.

Evans, John Henry. *Charles Coulson Rich: Pioneer Builder of the West.* New York: Macmillan, 1936.

Eventful Narratives. Thirteenth Book of the Faith Promoting Series. Salt Lake City: Juvenile Instructor Office, 1887.

Fragments of Experience. Sixth Book of the Faith Promoting Series. Salt Lake City: Juvenile Instructor Office, 1882.

Gates, Susa Young. *Lydia Knight's History.* Salt Lake City: Juvenile Instructor Office, 1883.

Gates, Susa Young, and Leah D. Widtsoe, *Life Story of Brigham Young.* New York: Macmillan Company, 1930.

Gems for the Young Folks. Salt Lake City: Juvenile Instructor Office, 1881.

Gibbons, Francis M. *Dynamic Disciples, Prophets of God.* Salt Lake City: Deseret Book, 1996.

———. *Joseph Fielding Smith: Gospel Scholar, Prophet of God.* Salt Lake City: Deseret Book Co., 1992.

———. *Spencer W. Kimball: Resolute Disciple, Prophet of God.* Salt Lake City: Deseret Book Co., 1996.

Grant, Heber J. *Gospel Standards: Selections from the Sermons and*

Writings of Heber J. Grant. Compiled by G. Homer Durham. Salt Lake City: Improvement Era, 1969.

Hafen, LeRoy R., and Ann W. Hafen. *Handcarts to Zion.* Glendale, Calif.: The Arthur H. Clark Co., 1960.

Hartshorn, Leon R., comp. *Remarkable Stories from the Lives of Latter-day Saint Women.* 2 vols. Salt Lake City: Deseret Book Co., 1973, 1975.

Hinckley, Bryant S. *Heber J. Grant: Highlights in the Life of a Great Leader.* Salt Lake City: Deseret Book Co., 1951.

———. *The Faith of Our Pioneer Fathers.* Salt Lake City: Deseret Book Co., 1965.

Huntington, Oliver B. "History of the Life of Oliver B. Huntington, 1878–1900." Typescript. Historical Department Archives. The Church of Jesus Christ of Latter-day Saints.

Jenson, Andrew. *LDS Biographical Encyclopedia.* 4 vols. Salt Lake City: Andrew Jenson History Co., 1901.

Jones, Daniel W. *Forty Years Among the Indians.* Salt Lake City: Juvenile Instructor Office, 1890.

Journal of Discourses. 26 vols. London: Latter-day Saints' Book Depot, 1854–86.

Labors in the Vineyard. Twelfth Book of the Faith Promoting Series. Salt Lake City: Juvenile Instructor Office, 1884.

Lake, Louise. *Each Day a Bonus.* Salt Lake City: Deseret Book, 1971.

Lee, Harold B. *Stand Ye in Holy Places.* Salt Lake City: Deseret Book Co., 1974.

———. *Ye Are the Light of the World.* Salt Lake City: Deseret Book Co., 1974.

Lightner, Mary Elizabeth Rollins. "The Life and Testimony of Mary Lightner." Typescript. Historical Department Archives. The Church of Jesus Christ of Latter-day Saints.

Littlefield, Lyman O. *The Martyrs.* Salt Lake City: Juvenile Instructor Office, 1882.

Lundwall, N. B. *Temples of the Most High.* Salt Lake City: Bookcraft, 1952.

McKay, David O. *Cherished Experiences from the Writings of David O. McKay.* Compiled by Clare Middlemiss. Salt Lake City: Deseret Book Co., 1955.

McKay, Emma Ray Riggs. *The Art of Rearing Children Peacefully.* Provo, Utah: Brigham Young University Press, 1966.

McKay, Llewelyn R., comp. *Home Memories of President David O. McKay.* Salt Lake City: Deseret Book Co., 1959.

Merrill, Melvin Clarence, ed. *Utah Pioneer and Apostle Marriner Wood Merrill and His Family.* [Salt Lake City:] Marriner Wood Merrill Heritage Committee, 1937.

Neff, Barbara. Autograph Book. Typescript. Historical Department Archives. The Church of Jesus Christ of Latter-day Saints.

Nibley, Preston. *Faith-Promoting Stories.* Independence, Mo.: Zion's Printing and Publishing Co., 1943.

Parrish, Mary Pratt. *Supplement to the Seagull, Home Builder Lesson Book.* Salt Lake City: The Church of Jesus Christ of Latter-day Saints, 1951.

Parry, Edwin F. *Sketches of Missionary Life.* Salt Lake City: George Q. Cannon and Sons, 1899.

Pratt, Parley P. *Autobiography of Parley P. Pratt.* Edited by Parley P. Pratt Jr. Salt Lake City: Deseret Book Co., 1985.

Pulsipher, Zera. Autobiography. Typescript. Special Collections. Brigham Young University.

Roberts, B. H. *A Comprehensive History of The Church of Jesus Christ of Latter-day Saints.* 6 vols. Salt Lake City: The Church of Jesus Christ of Latter-day Saints, 1930.

Romney, Thomas C. *The Life of Lorenzo Snow.* Salt Lake City: S.U.P. Memorial Foundation, 1955.

Scraps of Biography. Tenth Book of the Faith Promoting Series. Salt Lake City: Juvenile Instructor Office, 1883.

Smith, George Albert. *Sharing the Gospel with Others.* Compiled by Preston Nibley. Salt Lake City: Deseret News Press, 1948.

Smith, Henry A. *Matthew Cowley: Man of Faith.* Salt Lake City: Bookcraft, 1954.

Smith, Joseph. *History of The Church of Jesus Christ of Latter-day Saints.* 7 vols. 2d ed. rev. Edited by B. H. Roberts. Salt Lake City: The Church of Jesus Christ of Latter-day Saints, 1932–51.

Smith, Lucy Mack. *History of Joseph Smith.* Edited by Preston Nibley. Salt Lake City: Bookcraft, 1958.

Snow, Eliza R. *Biography and Family Record of Lorenzo Snow.* Salt Lake City: Deseret News, 1884.

Speeches of the Year. Provo, Utah: Brigham Young University, 1965, 1970, 1991. (This publication has been titled in different ways over the years, for example, *Brigham Young University 1990–91 Devotional and Fireside Speeches.*)

Tagg, Melvin S. "The Life of Edward James Wood, Church Patriot." Master's Thesis. Brigham Young University, 1959.

Talmage, John R. *The Talmage Story: Life of James E. Talmage—Educator, Scientist, Apostle.* Salt Lake City: Bookcraft, 1972.Widtsoe, John A. *In the Gospel Net.* Salt Lake City: Bookcraft, 1966.

Tullidge, Edward W. *The Women of Mormondom.* New York: Tullidge and Crandall, 1877.

Whitney, Orson F. *Life of Heber C. Kimball.* Salt Lake City: Bookcraft, 1967.

Widtsoe, John A. *In a Sunlit Land.* Salt Lake City: Deseret News Press, 1952.

———. *In the Gospel Net: The Story of Anna Karine Gaarden Widtsoe.* Independence, Mo.: Press of Zion's Printing and Publishing Co., 1941.

Woodruff, Wilford. *Leaves from My Journal.* Third Book of the Faith Promoting Series. Salt Lake City: Juvenile Instructor Office, 1881.

Zobell, Albert L. *Story Gems.* Salt Lake City: Bookcraft, 1953.

INDEX